creativity *in* fashion design

fb

Transparent Jacket

Inspiration for the
Spring 2010 menswear
line showing in Milan,
Italy by Calvin Klein.
Collection designed
by Italo Zucchelli.
Courtesy of WWD

creativity *in* fashion design

AN INSPIRATION WORKBOOK

Tracy Jennings, EdD

Dominican University

FAIRCHILD BOOKS   NEW YORK

Vice President & General Manager, Fairchild Education & Conference Division: Elizabeth Tighe

Executive Editor: Olga T. Kontzias

Senior Associate Acquiring Editor: Jaclyn Bergeron

Assistant Acquisitions Editor: Amanda Breccia

Editorial Development Director: Jennifer Crane

Development Editor: Sylvia L. Weber

Associate Art Director: Carolyn Eckert

Production Director: Ginger Hillman

Senior Production Editor: Elizabeth Marotta

Copyeditor: Susan Hobbs

Ancillaries Editor: Noah Schwartzberg

Cover Design: Andrea Lau

Cover Art: (Front) "Spring Things." Art by Brazilian artist Beatriz Milhazes. *WWD* (Back) Diane von Furstenberg, Spring 2010 RTW. *WWD*/George Chinsee

Text Design and Composition: Mary Neal Meador

Illustrator: Andrea Lau

Library of Congress Catalog Card Number: 010923005

ISBN: 978-1-56367-895-0

GST R 133004424

Printed in the United States of America

TP08

contents

preface   xv

acknowledgments   xix

introduction   1

1   creativity *and* fashion design   12

2   creativity *and the* environment   50

3   creativity *and* cognition   88

4   creativity *and* character traits   118

5   creativity *and* motivation   152

6   creativity *and the* design process   186

7   creativity *in the* industry   217

references   245

appendix   249

index   257

extended contents

preface   xv

acknowledgments   xix

introduction   1

   understanding creativity   2

   your dynamic inspiration notebook   3

     three-ring notebook   4
     digital notebook   4
     collect data   4
     generate ideas   7
     conceptualize ideas into themes   7
     combine themes into connections   7
     sketch your connection   7
     getting started   7

   the workbook format   10

   digital camera   10

   design integrity   10

   let's create!   11

1 creativity *and* fashion design   12

objectives   13

understanding creativity   13

what is creativity? 14

who is creative? 19

creativity as a confluence of traits 19

knowledge base   19

historical aspects of dress 22

cultural aspects of dress 22

textiles 23

legendary designers 23

silhouettes, terminology,
and sources of information 24

skills of the discipline 24

technology 24

audience 24

the human body 24

guiding principles 24

guiding principles of fashion design   27

golden ratio 27

elements and
principles of design 28

color theory 35

breaking the rules 37

critiquing fashion design   40

arbiters of design 40

critique criteria 40

learning experience 41

the design critique 45

summary   48

key terms   48

2 creativity *and* the environment   50

objectives   51

physical aspects of the
designer's environment   52

    workspace 54

    tools and equipment 54

psychological aspects of the
designer's environment   57

    supportive family and peers 58

    society's role 58

    societal norms 59

scanning the environment   62

    environmental scanning 62

    inspiration from a to z 63

change of environment   69

    a global perspective 73

    a change of mind 76

environmentally friendly designing   76

    fiber production 77

    textile production 77

    apparel design 79

    apparel manufacturing 82

    apparel packaging and shipping 84

    retail outlets 84

    consumer 84

    post consumer 85

summary   86

key terms   86

3   creativity *and* cognition   88

objectives   89

creativity-enhancing cognitive skills   89

    divergent and
    convergent thinking 90

    problem solving
    and problem finding 92

theory of multiple intelligences 97

technology 98

    ancient world
(3000 B.C.–A.D. 500) 101

    the middle ages
(500–1500) 101

    the renaissance
(1400–1600) 102

    baroque and rococo
(1700–1800) 102

    the nineteenth century
(1800–1900) 103

    the twentieth century
(1900–2000) 104

    the new millennium 104

    virtual design 106

    form and function 112

    innovators 112

    home-grown technology 115

summary 116

key terms 116

4   creativity *and* character traits 118

objectives 119

character traits associated with creativity 119

    tolerance for ambiguity 122

    freedom 122

    preference for disorder 123

    perseverance and
delay of gratification 123

    risk taking 123

    courage 124

    self control 124

    other character traits
of creative individuals 124

    polarities of traits 124

    fear 125

    passion for fashion 128

affective dimensions of design 128

    dimensions of personality 129

    emotions and feelings
    as inspiration 129

    expressing concepts 132

expressing traits through fashion design 132

    styling 132

    fabrics 138

    color's multiple personalities 138

meanings of dress 144

    culture 145

    group association 148

    self-esteem 148

summary 150

key terms 150

5 creativity *and* motivation 152

    objectives 153

    intrinsic and extrinsic motivation 153

        intrinsic motivation 153

        promoting intrinsic motivation 155

        extrinsic motivation 157

    motivations to explore 158

        imagination 158

        play 161

        reflection 165

        incubation 165

        the unconscious mind 165

        taking time 166

        intuition 166

        flow 166

        aha moment 168

    human motivations 168

        gestalt theory 168

        maslow's hierarchy 169

        fea consumer needs model 172

motivations to design   172

    niche markets 172
    attire for special needs 173
    fast fashion 175

community involvement   180

    corporate social responsibility 180
    the (red) campaign 180
    fair trade 180
    critics of corporate social action 182

summary   183

key terms   184

6   creativity *and* the design process   186

objectives   187

why a design process?   187

    a design process is not . . . 189
    a design process is . . . 189
    your design process 190

the holistic approach:
seven da vincian principles   193

    curiosity 197
    demonstration 197
    the senses 197
    ambiguity, paradox,
    and uncertainty 197
    art/science 197
    health and well-being 198
    connections 198
    holistic process summarized 198

the phase approach: the design process   198

    inspiration 199
    identification 199
    conceptualization 199
    exploration/refinement 200
    definition/modeling 200

communication 200

production 200

design process summarized 201

the creative problem-solving approach:
design as problem solving   202

understanding the challenge 202

generating ideas 203

preparing for action 203

creative problem
solving summarized 203

your design process, revisited 206

pitfalls for designers   206

procrastination 206

noncommittal design 207

throw-away design 207

the category trap 207

the puzzle trap 207

the number trap 207

the icon trap 208

the imagetrap 208

the design process:
champignons, a case study   210

summary   214

key terms   214

7   creativity *in* the industry   216

objectives   217

the fashion design portfolio   217

fashion design spreads 217

comprehensive portfolio 220

professional presentations   222

fashion design in context   224

trend forecasting and research 224

line concepts 224

line presentations 225

prototype development
and approval 225

production sample 225

production 226

creative collaborations   226

creativity in a group setting 226

creative teams 226

networking 230

the ethical designer   230

unfair and discriminatory
labor practices 232

environmental abuses 233

culture of disposable fashion 233

promotion of an
unrealistic body type 233

pervasive copying
and counterfeiting 234

treatment of animals 234

creative approaches
to ethical issues 234

the future of fashion   237

preparing for change 237

trend forecasting 238

my creative potential:
a stocktaking 238

summary   242

key terms   242

references   245

appendix   249

index   257

preface

Creativity in Fashion Design is a text about understanding creativity and applying this knowledge to innovative fashion design. It follows the assumption that the more designers know, the better able they are to connect ideas and turn them into inspiration for design. Creativity is often misunderstood. It seems mystical and out of one's control. It may be thought of as a gift that some have and some do not have. This book maintains that fashion designers and students of fashion design are naturally creative, and they can understand and utilize the components that lead to creativity. By understanding creativity, designers can actively seek characteristics and environments that foster it and avoid factors that inhibit it. This understanding empowers designers. They can take charge of their own creative destiny. In this time of rapid change and fast fashion, fashion designers must have an arsenal that allows them to act. They cannot sit back and wait for the muse. They must continually seek inspiration.

author

The author comes to this book as a fashion design educator and experienced fashion designer. In addition, fashion design instructors and students and a variety of professionals in the design industry were interviewed to determine their perspectives on creativity. These investigations led to several discoveries. Individuals are fiercely protective of their perceptions and understanding of creativity. This book is not intended to change those notions. The author recognizes that people want to take an individualized approach to their creativity. However, research has also uncovered that many people have an incomplete understanding of the complexity of the creativity construct, and this can cause misunderstandings in the classroom and missed opportunities for design. For example, students are often hesitant to try to understand creativity. In this way, they can declare any artistic expression to be creative. However, the complex and competitive apparel industry of today requires a more discriminating, calculated, and proactive approach. Designers can empower themselves, and creativity is their reward for hard work.

Successful practices should be encouraged and continued, and the author welcomes comments and discussion about productive creativity-fostering activities. Please send comments to tjennings@dom.edu. This book introduces designers to ways of looking at design that will augment, not replace, their current practices. Not every concept will resonate with every reader. That is okay. Readers are encouraged to formulate an understanding of creativity that incorporates multiple aspects but ultimately utilizes ideas that work for them.

how to use the book

This text can accompany pattern-making texts in a fashion design class or technique-based texts in an illustration class, or it can introduce the inspiration portion of a product development class. As a stand-alone text, it thoroughly presents inspiration-gathering processes and creativity-enhancing activities.

Creativity is a dynamic concept. It changes through our experience. An important component of the text is the *Dynamic Inspiration Notebook (DIN)* that students maintain in conjunction with this text-workbook. Students are encouraged to utilize their *DIN*s to apply and practice concepts presented herein.

The book provides many design assignments. All of them cannot culminate in a complete three-dimensional form in the course of one short semester. Instructors, students, and designers should choose how to address each of the suggested activities and challenges. Assignments can be altered to fit the dynamics, grade level, goals, and timing of a course. Although a preferred method is suggested, consider completing a particular assignment as:

- Thumbnail sketches
- An illustration of a fashion design
- A grouping of flats
- A sketch or illustration of a complete line or collection
- A portfolio spread
- An experiential piece
- A patterned piece as a component of the product development process
- A three-dimensional artistic piece, either draped or flat patterned, that is designed with the goal of personal expression
- A three-dimensional artistic piece that answers a need of a particular niche market
- An investigation of the design process
- A research project that includes thorough investigation into the subject of the piece

Undoubtedly, students have a preferred method of designing, but they are encouraged to give several types of assignments a try because they might learn a new concept that they otherwise would not have.

physical features of the book

It is a workbook. It is intended to be written in, carried around, and tossed in backpacks. The dimensions and soft cover liken it to a sketchbook.

theoretical connections

Constructivist theory has its origins in cognitive development research advanced by Jean Piaget and Lev Vygotsky. The Piagetian view is that learning is a process of human construction and reflection. Ideas result from a person's activity and interaction with the world. Relationships and social interests affect how one learns, and people and their environments cannot be separated. Constructivism asks learners to take charge of their own learning. In advocating that students and designers take part in a continual process of social and individual renewal, this book adheres to the constructivist philosophy.

chapter features

Each chapter presents several features that are intended to give a holistic view of creativity.

- *Voice of Experience* Interviews with a variety of industry professionals that include their perception of creativity

- *Activities* A variety of assignments, ranging from short answer to full design assignments that enhance and expand upon the content

- *Creativity-Enhancing Activities* Suggestions for fostering creativity

- *DIN Challenge* End-of-chapter assignments that synthesize the content

- *Quotations* Insights from fashion design students and instructors, intended to exemplify the individual nature of creativity

introduction

An introductory chapter explains how to use the book and *DIN* to develop and record their ideas as assignments are completed. It offers practical advice for setting up a *DIN* as a physical or electronic notebook.

chapter 1

Chapter 1 elaborates on the concept of creativity. In place of a formal definition, common characteristics are given. Designers are encouraged to establish a broad and deep knowledge base. This chapter also includes a discussion on the arbiters of fashion and information on the evaluation and critique of creative products.

chapters 2 through 5

Creativity is a multifaceted concept, for which there is no single formula. There is a good deal of agreement, however, that suggests that creativity results from an interaction of factors. Among these are the environmental, cognitive, character trait, and motivational aspects. This book presents creativity as a confluence of these traits, but, for clarity, they are presented individually in Chapters 2 through 5. Chapter 2 considers the individual's environment, from the state of the design studio through support from family, peers, and even society. It includes a discussion of gaining inspiration from the environment as well as challenges that designers face in contributing to practices that sustain a healthy environment. Chapter 3 looks at the cognitive aspects of creativity, which can involve divergent or convergent thinking. Chapter 3 also takes into account the role technology plays in the apparel industry. Chapter 4 presents character traits that have been known to foster or inhibit creativity. It considers the strong emotional connections that are associated with producing creative products. Chapter 4 also examines meanings of dress, silhouettes, and colors. Chapter 5 discusses what motivates us to create. Intrinsic motivation, like designing for the pleasure of it, is generally thought to be the most conducive to creative designing. Extrinsic motivation, designing for fame or money, for example, can be counterproductive to creativity. Also included in this chapter is a discussion on play and the importance of downtime in a designer's daily life as well as deriving meaning and pleasure from designing for groups with special needs and for larger causes.

chapter 6

Although there are several design process methods and techniques, and many experienced designers do not consciously follow a step-by-step process at all, understanding your own design process can serve as an underpinning that can be referenced in challenging design situations. Chapter 6 introduces the holistic, phase, and problem-solving approaches to fashion design. Designers are encouraged to be loyal to their own processes but also flexible and open to other practices.

chapter 7

Chapter 7 considers creativity and the industry. In today's professional world, designing is rarely a solitary endeavor. Designers must work in consultation and communion with any number of production, sales, and marketing professionals. Chapter 7 discusses creativity as it relates to working in teams. It offers suggestions for assembling a successful creative team, and it encourages building upon members' strengths and identifying common goals. An enhanced version of the portfolio is introduced.

the overriding theme

In summary, the premise of the book is that everyone possesses the potential to be creative, but not every idea is necessarily creative. Creativity is complex and multifaceted. It is a lifestyle that stems from dedicated study, determination, and passion.

acknowledgments

I am deeply indebted to the many, many people who enabled me to write this book. They include the editors at Fairchild Books, Olga Kontzias, executive editor, and her associate, Jaclyn Bergeron, who invited me to become a Fairchild author; Elizabeth Marotta, my production editor, who oversaw the transformation of the manuscript into a book; and especially Sylvia Weber, my development editor. This book could never have been completed without her careful attention to every detail and her patience and guidance with this first-time author. I also thank Elizabeth Greenberg for her keen eye for photographic research and Carolyn Eckert for her inspired art direction.

I wish to express my appreciation for the many fashion design instructors and students who generously gave their time and expressed their perspectives on creativity. My gratitude is also extended to those apparel design professionals who allowed me to enter their places of business and disrupt their busy days with my many questions.

Special thanks go to my inspiring students who allowed me to publish their designs, projects, portfolio spreads, and illustrations. Theresia Dschida and Caroline Borucki were especially generous with their time and talents. I also thank Erika Neumayer, Miriam Carlson, Denise Headrick, Susan Wu, Michael Shallow, Anastacia Chmel, Jackie Turmel, Lydia Wawryzniak and Jane Arvis. I also want to thank my family for their interminable support.

Comments and feedback from the readers and peer reviewers, selected by the publisher, were extremely helpful in focusing the content. I am indebted to Kristeen Buchanan, Stephens College; Penny Collins, Woodbury University; Linda Gardner, Alabama A&M University; M. Jo Kallal, University of Delaware; Van Dyk Lewis, Cornell University; Mary Kawenski, Rhode Island School of Design; Nancy N. Lyons, South Dakota State University; Lisa Barona McRoberts, Louisiana State University; Doris Treptow, Savannah College of Art and Design; and Theresa Winge, Michigan State University.

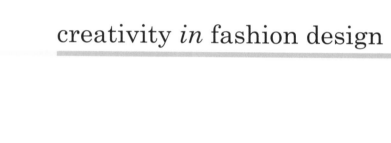

creativity *in* fashion design

"Sculptural layering and transparencies."
—Gilles Mendel,
    J. Mendel

Image of the inspiration board that fashion designer Gilles Mendel of J. Mendel used as inspiration for the Spring 2010 Ready to Wear (RTW) collection for New York Fashion Week. *Courtesy of WWD*

introduction

The world is changing rapidly—so rapidly that fashions that used to come into style once a generation are now fleeting. The marketplace is immediate and competitive. A short time after a style is seen on a Paris runway, it is in the stores and on the Internet at all price levels. Fashion used to trickle down from haute couturiers, but it now comes up in waves from urban streets, mass media, and an interconnected global web of ideas and cultures (Figure I.1). No longer is there the "must have" item of the season. Rather than following trends, people are dressing the way they see themselves. Fashion is becoming democratic. Consumers, with a mix and match aesthetic, want customized products that show their individuality (Binkley, 2010).

Fashion designers are not only asked to respond to these changes; if they are to maintain their relevance and livelihoods, they must lead them. To generate innovative apparel, designers are expected to immerse themselves in the zeitgeist of their time and connect this spirit to a spectrum of interrelated ideas past and present. Creativity and all it entails can be the driving force behind these innovative connections.

Figure I.1
Fashion today is an exciting explosion of influences and inspiration.
© iStockphoto.com/ Robert Churchill

1

understanding creativity

So what is **creativity**? It is connections and interactions. It is innovation and originality. More than these, however, it is what makes us human and what differentiates us from all other animals. Creativity adds to the richness and complexity of living, and when we are involved with it we feel that we are living life to the fullest (Csikszentmihalyi, 1996). "The excitement of the artist at the easel or the scientist in the lab comes close to the ideal fulfillment we all hope to get from life, and so rarely do" (p. 2). The fashion designer creating novel clothing designs could be added to the previous declaration. Fashion design is fun, invigorating, topical, and rewarding, but it is also hard work. It is challenging to develop new lines four to five times a year, and one can never rest on the laurels of the previous season. The designer continually strives for designs that are new, fresh, and original. An industry saying reminds us, "You are only as good as your next collection." Considering the demanding and changing world in which they work, designers cannot sit back and wait for ideas to come to them. They must be proactive about their designing. They must seek out situations that foster inspiration and do all they can to set the stage for innovative design.

The goals of this workbook are simple. They are to (1) inspire design and (2) empower designers. Creativity is used as the means of addressing these goals. Creativity is making connections and looking at things differently, and this can inspire design. Creativity asks us to look to character traits that foster new ideas, examine our motivations and thought processes, and establish a design-friendly environment, and this insight empowers designers. This is not a "how-to" book on being creative, though. There is no single best way to be creative, but designers can be intentional about innovative design. Today's understanding of creativity implies a purposeful generation of new ideas under direct control of the innovator (Von Stamm, 2008, p. 14).

Creativity is a highly positive term, but it is also misunderstood. There is a lot known about creativity, yet some hold that it is mystical and that through study of it, its magical powers will abate (Sternberg & Lubart, 1999). Some liken the concept of creativity to love, in that it is hard to define and that it is better not dissected, but this approach does not encourage individuals to take ownership of their creativity. By understanding creativity, designers can create environments that are conducive to innovation. They can practice concepts often associated with creative thinking, and they can determine what motivates them to design. Designers can identify character traits and design processes that have been found to foster creativity, and with this knowledge they can take an active role in finding inspiration for design.

Creativity in Fashion Design: An Inspiration Workbook is written for aspiring and practicing fashion designers. In the fashion design classroom, this book can be a valuable tool for the inspiration and design stages of garment generation. In a product development course, the book can offer constructive insight into the designer's role in the production process. The practicing designer can use the creativity concepts included in this book to inspire new avenues of design. Some academic fashion design programs and design houses focus on artistic expression while others express creativity through meeting the needs of a particular market. Most likely, you have found a design direction that works for you. This workbook is compatible with most design expression because the material contained herein does not attempt to tell designers what to create; rather, it gives them the underpinnings for understanding their role in the creative process.

Some may be concerned that learning the concepts of creativity will lessen the wonder and excitement inherent in fashion design. Designers have strong emotional connections to the products they create. That's often what gives them their drive and the willingness to commit long hours to the process. *Creativity in Fashion Design* is not intended to minimize this emotional connection or sterilize the process. Understanding creativity is not a prescriptive exercise. On the contrary, learning about creativity can contribute to enabling individuals to understand their own design process and realizing their full potential as designers. There is no right or wrong way to design or to create. This book is intended to augment your current successful design strategies and also inspire you to create some new ones. The exercises in this book are investigative and exploratory. In places, step-by-step instructions are included for concepts and activities. The directives are included for those who have not been introduced to that particular concept before and would like some first-time guidance. You are encouraged to experiment with the concepts and use the book in a manner that best suits you and your design process.

your dynamic inspiration notebook

As you read this workbook, you are expected to contribute to an inspiration notebook. Creating an inspiration notebook is a planned and intentional process that can be a valuable tool in inspiring design. Your *Dynamic Inspiration Notebook (DIN)* is a collection of ideas, clippings, tear sheets, images, photos, thoughts, notes, and sketches. Referring to its title, the *DIN* is characterized as (1) dynamic, (2) inspirational, and (3) a notebook. To be dynamic is to be vibrant, full of life, and vigorous, and the *DIN* is intended to be "alive" and teeming with ideas. Keeping up with the *DIN* enables you to have a constant rotation of fresh ideas and nearly limitless possibilities for combinations of those ideas. Every designer needs inspiration, a muse, or something to reflect on and ponder. The *DIN* is a planned way of creating that inspiration. It is intended to stimulate and motivate design. Entering pages into the *DIN* every day reminds the designer to be ever vigilant for ideas from a variety of sources. The word *notebook*—whether it describes a binder with loose leaf pages or a digital file—is used to imply that there is an intentionality to creating a *DIN*. As in a journal, individuals can add thoughts and feelings to the pages, but they also include assignments, notes, and research. It is intended to be organic, however, and not presented formally, as a portfolio might be.

The *Dynamic Inspiration Notebook* is a template for collecting, sorting, and combining ideas. It takes the idea-finding process a step further and provides designers with ways to maximize the creative potential of their selected information. The process of sorting and combining used in the *DIN* is modeled after data sorting and coding processes used in qualitative research (Rossman & Rallis, 1998). The *DIN* gives designers guidelines for working with the myriad ideas they accumulate. The *DIN* process aids the designer by:

- Making the journaling process intentional and habitual.

- Giving designers a clear plan on what to do with information after it is collected.

- Keeping information active and dynamic as contents are intended to be moved, used again, kept for years and reactivated, and/or deleted as the designer's sensibilities change.

- Encouraging connections among interrelated ideas.
- Encouraging connections among dissimilar ideas.

Undoubtedly, designers will develop their own inspiration processes as they gain more and more experience. Until then, there are six easy steps to creating and utilizing a dynamic inspiration notebook:

1. *Obtain* a three-ring notebook, or set up a digital notebook.
2. *Collect data* (images, thoughts, clippings, sketches, etc.) every day.
3. *Generate ideas* from the data.
4. *Conceptualize themes* from the ideas.
5. *Make connections* by combining themes.
6. *Create design(s)* suggested by combined themes.

three-ring notebook

You need a centralized location in which to keep all of your design materials together. Obtain a three-ring notebook that can accommodate 8½ × 11 inch sheets of paper. A soft-sided notebook works best as it is lightweight and fits easily in most backpacks and tote bags. This type of notebook is particularly handy because the cover can be completely flipped to the back while sketching. Also, purchase numerous pocket folders for your notebook that you can use for storing images until you have a chance to mount them on pages. Make copies using the *Ideas* template in the Appendix of this book. Punch holes in the pages and place them in your binder.

digital notebook

The *Dynamic Inspiration Notebook* can easily be created on the computer instead of in a binder.

Each completed *Ideas* page should be saved individually, and all *Ideas* files should be contained in one folder. Likewise, *Themes* and *Connections* pages should be saved and stored in self-named folders. Images utilized in your spreads can be scanned in or taken from the Internet. Digital photos can also be easily uploaded and stored in computer files. Software programs such as Adobe Illustrator, PhotoShop, InDesign or even Microsoft Word or PowerPoint can accommodate the kinds of files being used for your digital *DIN*. However, if you would like to manipulate the images, in addition to storing them, a graphic design software program such as Adobe Illustrator works best.

collect data

Each day, accumulate ideas, magazine clippings, thoughts, sketches, notes, and whatever else draws your interest, and place them in pocket or electronic folders. At the end of each day, mount the items in the space allocated on the *Ideas* pages. Your contributions to the *DIN* may be planned and on topic, as when including images and sketches gained from a trip to a museum exhibit. Other pages may include random collections of ideas that simply please or excite you (Figure I.2). Affix your images to the pages using glue sticks, mounting spray, or any other convenient method. A lightweight spray adhesive or removable tape is preferable because it will not permanently attach the item to the page. This allows for the possibility of moving and rearranging images. It is important to get in the habit of contributing to the

continued on page 7

IDEAS

List as many words as you can that embody the ideas on the spread.

Attach concepts in the space below.

1. _____
2. _____
3. _____
4. _____
5. _____
6. _____
7. _____
8. _____
9. _____
10. _____
11. _____
12. _____
13. _____
14. _____
15. _____
16. _____
17. _____
18. _____
19. _____
20. _____
21. _____
22. _____
23. _____

GOING GREEN

HATS!!

It's time for a revival of the CLASSICS

Figure I.2
Collect ideas, thoughts, and inspirations and place them in your *DIN*.

IDEAS

List as many words as you can that embody the ideas on the spread.

Attach concepts in the space below.

1. Sand
2. Sailing far away
3. Swimming
4. Rope trim
5. Active
6. Fun fish
7. Azure
8. String ties
9. Sails
10. Waves
11. Lighthouse
12. Espadrilles
13. Cerulean
14. Movement
15. Fuchsia
16. Romper
17. Rock and roll
18. Eighties
19. Retro
20. Neon brights
21. Tennis shoes
22. Punk
23. Repitition
24. Lines

Figure I.3

Generate *Ideas* from the data you have placed on the pages. List the ideas in the left hand column.

continued from page 4

DIN every day. The more accumulated ideas, the more possibilities there will be for connections and interactions. Also, the practice keeps your eye keen for details and inspirations.

generate ideas

As each page is filled, generate topics garnered from the pages and list them in the *Ideas* column on the far left of the two-page spread. List as many words as you can that embody the ideas evidenced on the pages. Try to use specific, not general, terms, and include fashion-oriented details like colors (puce, chartreuse, aubergine, etc.), silhouettes (a-line, bubble, sheath, etc.), and concepts (vintage, techno, retro, etc.). Also, include perceptions, such as friendly, exciting, active, and shocking. Generate an *Ideas* list for every several pages you complete (Figure I.3). Taking a moment to list your ideas will help you sort through all of the information that you have collected, and it also helps identify concepts that are important to you. It is a filtering exercise in which your raw, primary thoughts are caught in a net (the pages) and then sifted so vital ideas are captured and listed.

conceptualize ideas into themes

Make copies of the *Themes* sheet found in the Appendix and place them in your *DIN*. Review your *Ideas* lists and, on the *Themes* page, identify similar ideas and group them on one list to make a theme. The same idea can be used in more than one theme list. Title the theme (Figure I.4). The theme-finding exercise helps further identify ideas that are important to you. Similar ideas found repeatedly throughout the pages indicate a strong preference for a concept. The act of prioritizing ideas into themes also helps you develop your own personal style. Your design style will start to emerge as you build themes constructed from ideas that are relevant and important to you.

combine themes into connections

Make copies of the *Connections* sheet found in the Appendix and place them in your *DIN*. At the top of the sheet, list three themes in order to make a *connection*. These connections can be employed to inspire design. Combining similar themes can create a connection that is strong with detail and embellishment. Combining dissimilar themes allows for connections that you otherwise might not have thought of. This can lead to novelty and new design inspiration. Title your connection.

sketch your connection

In the space provided on the *Connections* page, sketch the design or designs inspired by the connection. Don't be concerned about creating polished illustrations at this time. Try to capture the essence of the contents of the three themes. Experiment with sketching both literal and figurative representations of the three themes (Figure I.5).

getting started

Let's get started with your *Dynamic Inspiration Notebook* today! Each chapter of *Creativity in Fashion Design* contains suggested assignments for the *DIN,* but you can begin now by collecting data about yourself, what you like, and what you are interested in and entering it in your *DIN*. This information will get you on the way

continued on page 10

THEMES

Revisit your IDEA spreads.
Group similar ideas and create a corresponding THEME

List like Ideas

1. Sand
2. Fish
3. Shells
4. Scales
5. Nature
6. Sails
7. Rope
8. Waves
9. Azure

Combine ideas into a THEME
and give it a title:
Nautical

List like Ideas

1. Fluffy
2. Soft
3. Ridges
4. Grooved
5. Pebbles
6. Smooth
7. Rough
8. Furry
9.

Combine ideas into a THEME
and give it a title:
Textured

List like Ideas

1. Dreamcatcher
2. Feathers
3. Headdress
4. Ecru
5. Beadwork
6. Body paint
7. Leather
8. Fringe
9. Animal

Combine ideas into a THEME
and give it a title:
Native American

List like Ideas

1. Shapes
2. Clean lines
3. Soft
4. Flowing
5. Solid
6. A-line
7. Symmetrical
8. Sheath
9. Smooth

Combine ideas into a THEME
and give it a title:
Simplicity

List like Ideas

1. Fuchsia
2. Neon brights
3. Romper
4. Dolman sleeves
5. Spandex
6. Rock and Roll
7. Ostentatious
8. Bangs
9. Bling

Combine ideas into a THEME
and give it a title:
The 80s

List like Ideas

1. Zebra
2. Snake
3. Tiger
4. Alligator
5. Dots
6. Spots
7. Stripes
8. Leopard
9. Scales

Combine ideas into a THEME
and give it a title:
Mixed Animal Prints

Figure I.4
Review your ideas. On
the *Themes* page, list
similar ideas and give
the list a title.

CONNECTIONS

Combine *similar* THEMES to add details and embellishment to inspiration OR
Combine *dissimilar* THEMES for novel inspiration

List three similar OR three dissimilar THEMES:

1.	2.	3.
Waves	*Car Wash*	*Monochromatic*

Combine THEMES into a CONNECTION and give it a title: *Urban Shores*

Sketch your CONNECTION:

Figure I.5

Make *Connections* with the themes. Combining
like themes will make a strong connection
that reflects your design style. Combining
unlike themes will break you out of established
patterns and lead you in a new direction. Title
your *Connection*. Sketch the concepts.
Illustration: Erika Neumayer

continued from page 7

to establishing your own design style. For example, a theme generated from the ideas "edgy," "shocking," and "vibrant" will evolve into a different design voice from a theme generated from the ideas "gentle," "mellow," and "soothing." And combining the two themes might inspire something really unexpected! So, to get started, create pages answering the question: *Who am I as a designer?*

the workbook format

Just as individuals must be proactive in their designing, readers should expect to actively form their understanding of creativity. Navigating this book will require full participation. This is a workbook, and readers are encouraged to carry it with them, write in it, and interact with the ideas presented. There are multiple opportunities to engage with the contents. Each chapter includes:

- An expectation that you will contribute to your *DIN* every day with both planned and spontaneous data. Many of the workbook's activities are contingent upon having a considerable amount of material in the *DIN*.

- Activities to be completed in the workbook and/or in your *DIN*. They are part of the instructional material and are instrumental in presenting the content.

- Activities that expand upon the content. They ask you to go beyond the stated material and explore, in depth, new avenues for inspiration and design.

- Creativity-enhancing activities that encourage you to practice fostering your creativity.

- A *DIN* challenge. This activity, found at the end of every chapter, synthesizes the material and connects content with *DIN* projects and other chapter activities.

Treat this workbook as you would a tool for enhancing your creativity. You are encouraged to write in it, make notes, add comments, and complete activities.

digital camera

As you begin accumulating images for your *DIN*, you will find that a digital camera can be a designer's best ally. It is said that a picture is worth a thousand words, and it is especially true when creating a designer's notebook. Get in the habit of carrying one with you everywhere. You never know when or where a great design idea is lurking. If creating a paper-based *DIN*, digital pictures can be printed and added to your notebook. If creating a digital *DIN*, pictures are easily uploaded and stored on the computer.

design integrity

As mentioned previously, it is essential that designers be connected to the milieu in which they live and work, and the *DIN* is intended to be used as a source of inspiration for design. This indicates that, inevitably, designers' products are impacted by what designers learn and see. However, this does not suggest that designers have the desire or the intention to expressly copy another's work. On the contrary, the *DIN* process is developed so that the inspiration for design is derived from the individual creating the design. It is true that inspiration is found everywhere, from attending a momentous art exhibition, to examining ordinary household objects, to viewing another designer's collection, but creative inspiration comes from the interaction of these ideas. "The fundamental mechanism of innovation is the way things come together and connect" (Burke, 1996, p. 5). It is these interactions, uniquely directed by each individual designer, that give a designer his or her personal style. These connections also help move the field forward by taking existing ideas and building and expanding upon them.

Designers should not violate the copyright of material they use in the *DIN*. Most images found in print and on the Internet are copyrighted. In general, designers can use these images for their own personal use in a compilation like the *DIN* or in collages and storyboards created for design assignments. Much of this data can also be used in the classroom to aid in discussions and presentations. Designers may not, however, use copyrighted images for works that will be published, disseminated, or sold.

let's create!

Creativity in Fashion Design: An Inspiration Workbook takes the fashion designer on a journey using creativity concepts as the impetus for design inspiration. This workbook considers creativity in terms of the knowledge, thought processes, motives, attitudes, character traits, and interactions with the environment that come together in the generation of innovative fashion design. This knowledge can empower the designer with the capacity to make associations and connections that will inspire design.

Let's create! Be creative! Enjoy creativity!

1 creativity *and* fashion design

Creativity is the backbone of fashion design. Its elusive, yet intriguing, characteristics make it a natural component of the enigmatic world of fashion, and the malleable and adaptive nature of the concept makes it uniquely applicable to the ever-changing apparel field. Creativity is a ubiquitous term that is called upon to address many of fashion's more difficult dilemmas and design problems. It is hard to imagine a cutting-edge fashion that is not also creative. Creativity is often a criterion for fashion design assignments in school, projects in design competitions, and fashions for runway exhibitions. But what is creativity, really?

Creativity is a common and maybe overused word, yet it is hard to define. Some view creativity as a problem-solving process, and others consider it a form of self-expression. Some consider it dependent on a group of psychological and motivational factors, and others consider it manifested by people and process. In actuality, it is all of these things and more. Despite an abundance of research confirming these creativity attributes, there is no definitive definition of creativity. One will not be found in this workbook either. The fundamental nature of creativity rebels against being limited by a universal definition. Individuals and groups can, however, develop their own understanding of creativity. Part of the allure of creativity is that designers feel a personal connection to it. The components of creativity apply to their distinct situations and specific design challenges.

understanding creativity

When fashion design students and instructors were interviewed to determine their perspectives about creativity, it was discovered that most were quite confident of their understanding of creativity; however, their definitions of the concept were not comprehensive, and they varied widely among members of the group (Jennings,

(opposite)

Piece of foam crumpled up.

Fashion designer Italo Zucchelli's inspiration for the Fall 2009 Calvin Klein menswear collection. *Courtesy of Fairchild/ Condé Nast/Calvin Klein*

OBJECTIVES

— To discover common components of creativity

— To be able to define creativity for yourself and your group

— To explore creativity as a confluence of traits that work together

— To recognize a knowledge base in the apparel field

— To identify the arbiters of fashion design

— To investigate the evaluation and critique of fashion design

13

2006). Within a class, group, or company, an understanding of creativity is essential so that all may work toward a common goal. If a professor calls for creativity on a fashion design assignment, it is beneficial for the entire class to have a unified understanding of the directive. If entries in a design competition are judged on creativity, designers want to comprehend what is asked of them. Also, by understanding creativity, designers can seek situations that foster it and avoid those that hinder it. Creativity is highly individual, and what resonates for you may not be relevant for another; but deepening your own understanding, and discovering others' perceptions, can aid the design process by (1) opening new avenues for inspiration, (2) ensuring that all involved in a particular project have a unified vision of the expected outcome, and (3) empowering designers to make the most of their creative potential.

what is creativity?

Although there is no universally agreed-upon definition of creativity, there are components that are intrinsic to the concept (Figure 1.1). Key aspects of creativity include (Cropley, 2002):

- Novelty
- Effectiveness
- Elegance
- Communication
- Emotion
- Surprise
- Ethicality

novelty

Synonymous with originality, **novelty** is considered to be a core component of creativity. It can be described as newness, uniqueness, and innovation. A novel design is one with a fresh approach, or one that departs from that which is familiar. In fashion design, novelty can be widely relative. What is novel for one group may be considered ordinary for another. Depending on the ultimate channel for the novel concept, an idea that veers only degrees from the familiar may be accepted more readily than an idea that completely departs from what is currently known. Examples of this abound when considering the cyclical aspect of fashion. Fashions have a tendency to evolve over a period of time rather than pop into existence. Novelty in fashion design may be more concerned with the degree of originality the target audience will accept, rather than a total departure from what is currently known.

Creativity is very important. You don't want to just come out with the same stuff all of the time because then you're not keeping up with anything. In this industry you have to be creative. It's very important to always be coming up with new things, putting a different twist on it. —*Fashion Design Student*

Figure 1.1
Gianni Versace
incorporates the
iconic images of
Marilyn Monroe and
James Dean in the
ironic juxtaposition
of pop culture and
couture in this novel,
elegant, surprising,
and — most would
say — creative gown.
Getty Images

effectiveness

Effectiveness connotes that the product works, achieves some end, or solves some problem. At the most concrete level, this considers whether the garment can be donned and used as bodily cover. Many garments have a practical application. A raincoat should protect the wearer from getting wet. A winter coat should keep the wearer warm in cold weather. Most garments are not created for pure practicality, though. Effectiveness may also be considered in the aesthetic, artistic, psychological, and/or spiritual sense. For example, business suits are made to cover the body, but they also are designed to project authority and ability. Athletic sportswear is made to stretch with limb and muscle movement, but it is also expected to be aesthetically pleasing to the wearer. A wearable art piece would be effective if it makes the desired artistic statement. The effectiveness of a fashion design relates to what degree the garment fulfills its reason for existing.

Effectiveness can also be related to the quality of workmanship found in an apparel item. If stitches break when the garment is worn, or if lining is showing where it should not be, the design cannot be described as effectively executed. Effectiveness of workmanship is related to the quality denoted by the brand. Couture garments are expected to have superior workmanship that often includes impeccable hand stitching. Even if the stitching in a couture garment is neat and even, it might not be considered effective if it does not contain the hallmark tailoring techniques of high fashion design.

elegance

When people think of elegance, they often think of red-carpet gowns and royal attire. The term is often used when describing the rich and famous. Considering fashion creativity though, elegance is not restricted to the expensive and exclusive. **Elegance** refers more to the overall composure of a garment than the price of the materials. An elegant garment looks as though its elements fell perfectly into place, and it is thought that no other design tactics could have served the purpose as well. It is not contrived or overwrought. It makes *beautiful sense*. Regardless of design influence—grunge and street attire can be elegant—an elegant garment looks easy, even if it is particularly complicated to pattern and produce. Elegance is the elusive quality of grace and chic that can make average designs spectacular and make striving designers noteworthy.

communication

Many in creativity research agree that for a product to be deemed creative, it must be communicated to others (Cropley, 2001; Csikszentmihalyi, 1996). The **communication** of creative products can include entering garments into design competitions, exhibiting fashions on the runway, and showing collections at markets. Communication can validate a creative idea. Can a garment be considered creative if no one other than the designer sees it? Individuals can produce products created solely for personal use, but when a product is disseminated, the industry benefits.

With communication comes evaluation and feedback. Designers can take what they have learned from others to enhance their designs. When designers continually improve their designs, through the nurturance and guidance of others, it makes a stronger, more relevant industry. Ideas build upon one another, they evolve, and this creates advances in the field. "The works (and the workers) so judged come to occupy the most important spot in the dialectic: They actually cause a refashioning of the domain. The next generation of students, or talents, now work in a domain that is different, courtesy of the achievements of highly creative individuals. And in this manner the dialectic of creativity continues" (Gardner, 1993, p. 38).

emotion

Emotion plays a vital role in fashion design, but sometimes creativity research overlooks this important **affective** or expressive aspect. Designers become emotionally connected to the design process and their products for several reasons. First, they often use personal aspects of themselves and their lives as design inspiration. For example, they have been known to draw insight from where they grew up, their favorite travel destinations, and family members' hand crafts, such as quilting, crochet, and knitting. In this way, designers' products are extensions of their lives and environments. With such close affiliations, designers are bound to be attached to their creative products.

In addition, designers often spend inordinate amounts of time and energy on their creations. Individuals often can be found in the design lab after hours and in the studio sewing while their peers are relaxing. The enormous devotion designers have to their craft is manifested in close emotional ties to their products. Every new design is a creative birth, and, as such, it is treated with regard and devotion. This personal investment can be a source of heartache when designs are harshly judged and critically evaluated, but it mostly gives designers joy and a sense of fulfillment that other means of employment cannot duplicate.

surprise

Few would venture to suggest that surprise alone could describe creativity. In fact, the terms **pseudocreativity** (Cattell & Butcher, 1968) and **quasicreativity** (Heinelt, 1974) were coined to suggest creativity that lacks discipline and does not fulfill any purpose other than to shock the observer. The element of **surprise** can contribute to the understanding of creativity, though, because of the intense response it causes. Designers do not want a lukewarm reaction to their work. Most want their designs to instigate an enthusiastic buzz of conversation. Adding the element of surprise, amazement, astonishment, or wonder to design can add excitement to a collection (Figure 1.2).

ethicality

Although it is not explicitly inherent in most definitions of creative design, it is generally understood that creativity is a positive force in the apparel industry. Creative designers, practicing ethical design tactics, do not intentionally cause harm to others or the environment. From the materials used to the human labor needed to produce apparel, **ethicality** considers what is fair and decent.

Which of the seven components resonate with you? Consider the concepts listed and add your own observations to craft your perception of creativity. Compare your ideas with others in your class or group. Define the term.

creativity is _____

_____

_____

_____

_____

_____

_____

How can each of the characteristics of creativity be represented in fashion design? Activity 1.1 asks you to find examples of creative fashion designs.

Figure 1.2
The paper-based material, Andy Warhol-inspired commercial print, and throwaway fashion aesthetic are surprising elements of the "Souper Dress" from the 1960s.
© *The Metropolitan Museum of Art/Art Resource, NY*

Understanding Creativity

The seven creativity characteristics are included in various definitions of creativity. Each can contribute to our understanding of the concept. Collect images in your *DIN* that embody each of the creativity characteristics. Can you find images that contain all seven attributes? Select one of the images you've found and place it here. State why it contains qualities of each creativity characteristic.

_____

_____

_____

_____

_____

_____

_____

_____

who is creative?

You are creative. Creativity is not reserved for the acclaimed and the famous. Unlike **talent**, which can be considered in terms of specific aptitudes that are innate in some and not in others, creativity is present in all human beings. Creativity is the energy that can be described as putting the heart and soul into talent. "It is regarded as a normally distributed trait that is found in everybody although to differing degrees in different people, highly in some, less in others, and somewhere in between for yet others. It is impossible to have zero creativity just as it is impossible to have zero intelligence" (Cropley, 2002, pp. 10–11). So, the challenge is not to acquire creativity, but it is to maximize the potential of the creativity that all individuals already inherently possess.

creativity as a confluence of traits

There are innumerable strategies, techniques, and systems for enhancing creativity. Many books and online sites are devoted to the topic. From the plethora of information available, it becomes obvious that there is no single method for enhancing creativity, and no solitary component can account for the complex process that leads to a creative product (Cropley, 2002, p. 146). Researchers (Gardner, 1993; Sternberg & Lubart, 1996) generally agree that creativity results from, and is enhanced by a confluence of interrelated and interacting traits. *Creativity in Fashion Design* recognizes that creativity is multifaceted. This chapter acknowledges the need for a broad base of knowledge of the apparel field. Additional chapters consider (1) the environment, (2) cognitive aspects, (3) character traits, (4) motivations, (5) design processes, and (6) the apparel field as influencing the dimension of fashion creativity. Optimum conditions for creative design exist when all creativity-fostering aspects are present. "Where this is not the case (probably the usual state of affairs) different combinations of favourable and unfavourable circumstances would hinder or facilitate creativity in different ways" (Cropley, 2002, p. 146). For this reason, some ideas may resonate more with some individuals and others more with other individuals. You are invited to take an individualized approach to fulfilling your creative potential, and this book is intended to assist in that effort.

Is your creativity multifaceted? Activity 1.2 asks you to consider components of your own creativity.

knowledge base

A **knowledge base** in the fashion design field does not guarantee creativity, but it is not possible to sustain a pattern of creative design without such a base. Of course, certain singular bursts of creativity can occur, but new insights are rare without an understanding of what is already known (Nickerson, 1999). "People who do noteworthy creative work in any given domain are almost invariably very knowledgeable about the domain" (p. 409). Popular quotations abound extolling the value in hard work and preparation. Thomas Edison's bon mot, "Genius is 1 percent inspiration and 99 percent perspiration," has certainly motivated many designers to work hard at the underpinnings of creativity. Similarly, Louis Pasteur noted that groundwork is a necessary part of the innovation process when he declared, "Chance favors the prepared mind."

Your Creativity Sphere

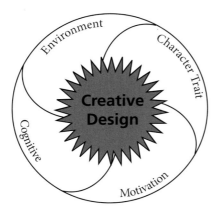

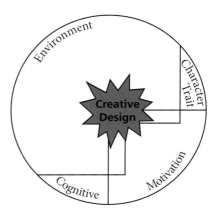

Designer A

For designer A, all creativity components combine together in nearly equal proportions to provide optimum conditions for multifaceted solutions to design problems. The resulting fashion design is creative.

Designer B

Designer B has high motivation and a very nourishing environment, but fear of failure (character trait) and a lack of a broad knowledge (cognitive) base are inhibiting the creative process. The resulting creative design is not all it could be.

Your Creativity Sphere

Consider your knowledge base, environment, cognitive methods, character traits, motivation, understanding of design processes, and relationship with the fashion industry. Are all of these facets fostering your creativity? Complete your creativity sphere by labeling the significance of each component. Allow the most space for those aspects that have the greatest influence on how you design.

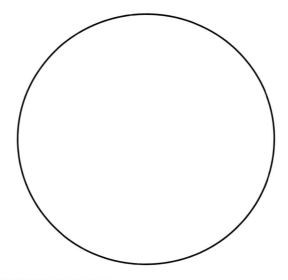

Contextual knowledge makes a designer's work easier. Imagine the products generated by a designer who did not have an understanding of how a garment is donned and worn! With the exception of certain ironic and statement pieces, a fashion design, no matter how innovative, would not be considered a success if it could not be put on the body. Neckline openings must be large enough to accommodate head size; sleeves must be designed and patterned so the wearer is not immobilized; and skirt sweeps must be generous enough to allow for wearers' strides. A basic knowledge base enables individuals to make garments that are viable, but the combinations and associations that can be made with a strong base can inspire creative design. For example, designers often look to the past for inspiration. Individuals familiar with the Renaissance period may be inclined to incorporate components of the corset in each of their lines. However, designers versed on dress through the ages can draw inspiration from ancient Roman togas for one collection and Elizabethan ruffs for another and combine aspects of the toga and the ruff for yet another. Each bit of knowledge enables a connection to be made and each connection is a new opportunity for fresh ideas (Figure 1.3).

Figure 1.3
A person with three bits of knowledge can make three connections, but a person with six bits of knowledge is able to make fifteen connections, and this aspect multiplies exponentially as more knowledge is gained. *Courtesy of the author's collection*

Creative people think in a circular fashion rather than a linear fashion. So, they can make connections from seemingly unrelated information. But, there is a relationship in everything, in every experience, and everything that they do. —*Fashion Design Instructor*

Figure 1.4
Women of the late 1800s increasingly worked outside the home and participated in recreational athletic activities. This tendency contributed to the pared down fashion silhouette of the time. Although the expansive crinoline had fallen out of style, women were loathe to discard the dresses that covered them, so they pulled excess fabric to the back for a bustled silhouette. The Charles Worth gown below features the generously draped bustle and elaborate embellishment of gowns worn at French and English courts during the period. © The Metropolitan Museum of Art/Art Resource, NY

A fashion designer's domain-specific knowledge should include:

- The historical aspects of dress and the underlying conditions that lead to developments in fashion.

- An appreciation of the cultural aspects of dress and their inherent meanings.

- An understanding of the origins of, uses for, and care of fabrics and textiles.

- An awareness of legendary designers and the impact they made on the field.

- Familiarity with silhouettes, style terminology, and sources of information.

- Knowledge of the skills of the discipline, such as patternmaking, dressmaking, and tailoring.

- An aptitude for the technology used and developed in the field.

- An extensive understanding of one's customer base or audience.

- An understanding of anatomy and the proportion and movement of the human body.

- The guiding principles that underpin all design.

This knowledge is not gained quickly. It takes patience and devotion to develop a deep and broad base. Most disciplines are never really mastered, but continual learning always keeps the material fresh and exciting. Acquiring an ever-increasing body of knowledge gives the learner confidence, even as it stimulates inspiration. University courses within fashion design programs address many of the aspects listed here, and industry experience expands on the knowledge gained from coursework.

historical aspects of dress

Designers look to history for several reasons. First, there is no reason to reinvent the wheel, as the saying goes, each time a garment is made. Past eras reveal much in the way of clothing construction, sewing techniques, textiles used, and skills developed, and many of these tactics still have relevance in the apparel field today (Figure 1.4). The aesthetic aspects of dress are also explored. Dress is often considered as an art form that can reveal much about the cultural sensibilities of an age. When approaching the study of historical costume, designers rarely look at the dress of a period in isolation. They also consider the circumstances of when it was worn. Economic conditions, political climate, social structure, religion, technology, and other aspects are investigated, and these components can inform how certain items can be viewed and utilized today.

cultural aspects of dress

As with the study of historical dress, cultural aspects of dress are considered within the broad context of how a garment is developed and worn (Figure 1.5). Many cultural traditions evolve out of necessity, and skills in fabric construction, dyeing, and printing often originate from the indigenous natural resources available to the people. Designers want to ascertain, and be respectful of, the meanings behind the cultural aspects of dress. In this way, when they reference cultural facets in their designing, they honor the embodied traditions of the work.

textiles

Fibers have inherent properties that determine their end uses. For example, hydrophilic fibers, such as cotton and wool, absorb moisture so, most often, they are comfortable to wear. Hydrophobic fibers, such as polyester and acrylic, do not readily absorb moisture, so they are prone to static and can feel clammy against the skin. Fiber and fabric properties suggest how garments will drape, feel, and be worn, and also how they can be cleaned. Designers wanting to avoid returns at retail will familiarize themselves with fiber and fabric characteristics, so they can choose fabrics that are compatible with the ultimate end use of the product. In addition, new textile innovations are continually being introduced that can increase a fabric's comfort, performance, and/or aesthetics. Designers need to keep abreast of these developments.

legendary designers

When you think of iconic designers, Christian Dior, Miuccia Prada, Narciso Rodriguez, Tracy Reese, or Carolina Herrera may come to mind. Or it could be American designers Calvin Klein and Ralph Lauren. Regardless, a league of fashion designers has paved the way for designers today. For example, Coco Chanel is often credited with ridding women's fashion of constricting corsets and introducing menswear fabrics into women's apparel (Figure 1.6). Each designer that has come before or is in the limelight today has made a contribution to what we know as contemporary fashion.

Figure 1.5 (above) Traditional Japanese kimonos are made from a single, narrow length of cloth. The meticulously screened silk fabric was considered a precious resource, so the entire length was used. No fabric was cut away as waste. This Christian Dior creation is an amalgam of Japanese influences, but the drape of a single length of uncut silk fabric acknowledges the kimono as its inspiration. *Courtesy of WWD/Giovanni Giannoni*

Figure 1.6 (left) Coco Chanel ushered new styling into the twentieth century. She advocated simplicity and comfort over the structured silhouettes that came before. Her soft tailoring complemented, rather than restricted the female form, and it epitomized the independent modern woman. *Courtesy of Condé Nast Archive*

silhouettes, terminology, and sources for information

Terminology forms the language of the field. There are categories of silhouettes (e.g., tent, hourglass, trapeze), garment styles (e.g., jodhpurs, culottes, peacoat), and garment details (e.g., convertible collar, French cuff, welt pocket). Fibers, fabrics, and finishes all have descriptors that reveal specific details about their properties. Although individuals will want to become acquainted with the terminology most often used in their areas, the information available is copious. It is just as important to know how to find information when you need it. Designers need to know how to search library databases and online resources. They may also consider obtaining desk copies of references such as *The Fairchild Book of Fashion Production Terms (2011)*, *The Fairchild Dictionary of Fashion* (2003), and *Fairchild's Dictionary of Textiles* (1996).

Activity 1.3 invites you to discover some of those databases that contain vast amounts of helpful information for designers.

skills of the discipline

Skills of the apparel design discipline include patternmaking, grading, marker making, cutting, sewing, technical designing, and pricing. In general, the smaller the company, the more probable it is that designers will have to perform these tasks also. In most average-sized or larger companies, however, designers are usually not expected to have advanced expertise in all of these areas, but they will want to have an understanding of what each job entails. For example, it is the marker maker's job to maximize the usage of fabric in a garment. If a designer consistently designs styles that necessitate unwieldy pattern pieces, the marker maker may not be able to make an efficient marker. Too much fabric will then be required, and the cost of the garment may rise beyond the manufacturer's price point. A good designer is a team player who enables all the members of the product development chain to do their job well.

technology

Technology is found in nearly every aspect of the apparel field. From new developments in fiber and fabric technology to upgrades in production and presentation software, technology is ever-present and continually advancing. Apparel designers are lifelong learners. They realize that their learning does not stop after they are out of school. They will continually have to upgrade their skills and refine their knowledge to keep up with progress in the field.

audience

Today's consumers are informed. They know what they want, and they usually have choices in where to get it. Product developers research their markets so they can align their products with the needs of their consumers. Even concept pieces, aesthetic designs, and wearable art are created in response to a need or void. Sometimes it is researched and sometimes it is intuitive, but perceptive designers always respond to their audience.

the human body

Most fashion is meant to be worn on the body, and that simple fact can present the designer with innumerable challenges, one of which is that the body is three-dimensional and most fabrications are not. Knowledge of anatomy and kinesthetics, or body movement, can provide guidance for designers attempting to contort a

continued on page 27

Searching Online Databases for Information and Inspiration

The Metropolitan Museum of Art and the Victoria and Albert Museum are great resources for apparel-related information. Both museums also maintain vast searchable databases of art works, costume, furniture, glass, metalwork, jewelry, textiles, ceramics, and more that provide nearly limitless avenues for design inspiration. Individual database records usually contain an image, origination date of the piece, and background information about the object. The museums' online sites include many additional features, such as educational sections (e.g., caring for your textiles), audio and video recordings (e.g., analysis of a costume designed by Nicholas Roerich for the ballet *The Rite of Spring*), and opportunities to interact and contribute ideas (e.g., in advance of the exhibition *Wedding Dresses,* the Victoria and Albert Museum invited viewers to upload three photographs showing their wedding fashions).

Take an online visit to the Metropolitan Museum of Art (www.metmuseum.org) or the Victoria and Albert Museum (www.vam.ac.uk), and investigate the site. After you become familiar with the museum's online offerings, respond to the following:

• What is the layout of the site? Could you navigate it easily and find the information you were looking for?

_____

_____

• List three features that you were surprised to find there.

_____

_____

_____

• List three pieces of information that you were able to add to your fashion knowledge base.

_____

_____

_____

• Add three images from the site to your *DIN*. List the ideas here.

_____

_____

_____

• How can the site enable you to gain information and inspiration and foster your creativity?

_____

_____

continued on page 26

continued from page 25

ACTIVITY 1.3

Of course, there are many more museums that can inform and inspire. Many focus specifically on a particular art style or culture, for example. Do your own investigation and identify three or more additional museums with online databases and resources that can benefit you as a designer. Share your results with the group, and create a resource list for all to refer to.

Database	Description	Website Address
Metropolitan Museum of Art	New York City museum with huge costume collection as well as artistic, historical, and cultural pieces	www.metmuseum.org
Victoria and Albert Museum	London museum that is great for art and design. Very broad and diverse collection.	www.vam.ac.uk

An entire collection can be inspired by one great find! This intricate ship pendant conjures visions of a sailor-inspired line of designs. The chains, masts, sails, and waves can be incorporated in numerous creative ways to expand on the concept. © V&A Images, Victoria and Albert Museum

continued from page 24

fabrication to fit the curves and swells of the body. Muscle and bone structures give clues to how the body moves and to the amount of fabric allowance required so as not to impede motion.

Knowledge of the human form also assists the designer in knowing what looks good on the body. Fashion illustrations are sketched with reference to the length of the human head. An average, real-life figure stands seven to eight heads tall. On the contrary, the **fashion figure** is often illustrated to be nine and one-half heads tall. It is an elongated, exaggerated, and stylized version of the human figure. Also, the fashion figure's proportions, subject to the whims of fashion trends, are frequently altered (Abling, 2007, p. 8) (Figure 1.7). The human form is distorted further when styles created for distinctive body types, such as plus size and petite figures, are illustrated with little or no relevance to the intended wearer's silhouette. Designers should refer often to real body proportions to ensure that their designs are flattering on the body as well as in a fashion sketch.

guiding principles

There are time-honored guidelines for design. They include the golden ratio, the elements and principles of design, and color theory. These principles, relevant to nearly all design, form a solid underpinning that the designer can rely on and refer to.

guiding principles of fashion design

Exploration of the guiding principles of design also offers potential new avenues of inspiration. They should be considered tools, not rules (Hunter, 2007, p. 100):

> They may also be viewed as a checklist, against which a designer can constructively critique his or her work. There are no "right" or "wrong" options. Ultimately, it is the designer's good taste, ability to "interpret" fashion trends into what their target customer wants, and skill in pulling the components together that results in winning designs.

golden ratio

The discovery that the structure of the human body followed a certain rule of proportions heavily influenced ancient Greek art (Figure 1.8). Classic Grecian

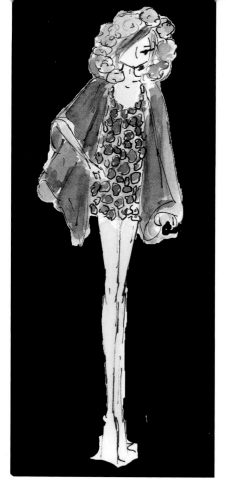

Figure 1.7
Fashion illustrations emphasize mood, attitude, and fantasy. *Illustration: Miriam Carlson*

Figure 1.8
The Nashville Parthenon is a replica of the Parthenon in Athens, Greece. Like the original, it prominently features aspects of the golden ratio. The many rectangles seen in the façade, the space between the columns, for example, meticulously adhere to the length/width ratio and repeat the pleasing proportion. *© Mark E. Gibson/ Corbis*

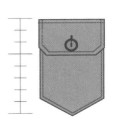

Figure 1.9
Look at the decorative stitching on jean pockets. You will find that the stitching is most often placed in accordance with the golden ratio. Examine pocket flaps and pocket shapes for this same rule of proportion.

Figure 1.10
Appliqués, embroidery, and other design features are pleasing to the eye if placed according to the golden ratio.

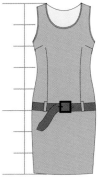

Figure 1.11
This guideline has numerous applications in fashion design. For example, consider the length of a three-quarter sleeve in relation to the length of the arm; the width of a skirt border in relation to the length of a skirt; or the placement of the hip styleline in relation to the length of the dress, shown here.

Figure 1.12
Consider the length of the dress in relation to the height of the figure. The context of a design becomes especially important in photography. For example, will the length of the train on a bridal gown disrupt the pleasing proportion of a picture?

sculptures are still enjoyed today, in part because their proportions are so pleasing to the eye. That same rule of agreeable proportions found in the arts can be found throughout nature—in the exquisitely balanced wings of a butterfly, for example. This dominating principle of proportion translates to a ratio of roughly three parts to five parts of an eight part whole. So, if you divide any length by eight, three of the parts will be in pleasing proportion to the remaining five parts. This guideline is called the **golden ratio** or *golden mean,* and designers can utilize it to gain insight into creating harmonious designs.

Consider four levels of proportion when referencing the golden ratio (Ericson, 2009, pp. 37–41):

- The proportions within one part. For example, compare a pocket's width in proportion to its length (Figure 1.9).
- The proportions among parts. For example, examine design features within a garment, such as the size of embellishments in relation to one another (Figure 1.10).
- The proportion of one part to the whole. For example, look at the length of the bodice compared to the length of the entire dress (Figure 1.11).
- The proportion of the whole garment in relation to its context. For example, take the height of the person into consideration when determining the length of a garment (Figure 1.12).

The golden ratio is derived from the Fibonacci series of numbers. See Activity 1.4 for further explanation of the principle and for insight into how the Fibonacci series can inspire design.

elements and principles of design

Like the golden ratio, the elements and principles of design are guidelines that are referenced in many disciplines, including architecture, art, visual merchandising, interior design, and fashion design. The **elements of design** are the raw components integral to every design. Line, color, shape, texture, and pattern serve as the foundation upon which fashion styling can be built (Figure 1.13).

line

Line refers either to the boundaries of a garment or to the style lines, seaming, and detailing that partition areas within a garment. The placement, spacing, and direction of a line can draw the eye to, across, or around a given area; thus, it can create visual illusions that can make a body appear shorter, taller, slimmer, or wider.

color

Color refers to the eye's interpretation of the white light reflected from a given surface. Specific colors are the result of the interaction of their attributes, namely hue (basic color family), value (lightness or darkness), and chroma (brightness). Color can evoke psychological and emotional responses and can also create optical illusions. In fashion, a collection's color palette must be appropriate for its designated end-use, season, location, and target customer.

texture

Texture refers to the surface appearance and **hand**, or feel, of a fabric. A fabric's texture is dictated by its fibers, yarns, construction, finish, and surface design.

continued on page 31

Using the Golden Ratio to Make Connections to Math and Nature

The golden ratio is derived from the Fibonacci series, which is a series of numbers whereby each new number results from adding the two previous numbers. For example, in the following list of numbers: 0, 1, 1, 2, 3, 5, 8, 13, 21, 34, the sum of 3 + 5 is 8, the sum of 5 + 8 is 13, and the sum of 8 + 13 is 21 (Ericson, 2009, pp. 37–41). The principle is achieved by calculating the ratio between any two sequential numbers in the Fibonacci series. Select a number from the series and divide it by the number before it. The resulting decimal figure will always be close to 1.618 or roughly three parts to five parts.

A spiral is created when the Fibonacci sequence is visualized as squares on a grid. The sides of each square on the grid correspond with a Fibonacci number and the spiral is created by drawing arcs connecting the opposite corners of each square. This spiral is found repeatedly in nature, as in the distribution of seeds of a sunflower, the growth pattern of a pine cone, or the expanding curve of a nautilus shell, and it can also have interesting applications in fashion design. For example, the width of a flounce on a skirt could increase proportionately as it winds around the body.

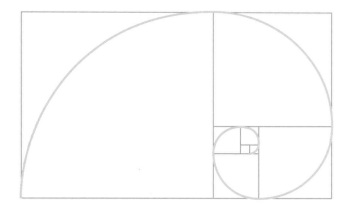

Don't hesitate to look to other disciplines, such as science and math, for inspiration. How will you interpret this graceful curve in your fashion designs?

Basic mathematical formulas are discovered in familiar rhythms found in nature. The Fibonacci sequence is revealed in the growth of the nautilus shell, the scales of a pineapple, and the florets of a flower, and it can also be the impetus for the flowering of a fashion design.
© iStockphoto.com/ Michael Siu

continued on page 30

continued from page 29

ACTIVITY 1.4

Select the sunflower, pine cone, nautilus shell, butterfly, or another article from nature. Take a close look at how the Fibonacci sequence is characterized. Make use of the thumbnails below to sketch series of designs inspired by these natural arrangements and the golden ratio and/or spiral.

Sketches

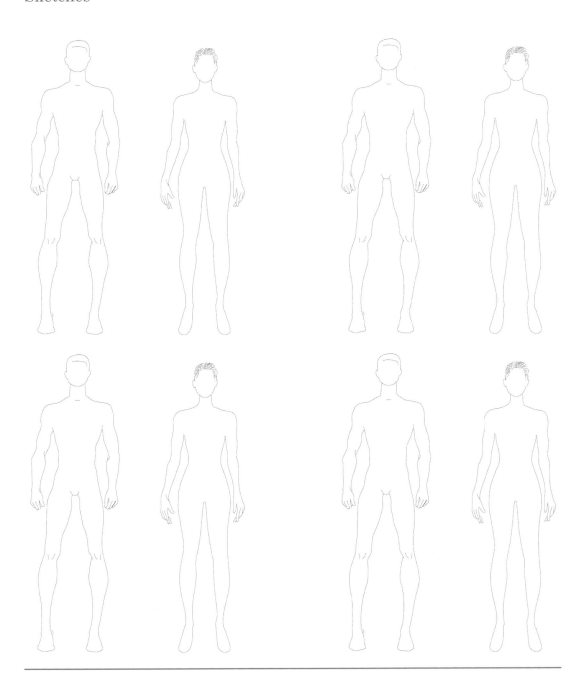

continued from page 28

Figure 1.13

How do the elements of design – line, color, shape, texture, and pattern – enhance the design of this creation by Alexander McQueen? *Courtesy of WWD/Mauricio Miranda*

Common terms used to describe fabric texture include: crisp, dry, lofty, nubby, scratchy, smooth, silky, spongy, and rough. A fabric's texture significantly influences its end use and should be considered prior beginning the design process.

shape

Shape refers to the form resultant from perceived boundaries external to or within a garment. **Silhouette** is used to describe a garment's outer shape. Commonly encountered garment silhouettes include: A-line, hourglass, wedge, and tube. Consistent shapes, created within a garment with style lines, trimming, and pattern pieces, such as pockets and collars, can contribute to an overall harmonious design.

patterns

Patterns are created by arranging shapes, lines, textures, prints, and/or design elements. They can be scaled to be in proportion to the wearer and the shapes within a garment. Large prints are broken up and distorted by lots of seaming. Small prints are often used for children's wear because they are compatible with a small body frame. In general, complicated prints complement simple shapes, and simple patterns are applied to garments with lots of seaming and detailing.

The **principles of design** are applications of the elements. They can be manipulated and combined to create unique and interesting fashions. Design principles include proportion, balance, emphasis, harmony, and repetition.

How can you apply the principles of design to make interesting and novel designs? Activity 1.5 asks you to investigate the individual principles.

proportion

Proportion refers to the scale of each of the garment's elements in relation to each other, the garment as a whole, and to the body. Designers often modify proportions to achieve varying standards of beauty. The impact of proportion can be manipulated through the use of color, texture, and pattern. Pleasing proportions can be achieved by referring to the golden ratio.

balance

Balance is the distribution of visual weight within a garment. Every garment displays one of two types of balance: formal (symmetrical) or informal (asymmetrical). Formal balance can make a garment appear reserved and static because the entire composition is comprised of uniform, repeating units. Informal balance can create additional visual interest because a composition can contain a series of varied units.

emphasis

Emphasis refers to designating a focal point of a garment. A designer will emphasize certain aspects of design in an attempt to draw the eye to that location. All elements of the design should reinforce the chosen focal point. Too many focal points can confuse the viewer and make a design look busy and unprofessional. A design with no focal point can be uninteresting and lackluster.

harmony

Harmony and *unity* refer to the cohesion of all elements of a design. A harmonious design is one in which all component parts complement and reflect one another. A garment is said to have unity when all elements and principles of design are in agreement.

repetition

Repetition refers to the frequency of use of a motif, a line, or an element in an apparel item. It can be used to create **rhythm** or movement within the garment. This rhythm can be either progressive or uniform. Progressive rhythm indicates gradation or sporadic variation in size and/or placement of elements. Uniform rhythm is achieved through the exact repetition of a particular element. Care should be taken in the use of uniform rhythm as it can easily become monotonous.

continued on page 35

ACTIVITY 1.5

Elements and Principles of Design

Find an image that represents each of the following principles, and place the image in the space provided on the left. Also, complete the sketch using your own ideas to represent the principle.

On the lines under the images, identify which design elements were used to create the principle in the clipped image and your sketch.

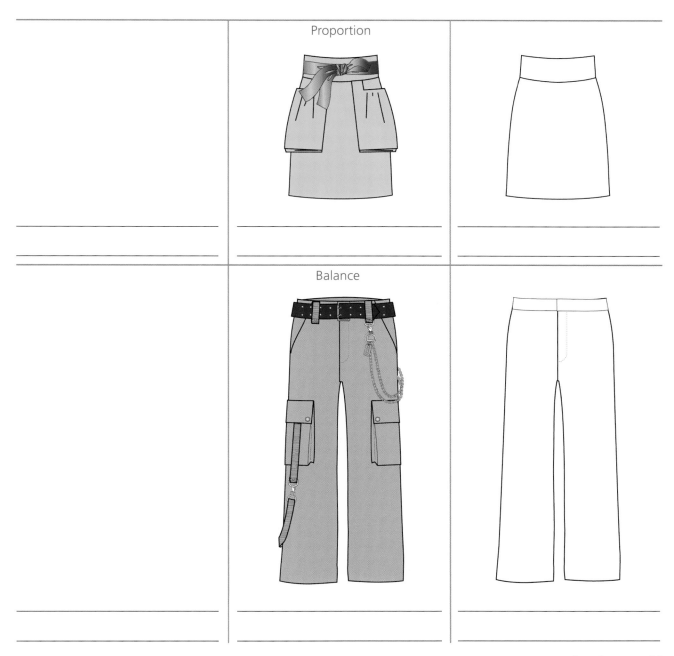

Proportion

Balance

continued on page 34

continued from page 33

ACTIVITY 1.5

Emphasis

Harmony

Repetition

continued from page 32

color theory

Color is of primary importance to fashion designers. They use it to make a statement, tell a story, attract attention, and energize styling. Color creates a garment's first impression, and consumers rarely purchase an item if they do not like the color, even if the styling and fit are satisfactory. The conscious selection of a harmonious color palette is one of the first tasks in the process of creating a fashion design.

color science

Light consists of a series of wavelengths, such as X-rays, microwaves, and radio waves that make up the electromagnetic spectrum. Only a narrow range of the spectrum is visible to the human eye. This portion contains the wavelengths that we recognize as color, and variations in those wavelengths cause us to see different colors. The shortest is perceived as violet; the longest is seen as deep red; and blue, green, yellow, and orange are found between them. When these colors are situated in a circle, you can see a natural progression from one color to the next. By mixing two adjacent colors on the circle, all variations from one color to the next are possible (Figure 1.14).

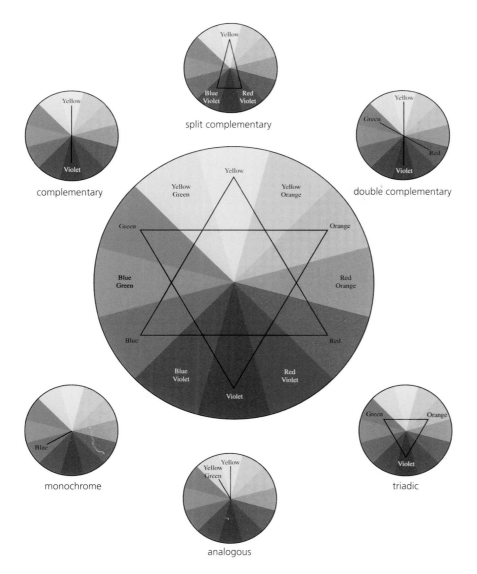

Figure 1.14
The standard color wheel shows that the primary hues — yellow, red, and blue — are equidistant from each other. Opposite each primary hue is the secondary hue that is its complement. Various color schemes can be utilized to create cohesiveness in a line. Configuring an unusual color scheme can lend excitement to a collection.

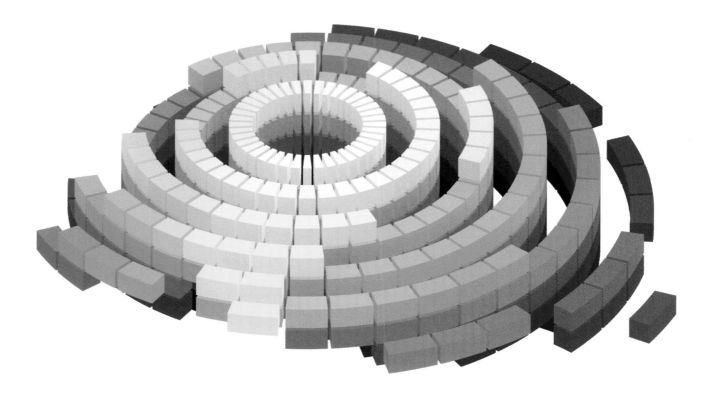

Color is considered to have three qualities: (1) hue, (2) value, and (3) chroma (Figure 1.15). The term **hue** is often used interchangeably with color. It is determined by wavelength. White, black, and gray are considered to be neutrals because they lack hue. **Value** is the lightness or darkness of a color. It is most often referenced with a comparative gray scale that ranges from pure black (value 0) to pure white (value 10). Colors with the same lightness as the corresponding gray on the gray scale are given that value. If white is added to a color to achieve a lighter value, it is referred to as a **tint**. Pink and mint are examples of tints. If black is added to a color to decrease the value, the darker color is referred to as a **shade**.

Chroma is a term used to describe a color's saturation, intensity, or purity. A hue at 100 percent strength is fully saturated. A hue with extremely low saturation appears gray. Utilizing subtle contrasts in intensity can add interest to a design. For example, pairing a saturated blue suit with a shirt of equal value but lesser intensity can create a striking and sophisticated look.

Objects have no inherent color. Color is a function of human perception. Wavelengths of light pass through the retina of the eye and are sent as signals to the brain. The brain interprets these signals as color. Many factors contribute to how a color is perceived, and color matching is always a challenge for designers. In an attempt to maintain color consistency in a line, fabrics from different lots are carefully dyed using the same chemical compositions. However, the colors of fabrics that have been dyed to match can still appear dissimilar if they are made from different fibers. Lighting, too, has impact on color. Two colors that appear to match in sunlight may look very different under fluorescent or incandescent lighting. This phenomenon is called **metamerism**. Color standards, by which all components of a line are evaluated, are established to minimize problems with color matching. Designers need to be on the lookout for potential causes of variations in color because mismatched items will prompt returns at the retail level.

color schemes

Basic color schemes include (see Figure 1.14):

- **Monochromatic**. In a monochromatic color scheme, only shades and tints of one hue are used in a color plan.

- **Analogous**. Two or three contiguous colors on the color wheel are used to create analogous color schemes. For example, blue and green and the intermediate colors between those hues can be used to create an exciting color story.

- **Complementary**. This color scheme is produced by utilizing colors that are opposites on the color wheel. Interesting variations on the complementary scheme are created by using two complementary schemes at the same time (double complementary) or utilizing colors that are adjacent on the color wheel to one of the selected colors (split complementary).

- **Triadic**. Triadic color schemes utilize three colors that are equidistant on the color wheel.

- **Achromatic**. An achromatic scheme is one in which only neutrals are used. White, black, beige, and gray are considered to be neutrals.

Activity 1.6 invites you to explore the many varied possibilities using the basic color schemes.

color story

Each season, designers thoughtfully identify a color theme for their collections. The theme, referred to as a **color story,** connects the various pieces of a line, unifies the designer's message, gives indications for how items can be worn together, and tells a story. Of course, trends influence which colors will be used. Each season has its hot colors, which may be prompted by world events, an art movement, or even the automobile industry. Car colors are usually decided three years in advance of the vehicle's release date in order to allow time for production. Designers also look to their customer base and niche market for additional clues in establishing a winning color story. Age, life stage, and fashion level of the consumer, geography and climate, and the garment's function should be considered when establishing colors for a season (Keiser & Garner, 2008, p. 151).

Color is both a science and an art. It can be analyzed for nuances in value or saturation, for example, but it also invokes emotional responses and is imbued with symbolism. Chapter 4 takes a look at the expressive aspects of color and considers them in psychological and cultural contexts.

breaking the rules

The most salient rewards resulting from a thorough knowledge of fashion's guiding principles stem from the insight and confidence you can gain with increased exposure to ideas and information. This knowledge emboldens you to challenge and experiment with the design guidelines. For example, not every fashion design adheres to the golden ratio. The surprise of nonconforming design proportions can

continued on page 40

Color Schemes

The color wheel provides a way of looking at the relationships among colors. Analyzing these interactions can give us ideas for using color in creative fashion design. Find fashion examples of the color schemes below and on page 39:

Place each image in the space according to the label. Using colored pencils, complete the corresponding color wheel so that it represents the color scheme of the garment in the image.

Monochromatic

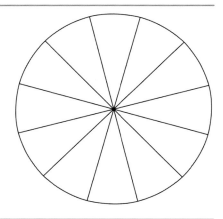

Complementary

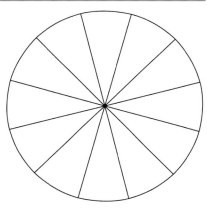

Triadic

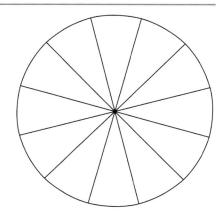

Double complementary

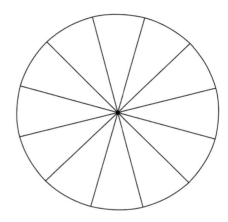

Split complementary

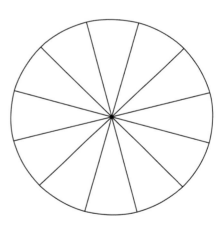

Analogous

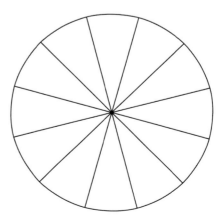

continued from page 37

make a garment interesting and palatable or awkward and ungainly. The designer's challenge is to ascertain when subverting the rules will result in improved design. "Every rule is waiting to be broken. Just remember the two rules for breaking a rule: one is to fully understand it; the other is to know why you want to break it" (Leland, 2006, p. 101).

critiquing fashion design

Given the highly personal nature of creative products, you may wonder if every product that is produced is creative. Harvard researcher Howard Gardner (1993) does not think so. He asserts "that nothing is, or is not, creative *in and of itself.* Creativity is inherently a communal or cultural judgment" (p. 36). Communication is one of the defining terms listed in this chapter, and many agree that one way to validate creativity is to communicate ideas and products to others in the field. It is a matter of discussion, however, as to which qualifications are necessary to evaluate those products.

arbiters of design

Creativity is **subjective** and open to interpretation by others. The **arbiters of fashion**, or those professionals in the apparel field who judge creative products, include esteemed designers and industry practitioners, editors of noted fashion publications, and university professors. Their experience includes having been exposed to a large number of fashion pieces, usually over an extended period of time and in a variety of circumstances. These experts can place the fashion item in context. They know what has preceded it, and they understand how the item is situated within the zeitgeist. But these experts are not without bias. Despite their honest and concerted efforts to be objective, their approach is bound to be influenced by their experiences. True professionals realize their partiality, and they disclose their interests before agreeing to be on an editorial panel or, if their interests are too closely connected to the products being evaluated, they recuse themselves entirely from that particular event. Press outlets, design competitions, and the like attempt to counter prejudice by assembling a varied panel of editors or jurors. The popular television show *Project Runway* convenes a panel of four industry professionals to judge the creations made by contestants on the show. The backgrounds of those judges—a fashion designer, a fashion editor, a fashion model, and a guest judge who brings in his or her own particular expertise—are varied, but extensive. You can imagine that, when combined, their reactions and interactions can elicit an analysis that is at least fair and encompassing, if not impartial.

In the *Project Runway* example, the judges appear to know the contestants, their talents, and their struggles. They are aware of the effort that each individual has put into the design challenge. In most exhibitions, however, the human element is removed from the jurying process, and the design must stand on its own merits.

critique criteria

Considering that each person comes to a judging with his or her own biases, it is remarkable that consensus among jurors can usually be readily achieved. Regardless of their individual backgrounds, arbiters are often united in their assessment of a particular fashion product. This would suggest that there are commonalities in what judges look for in design. These aspects could include the creativity descriptors that opened this chapter: novelty, effectiveness, elegance, communication, emotion, surprise, and ethicality, but the criteria could also be more specific and germane to the singular task at hand. Arbiters will want to assess how well the design responds to the design challenge. Creativity may also be indicated if a product exemplifies (adapted from Goff & Torrance, 2002):

- *Vividness of ideas:* The design displays a vibrant or exciting point of view.
- *Conceptual incongruity:* The design displays ideas that seem strange, absurd, or even inappropriate. It may be humorous or make you smile.
- *Provocative questions:* The design causes you to think and consider different points of view.
- *Different perspectives:* The design is presented from a perspective that is not common to most people.
- *Movement:* The design suggests movement or action.
- *Abstractness:* The design goes beyond conveying what is literal and asks the viewer to interpret its meaning.
- *Context:* The design tells a story, or the background to the creation is presented.
- *Synthesis:* The design combines multiple inspirations in a single presentation.
- *Fantasy:* The design is derived from mythical, fabled, or fictional sources.

Arbiters may not be specifically looking for these criteria, but when they see these creative elements presented in design, they react positively. The creativity-enhancing technique, brainstorming, in Activity 1.7 is one way to incorporate these varied aspects into design. The technique encourages the production of new and unusual ideas.

learning experience

Arbiters of design do not always get it right. At the time of his death, the now-esteemed painter, Vincent van Gogh, was penniless, and his talents were not appreciated. Only after a sufficient number of arbiters in the field of art had time to contemplate his complete body of work was it recognized that van Gogh's expressionistic paintings made important contributions to the field. Sometimes designers are ahead of their time or just out of sync with the zeitgeist. That does not necessarily indicate that their products are uncreative; it may suggest only that their designs do not appeal to a particular group of arbiters. Fashion is a changing concept that depends on the context in which it was generated. It is often instinctive and sensed intuitively, rather than logically analyzed (Jones, 2005, p. 174).

This does not imply, though, that the opinions of others are not valid. Much can be learned from feedback and constructive criticism, even if it is sometimes critical and unflattering. Reworking a design to incorporate arbiters' suggestions is a mature response to constructive feedback. It is said that nothing dies harder than a bad idea, and feedback from jurors can be the impetus a designer needs to release hold on an idea that is just not viable.

The designer always has the choice of rejecting arbiters' comments, however, and not every comment needs to be acted upon. Experienced designers evaluate

continued on page 45

Project Runway — Sitting in on a Televised Jury Review

> It is crafted well, cut well, but the asymmetry and the texture takes it out of the mundane.
>
> —Michael Kors

Michael Kors on creativity: I equate [the current economic climate] to late-seventies New York. I was young, excited, and I had no idea that I was moving to New York just as the city was on the verge of bankruptcy. Crime was at its worst. The world was ending. But it was actually a very creative moment for New York. Creative people—whether its fashion, film, music, art—are going to have to try a little harder (Foley, 2009).

Edited excerpts from the juror review of the All Star Challenge on the August 20, 2009 episode of the television show Project Runway.

Jurors include Heidi Klum, Michael Kors, Nina Garcia, and Diane von Furstenberg. Among the contestants were Korto, Daniel, and Sweet P.

Tim Gunn introduces the challenge: to create a collection of three looks on a budget of $1200. One of these is a look with unconventional materials found in a restaurant. Twenty-five percent of this new look can consist of fabrics from the designers' other two looks.

After the looks have been completed and shown on the runway, the jurors discuss the designs with the contestants.

Daniel speaks about his collection, and the judges give their reactions.

Daniel: I was really inspired by soft structure, this really strong athletic vibe, and combining them, but still giving a young sophistication. It still needs to be polished. It still needs to be edgy. It still needs to be urban, and very confident. That's how I look at it.

Heidi: I can totally see this dress at [a movie] premier. Absolutely.

Diane: You have a lot of clarity. You have a lot of confidence, and that dress is beautiful.

Michael: I love the idea of the athletic t-shirt with the bubble skirt. The hem on the bubble skirt is not so perfect, but I think the best thing about this whole collection [is that] you know who your girl is. I see a very clear picture of who you are dressing, and, most importantly, I really saw a focus.

Korto and the judges have the following conversation:

Korto: I love great, rich fabrics that can be inexpensive but still look very expensive. And just celebrating the woman's body, the real woman's body.

Nina: I think you never shied away from color, texture, prints. I celebrate that because . . . not many designers . . . go there.

Michael: I like the asymmetry . . . on the bustier. These are clothes that are going to look great on women. They are going to want to wear them. I mean it's that simple.

Diane: All of the clothes actually look like they would flatter the body and add to the body, and [they] have a signature.

Sweet P tells the judges about her line, and they respond.

The television show *Project Runway* displays a convincing approach to the design critique. Judges are quick to point out successes, but they also note when a composition does not hit the mark. © *Brendan McDermid/Reuters/ Corbis*

Sweet P: I like really feminine, romantic. Kind of simplistic in shape, but gorgeous clothes.

Diane: . . . It definitely carries your name very well. It's very sweet. It's very candy, but it's fun . . .

Michael: [T]he most important thing about this show is that you can look at their clothes and know that they are yours. [When the model] turned the corner, and if I didn't have the book, I would still know that Sweet P is starting.

Heidi: It's not particularly me. I like to dress harder, but I think that . . . a lot of customers would want to have your clothes.

The judges talk among themselves to determine the contest winner. Following are some of their observations.

Diane: Each one, individually, had a signature of their own and a point of view.

Nina: There was a real evolution.

Michael [Commenting on Daniel's work]: I like the idea that he thought about subtle things . . . about the way that dress was seamed . . . about the inset on the trouser. Those are the things that I think turn women on.

Heidi [in reference to Korto's designs]: I think that all of her clothes are so wearable.

Michael: I think it's a brilliant thing that everything she makes, a woman would want to put on. And, it is crafted well, cut well, but the asymmetry and the texture takes it out of the mundane.

Diane: She sees the body, and she designs around the body.

Diane [On Sweet P's line]: She has a message, and she carries that message . . . She has a signature.

Nina: I thought she told a story with her collection.

Although only one designer can be chosen as the winner (that is Daniel), all the contestants have had an opportunity to tackle a challenge to innovate with their unique personal style. The judges have called attention to criteria that make each designer's work worthy of a professional.

Creativity-Enhancing Exercise: Brainstorming

Designers are on a continual hunt for inspiration. They are constantly on the lookout for new ideas, but they may inadvertently disregard a plausible idea because it seems too far-fetched. The brainstorming technique popularized by Alex Osborn asks participants to consider all ideas, no matter how strange and implausible they may seem. These unrestrained ideas will, in turn, stimulate additional uninhibited ideas. Criticism is not allowed during brainstorming sessions. The assumption is that by generating a large quantity of ideas, there is a greater likelihood that one, or a combination of them, will be viable. Before brainstorming, the problem must be focused and clearly defined. There are four basic rules for brainstorming (Osborn, 1963):

- Focus on quantity
- Withhold criticism
- Welcome unusual ideas
- Combine and improve ideas

Brainstorming can be used effectively in a group setting, such as a critique, with participants offering a multitude of possible solutions to design problems and dilemmas. After idea collecting, good ideas can be considered, combined, and enhanced.

Although it is usually thought of as a group process, individuals can brainstorm successfully, and the technique is quite compatible with the *DIN*. You have already been entering thoughts, impressions, and ideas into your *DIN*, but most likely they have been either consciously or unconsciously edited. In this assignment, attempt to suppress the internal governor that causes one to say, "That will never work."

Your brainstorming assignment is to

1. Identify a specific design challenge. For example, select a bestselling book. Imagine that the author is attending a black tie event to promote the book. Create a formal gown or tuxedo inspired by the book jacket artwork that the author can wear to the event.
2. Fill at least six pages in your *DIN* with all of your thoughts, found images, and sketched ideas that relate to that problem.
3. Enter everything, edit nothing. Make a concerted effort to include ideas that you would not normally consider.
4. Let the ideas on the pages simmer for a day or two. Do not try to make use of them immediately.
5. Revisit your pages. Combine similar ideas to make a strong concept. Let weak ideas fall away.
6. Sketch your response to the design challenge in your *DIN*.

Design Challenge

continued from page 41

feedback and incorporate only those ideas that reinforce their message. Individuals should always remain faithful to their personal style. Even if arbiters' comments are valid and well-intended, a designer may decide to reject those suggestions in order to stay true to an original design idea. Indecisive designers, with vacillating design styles, will have some difficulty knowing which arbiters' suggestions to act on and which to disregard. A designer with a strong vision, well-defined personal style, and clear concept will have no problem identifying those ideas that will strengthen a design statement.

Design assessment is not reserved for professionals with years of experience. You can formulate **rubrics**, or judging criteria, for how you would like to evaluate creative design. Critiquing another's work is a learning experience and a great way to discover techniques, artistry, and differing viewpoints. In Activity 1.8, you will formulate a rubric with criteria that can be used to evaluate your designs.

the design critique

The design **critique** (or crit) is the assessment of your work by a group of peers or professionals. Although conducted in a variety of ways, from a classroom fitting on dress forms to a roundtable discussion with buyers, a sales force, or other stakeholders in attendance, the critique asks designers to open themselves up to evaluative comments from others. If the designer does not welcome open discussion and honest feedback, the crit can be a daunting and intimidating experience. In alternate applications, the word criticism means disapproval, and this may be why some fear the critique setting. **Criticism,** in the context of a design critique, however, denotes analysis, review, and appreciation, and not denigration. A design critique is intended to be an exchange of ideas and a learning event for all involved (Figure 1.16). Criticism should exhibit goodwill and have each designer's best interests at heart. The critique is:

• Collaborative

• Successful only with an engaged and interested group

• Interpretive, asking what the is design about

• Evaluative, asking whether the design is good and why

• An attempt at looking objectively at a subjective piece

It is not:

• A personal attack

• Mean-spirited or embarrassing

• Intentionally frustrating or stress-producing

• Being on the defensive

• One-sided

Creativity is a big consideration when I turn in an assignment. I want it to be creative when we critique ourselves. You like positive feedback. You don't want to make something plain because it is boring. You have an opportunity. You bought all of this fabric. You spent all of this money and time so you want something that you're proud of. Creativity makes that. Creativity is definitely up there. It's very important. —*Fashion Design Student*

Everyone participating in the critique wants your design to be the best it can be. Carefully considering feedback is one of the best ways for you to improve design execution. Be open to suggestions, take notes, and incorporate those ideas that enhance your vision. *Designer: Jane Arvis*

Designing is often a solitary endeavor, and critiques are an opportunity for individuals to communicate their ideas and practice asserting their design styles. Designers will also discover how others interpret their designs. Seeing a fashion through the eyes of others enables designers to look at the space between a design's desired effect and the actual result. For a critique to be effective, it must be honest. This asks participants to praise a garment's strengths, but also to be analytical enough to point out weaknesses. They should be informed and should have done the research required to perform the evaluation. For example, if the challenge was to create a design inspired by some past era, those critiquing should familiarize themselves with the context of that time period.

Critiques can elicit emotions. The merits of a particular fashion design can inspire lively, and sometimes heated, debate. For the betterment of the piece, designers should strive to detach themselves emotionally and refrain from becoming defensive. The critique can be an opportunity to improve design skills and practices. A committed group can make the design critique a rejuvenating, productive, and even fun experience.

Create a Fashion Design Rubric

Criteria for fashion design vary from assignment to assignment and competition to competition. Individuals are better equipped to respond to design challenges if they understand how their garments will be evaluated. One example of judging criteria is listed in conjunction with the Alpaca Owners and Breeders Association's recent student design competition. Design entries were assessed on the following criteria (AOBA, 2009):

- Essay (understanding the design challenge): 10%

- Level of creativity: 15%

- Commercial viability: 10%

- Illustration and rendering ability: 10%

- Craftsmanship and professionalism of the presentation: 15%

- Awareness of contemporary design trends: 5%

- Technical consideration: 5%

- Appropriate fabric selection: 10%

- Consideration of necessary details and trims: 5%

- Visual appeal: 15%

Collaboratively, create a design rubric that can be used in the critique of one of your design challenges or assignments. To get you started, a sample rubric is included here. Assign a point or percentage value to each level.

Fashion Design Evaluation Rubric

The work: Please rate the design concerning what extent it exhibits:	Does not address this aspect	Does not adequately or consistently answer this challenge	Answers the challenge, but it is typical and does not stand out as significant	Exhibits an above average level of proficiency in this area	Is remarkable, significant, and perceptive
(Criterion One)					
(Criterion Two)					
(Criterion Three)					
(Criterion Four)					
(Criterion Five)					
(Criterion Six)					
TOTAL					

summary

There is no universal definition for creativity, but a common understanding of the concept can mitigate misunderstandings within a group and enable all to work productively toward a common goal. Designers can use what they know of creativity to seek situations that foster creativity and avoid those that hinder it. Part of creativity's allure is that it is personal and adaptive. Even so, many agree on its core components and that it results from a confluence of traits.

A strong base of knowledge in the domain can inspire designers. Industry-related principles guide their design process, but these principles are tools, not rules, and they exist only to assist designers. Arbiters of fashion design can also contribute to designers' success. They work hard to prevent their experiences from coloring their evaluation of creative products. Designers use feedback gained from arbiters and critiques to make their collections stronger. Incremental improvements and innovation in design make the entire industry more vital and viable.

KEY TERMS

creativity	knowledge base	proportion	metamerism
novelty	fashion figure	balance	monochromatic
effectiveness	golden ratio	emphasis	analogous
elegance	elements of design	harmony	complementary
communication	line	unity	triadic
emotion	color	repetition	achromatic
affective	texture	rhythm	color story
pseudocreativity	hand	hue	subjective
quasicreativity	shape	value	arbiters of fashion
surprise	silhouette	tint	rubrics
ethicality	pattern	shade	critique
talent	principles of design	chroma	criticism

DIN Challenge: Creativity in Fashion Design

A deep and broad knowledge base is essential for creativity. It is hoped that this chapter increased your knowledge of creativity and the apparel design field. Referring to the entries you have made in your *DIN* thus far, determine the *Ideas* from the chapter that have made the greatest impact on you. Connect *Ideas* to *Themes* and design a look or series of looks based on the *Connections* you make. Critique your designs with a group of supportive participants.

Notes for Discussion

_____

_____

_____

_____

_____

_____

_____

_____

_____

2 creativity *and* the environment

The environment plays a vital role in creative fashion design. It is more than a passive setting in which the designer works. Rather, designers actively interact with their surroundings, and fashions are reflections of available resources, support from families and peers, and exposure to rich and varied locations. Even the society in which the designer works contributes to the creativity that is produced. "No one is immune to the impressions that impinge on the senses from the outside" (Csikszentmihalyi, 1996, p. 127).

Designers can be intentional about immersing themselves in creativity-friendly surroundings. "**Creativogenic**" (Cropley, 2001, p. 150) and "**congenial**" (Csikszentmihalyi, 1996, p. 355) are terms used to suggest environments that foster creativity. An atmosphere that is accepting of differences, enabling of self-directed work, and open to a variety of responses to a design problem encourages designers to explore alternative and innovative fashion designing. A creativity-fostering environment advocates experimentation, spontaneity, and flexibility. It also includes generous positive feedback and encouragement (Cropley, 2001). In addition, considering the symbiotic relationship that designers have with their surroundings, it is obvious that they have a stake in maintaining a healthy environment. Eco-friendly and sustainable design can be rewarding, while it also offers many new avenues for design inspiration.

Environment is a comprehensive term with varied components. A **microenvironment** is the immediate setting in which you live and work. This includes physical aspects of your workspace and your intimate social milieu. You can control, and alter to your creative advantage, much of what is contained in your microenvironment. You can regulate the atmosphere of your studio, and surround yourself with a supportive network of friends and co-workers. Social and cultural contexts are part of the designer's **macroenvironment** (Cskiszentmihalyi, 1996, p. 139). They include the values and mores inherent within a society. A group's **mores** refers to its conventions, customs, and particular way of life. Although designers are less able to

OBJECTIVES

— To recognize environmental influences on creative design

— To explore environments that can foster and inhibit creativity

— To investigate the role that family, peers, and society may play in creativity

— To investigate how environmental conditions and factors can be used as inspiration for design

— To explore full-cycle sustainable design, and to discover how designers may be able to incorporate environmentally friendly design in their own lines

control some aspects of their macroenvironment, they can immerse themselves in their own and other cultures and use that knowledge and understanding to inspire design. A change in environment is one of the quickest and most productive ways to gain new insight and inspiration.

physical aspects of the designer's environment

A designer typically works in a lab, studio, or workroom. Although these terms are often used interchangeably, there are subtle differences in the work atmospheres of each. A school or university design and sewing room is often referred to as a **lab**, primarily because of the investigational work that is being done there. A **studio** is a creative hub for a designer. It contains all of the materials necessary for designers to do their work, but it includes little or no production sewing equipment (Figure 2.1). A **workroom** is most often contained within an industry setting. The designer may work in a portion of a larger area, which also contains industrial cutting and/or sewing equipment.

Taking a look at the physical aspects of the fashion designer's studio or lab, it may be surprising that neutral furnishings may be preferable to a highly stylized decor. They are blank slates, inviting of all design styles, and they are compatible with fashion designers' frequent changes of creative direction. Although a decorated space is attractive, its stagnant point of view does not encourage exploration into alternative design styles. Dynamic, changeable walls with multiple bulletin boards or other surfaces that allow for the posting of photos, illustrations, swatches, and editable color stories are more conducive to inspiring design (Figure 2.2). They offer flexibility and an opportunity for editing. Walls or bulletin boards that accommodate changing design and color schemes can be used as large, interactive versions of the *Dynamic Inspiration Notebook* (*DIN*). Everyone in a class or group can participate in inspiration-gathering and posting of ideas. New ideas can be added, and projects for which time has passed can be taken down. However, just as a website soon becomes outdated if it not revised often, a bulletin board loses its ability to inspire if new and relevant material is not continually added. Activity 2.1 suggests that you maintain a bulletin board of inspiring images in your classroom.

Figure 2.1
The designer's studio is always a hub of activity. Inspiration is all around, so managed clutter is often preferred over a pristine workspace.
© *Chuck Savage/ Corbis*

Figure 2.2
Bulletin boards are assemblages of design inspiration. They offer flexibility in that items can be added, removed, and arranged easily. They also allow the designer to stand back and view assorted concepts in relation to one another. © *Image Source/Corbis*

ACTIVITY 2.1

Inspiration Bulletin Board

Your instructor will assign a different student each week to revise and update the bulletin boards in the fashion lab. The displays are not intended to be professional presentations, but rather they should be a scrapbook of ideas. The board content could relate to a particular assignment, contain updates on designer collections, or contain images intended to give everyone a fresh perspective.

Ideas for Bulletin Board

_____

_____

_____

_____

_____

_____

I like a warehouse kind of feel so it doesn't look as though it has been put together. For me, it's just open space, and **you bring the creativity**. That's what I like—not too much fancy stuff because it's all about the people and what they are offering. *—Fashion Design Instructor*

Designers may also want to bedeck their work space with items that have symbolic meaning to them. This personalization helps develop the designer's **voice** or personal style. When discussing the home, creativity professor and author Csikszentmihalyi (1996, p. 142) suggests that a "supportive symbolic ecology" helps one feel safe and enables individuals to drop their defenses. He asserts that, "a home devoid of personal touches, lacking objects that point to the past or direct toward the future, tends to be sterile. Homes rich in meaningful symbols make it easier for their owners to know who they are and therefore what they should do" (p. 142). One can easily imagine the relevance of this sentiment to the design studio. A workroom that houses stimulating fabrics and artifacts can offer both direction and inspiration. An environment that "reinforces one's individuality cannot but help increase the chances that one will act out one's uniqueness" (p. 143).

workspace

Although the aesthetics of the studio should be accommodating and inviting, it is equally important for designers to have a practical space to work. An effective workspace provides natural lighting; good air quality, including ventilation and temperature control; and the table space necessary for patternmaking and fabric cutting. Cramped quarters and uncomfortable room temperatures can inhibit creativity by distracting the designer from the task at hand.

The workspace should be organized, but not so orderly as to discourage individuals from diving into a project. Designing is often a disordered and organic process, and designers should not fear making a mess. Tile or polished cement floors are efficient in fashion workrooms because they are easy to sweep and wipe clean. Carpeting is not recommended because threads and fabric scraps can tangle with the carpet fibers and become difficult to vacuum up. Also, straight pins can get caught in a carpeted floor and create a safety hazard, but they can easily be picked up off of hard-surfaced floors with a magnet.

tools and equipment

A well-stocked studio includes the tools of the trade. A computer, sharp fabric shears, paper scissors, pattern drafting paper, 6- and 18-inch rulers, curves, punches, and notchers are all essential tools of the designer/patternmaker (Figure 2.3). Searching for and substituting tools can be time consuming and frustrating to the point of impeding the design process.

Although garments are often manufactured outside of the design studio at sewing contractors, some are still equipped with a number of sewing and stitching machines used for sewing samples and first garments. There are numerous industrial and home sewing machines on the market. The type of sewing work being done and

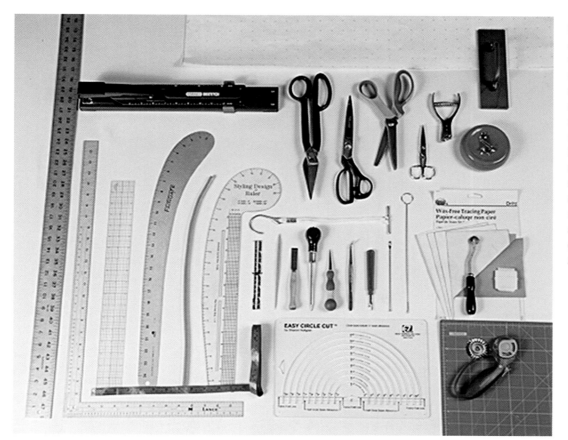

Figure 2.3
A wide array
of sewing and
patternmaking tools
can be found in a
designer's studio. A
rotary cutter, with
mat, is particularly
handy for cutting
quick samples. It cuts
sharp, clean lines,
and the grid on the
mat helps keep fabric
and patterns on
grain. *Photographer:
Eileen Molony*

economy often dictate the kind and amount of sewing equipment in a lab or studio. The most basic design environment contains a steam iron and a multipurpose sewing machine. An industrial workroom could include many additional machines, each dedicated to a specific sewing operation.

Supplying a design studio with basic equipment can remove impediments to creativity, but stocking extra accoutrements can actually inspire a designer and encourage new ways of working. Embroidery, machine knitting, and quilting equipment provide innumerable fresh avenues to explore. Additional presser feet and attachments for the sewing machine can be acquired to add flexibility, variety, and professionalism to sewing. Ruffling, cording, roll hem, shirring or gathering, and bias binding attachments are among the optional equipment available for industrial sewing machines. Also, consider supplying the design lab with an assortment of additional supplies, notions, ribbons and tapes, interfacings, grommet punches, buttons, and other sewing paraphernalia to inspire design

I want cement floors. I don't want to worry about spilling dyes. High ceilings so we're not limited. I don't want the limitations of the aesthetics because then you already have them. Raw space, lots of tables, and then all of the tools you would ever need. —*Fashion Design Instructor*

c

d

a

b

Figure 2.4

Sewing machine and workroom tools can inspire innovative design (a and b). A shirring foot attachment (a) for the industrial sewing machine aids in gathering yards and yards of ribbon and makes the tedious ruffling process quite easy (c). To make the skirt, fabric and yarn scraps were stitched to a water soluble stabilizer (b). After remnants are securely joined with thread, the stabilizer is rinsed away, leaving an airy net-like fabric (d). The dissolvable film enables environmentally-conscious designers to make use of scraps that would otherwise be discarded. *Skirt designer: Erika Neumayer. Photographer: Eileen Molony*

(Figure 2.4). Activity 2.2 asks you to experiment with one of the items mentioned here in order to inspire your next design.

The dress form is another indispensable item for the fashion design work space. A **dress form** is a three-dimensional figure, usually covered in linen, used to pin or drape fabric in the creation of an apparel design. This can be contrasted to the **mannequin**, which is a stylized, ornamental, or lifelike figure that is used to display finished products. Live models are sometimes called mannequins, also. Dress forms come in numerous sizes, styles, and price ranges. The word *dress* in this context refers to *apparel* or *clothing*, not a woman's chemise, so the term *dress form* encompasses men's and children's figures as well as women's. A well-stocked workroom could house dress forms in every apparel size that is sold by the company. Designers working in a smaller studio will generally try to procure at least one form in the size in which they develop their sample patterns. Most body forms have the center front, center back, princess seamlines, and side seams marked vertically with seaming or stitching. The waistline, and sometimes bustline and hipline, are marked horizontally with twill tape. Dress forms should contain enough padding so pins can be inserted at all angles without slipping or falling out. A designer working on custom-tailored garments might consider an adjustable or variable-sized form. This type of form can be altered to match the measurements of the client.

Take stock of the equipment in your work space. Does the studio contain the essential tools of the trade? What tools are necessary to do your work? What tools would inspire design? Make a wish list of items for future requisitions.

_____

_____

_____

Creativity in the Design Lab

Acquire a tool for your lab or an attachment for your sewing machine that you have not worked with before. Practice using it to gain proficiency, and then create a design or series of designs that are inspired by your newly attained expertise.

Tool   Design Possibilities

1. _____   _____

2. _____   _____

3. _____   _____

4. _____   _____

5. _____   _____

6. _____   _____

7. _____   _____

8. _____   _____

psychological aspects of the designer's environment

Maintaining a well-equipped lab allows designers to experiment and elaborate instead of having to compromise and make allowances. Equally important as the physical state of the lab, however, is that designers feel comfortable and welcome in their work space. A flourishing environment is one where creative individuals feel in control of their surroundings and in sync with their own habits and rhythms so that they can forget the rest of the world and concentrate on the task at hand (Csikszent-mihalyi, 1996, pp. 127–128). Some individuals do their best work before breakfast, and others prefer to work late at night. Workers need to be comfortable in, and compatible with, their own work space. Expanding workroom hours to nontraditional times and involving workers in design room decisions are two ways to create a designer-friendly studio environment.

A stress-free setting with encouragement and an opportunity to experiment is conducive to creative design. Tension and anxiety can interfere with your ability to remain attentive to the problem at hand, and external pressures can make it difficult, if not impossible, to concentrate. In an educational setting, students should feel secure enough in their learning environment to explore without fear of ridicule or excessive sanctions for less than successful work (Cropley, 2001). Continual and rigid evaluation of design products can inhibit the experimentation necessary to achieve creative breakthroughs. Some students may be hesitant to explore that risky avenue because, if it does not prove viable, their grade will be marked down. It is hoped that there is room in every curriculum for open investigation and experimentation.

supportive family and peers

Social support networks are positive contributors to a creativity-friendly environment, and they often provide the designer with the motivation to continue an extended project (Csikszentmihalyi, 1988, pp. 325–339). Positive reinforcement can come from one's family and friends. Even if they do not consider themselves to be creative, family and peers can provide nurturing environments where innovation is encouraged. Parents can offer a safe place to work, where a designer can practice without the fear of making a fool of oneself. Unqualified support from family can propel a designer to aim further in the experimentation stage. Peers, too, can be encouraging, and sometimes a designer needs this reinforcement in order to have the courage to try something new. Friends can be counted on to offer honest feedback that is free from negativity. Stable personal relationships may offer a designer license to venture into less stable and more experimental areas of design (Figure 2.5).

society's role

The society in which you live and work also plays a role in influencing fashion. "Certain environments have a greater density of interaction and provide more excitement and a greater effervescence of ideas; therefore, they prompt the person who is already inclined to break away from conventions to experiment with novelty more readily than if he or she had stayed in a more conservative, more repressive setting" (Csikszentmihalyi, 1996, p. 129). Social, economic, political, and religious factors combine to determine the degree of innovation advocated by a society. Throughout history there have been cultures and civilizations that have fostered creativity and those that have inhibited it. In large part because of increased

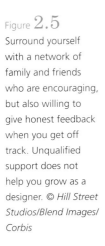

Figure 2.5
Surround yourself with a network of family and friends who are encouraging, but also willing to give honest feedback when you get off track. Unqualified support does not help you grow as a designer. © Hill Street Studios/Blend Images/ Corbis

Figure 2.6
Creativity is a social
process fostered by
a number of factors,
including vibrant
activity in the field,
diversity, openness,
and freedom to
express ideas. Many
find the bustle of
a busy Soho street
in New York City
stimulating. © *Mark
Peterson/Corbis*

cross-cultural influences, art and architecture thrived for Greeks during the Hellenistic period. Science and technology, as well as art and culture, flourished in Florence, Italy during the European Renaissance. During that time, a new attitude toward beauty and artistry assigned creative individuals a higher status and greater independence than was previously known. However, there have also been periods that were not as supportive of creative growth. The Middle Ages are sometimes referred to as the Dark Ages, in part because of the comparatively few cultural advances of that period.

Modern artists, writers, musicians, and designers have long been known to search out societies that they believe to be conducive to creating original works. Creative individuals seek a mix of influences, and they gravitate toward environments that are invigorating and varied (Florida, 2002, p. 227). They often look for a diverse community that is open and tolerant, and also one that exhibits a "vibrancy of street life, café culture, arts, music, and people engaging in outdoor activities" (p. 232). Although there are several commonalities, it should be noted that inspiring enclaves are unique to individuals, however, and what is stimulating to one may be too congested or too bucolic for another (Figure 2.6).

societal norms

Everyone functions within the norms and customs of a society. This most often works to society members' advantage in that they can navigate efficiently through

continued on page 62

Melissa Gamble Director of Fashion Arts and Events for the City of Chicago

Creativity is . . . originality. Something that's truly an original thought, an original work, an original approach to something. It could be inspired by something else or inspired by something in the past but with a fresh take on it.

My position within the Chicago Department of Cultural Affairs was to support fashion and raise the visibility of the industry here. The position was created in 2005. Before that, the city didn't have any kind of fashion program. The Mayor of Chicago and the Commissioner both view fashion as an art form, and, as such, they wanted to create some kind of program that would support the designers that are here in the city.

Fashion fits in well with the department's mission. The mission of the fashion initiative is to raise the visibility of the fashion industry here and to create more opportunities for the designers living and working in the city. They've done that through events and promotions showcasing the designers, boutiques, and shopping. They try to find the different resources that designers need in order to stay here in the city. So, it's everything from the www.chicagofashionresource.com website, which is a central portal for designers, boutique owners, and consumers, to creating a design incubator.

The Incubator, housed in the Macy's building on State Street, is a supportive environment for new designers. Designers are provided workspace—they pay nominal rent each month—and they're given mentors from the business community and the Incubator board. The designers attend workshops on developing their business, and they are also provided with some financial counseling. Mentors help the designers in finding sources, developing their collections, finding contractors, and all those things that young designers really struggle with. The goal is to give them many resources so they can focus on creating, thinking about their brands, and developing their lines.

A lot of designers work incredible hours and go a million different directions because they are required to do everything. The designer is the business person, the accountant, the marketing person, the public relations person, and then, if there's time, the designer. I've heard a lot of designers say that they spend the majority of their time on business-related items and a very small amount of time on actual designing.

> # There are so many people out there who want to see new designers succeed.
> — Miriam Cecilia Carlson

Miriam Carlson, a designer-in-residence at the Incubator, describes what it means to a new designer to have the support of the city, industry professionals, and her peers.

The Incubator helps us designers create a strong business foundation for our lines. To provide the business foundation, the board brings in lawyers and trademark specialists, and they have someone talk to us about business insurance. Someone else helps us with costing our garments. We get practice presenting our line to showroom reps. We've had two different branding specialists come in.

The incubator is on the eleventh floor of the Macy's building. We have a corner of the floor. There are several long tables for cutting and patterning and several industrial

CHICAGO FASHION INCUBATOR
at macy's on state street

sewing machines, several sergers, and industrial irons. There are even threads and zippers available. We have closet space as well and really everything we need to create our samples. They provide dress forms, but most of us use our own. There are three offices with two designers sharing each office. There's a show-room/conference room where we hold our workshops and different events. There are racks on the walls where we can hang garments when we are showing our line to a customer or buyer.

There are so many people out there who want to see new designers succeed. So many people come to the Incubator and share their time. They let us e-mail them. They answer our questions. In the community, people recognize that we are new and don't have the capital yet, and people are willing to work on differ-ent levels with one another. There are photographers working at a lower rate, hoping that we will come back to them when we're in a better place. Models do the same thing.

I try to give when I can, too, by taking on fashion design interns who are still in school. The Incubator is a great place to learn, and I like being able to bring students into that environment. They see what it takes to start a clothing line, and the internship helps them know if starting a line is something that they want to do. They get a taste of what it is to be a designer.

There are six designers at the Incubator every year. One of the first things I noticed about the Incubator was the support that I got from all of the other designers. When we are still in school, we build up support with our classmates. We help each other out and answer each others' questions. When we leave school, we are by ourselves again. It's hard to work by yourself and get that work ethic going. Here, the designers get along great, and we're so excited for one another. The Incubator board has an amazing selection process. They choose designers that complement each other. We don't directly compete with one another. We each have a unique niche. We all get along fantastically. Just the other day I was making a pair of men's pants. One of the other designers makes tons of men's pants so she helped me. She was working on a sleeve pattern and was having trouble getting a good fit. I was able to help her to get the slope right on a set-in sleeve. That was perfect, because her expertise and my expertise worked together.

I create a couture collection, and from that I create a ready-to-wear collection that can be sold to different boutiques. I also really enjoy working on custom designs. With wholesale, we only get paid twice a year, so the custom side can subsidize sales throughout the year. Right now all of the designers at the Incubator are kind of swarming around, trying to figure out our next move. We will only be at the Incubator for a few more months, but we'll be prepared when the time comes to leave.

a

b

continued from page 59

daily life and common social situations. Many take comfort in the repetition and rhythms of conventions, such as the etiquette and manners practiced in daily discourse. Designers, knowledgeable of mores and customs, can make informed design decisions. They can tailor fashions that are consistent with the ethos of the group. However, if fashion always safely stays within the confines of what is universally suitable and accepted, it can quickly become stale and predictable. Fashion is driven by change, but there are limits to the amount of change that is accepted by a particular group. With too little change, the fashion will appear mature and tired. If there is too much change too quickly, the fashion may appear too radical and extreme. Therein is a challenge for designers. It is up to designers to consider to what degree they want to challenge the unwritten guidelines established by certain segments of society. They weigh the need to make a particular design statement with the repercussions of not complying with established standards. The consequences of not staying within traditional confines can vary greatly and sometimes unpredictably. The intended target audience could be delighted with the new ideas that have been introduced, or they may be outraged and refuse to purchase the product.

Despite the challenges of designing within the norms of a society, the designer should not yearn for an atmosphere with no constraints and boundaries. Contrary to what one might imagine, designers need limits. Knowing those limits allows a designer to focus in on specific design problems and keeps unrelated distractions at bay. Boundaries give the designer direction and control. For designing on the cusp of what a group will accept, those boundaries can also be a source of inspiration. For example, gender roles are fairly well defined in most countries. In the United States, men are seldom seen wearing dresses. A designer wanting to address the gender constraints of a particular group will be guided and inspired by the gender roles and traditions of that group (Figure 2.7).

scanning the environment

It may not be possible to change aspects of the society one resides in, but designers can learn a great deal about their surroundings, and this knowledge can provide design direction. As one apparel designer states, "A good part of our work comes from being informed. One of the few ways you can be different from other deisgners is to be aware of the surroundings" (designer Loretta, as quoted in Manlow, 2007, p. 256).

environmental scanning

Environmental scanning is the process of gaining and interpreting data from a variety of disparate sources in order to identify trend directions for a particular group or consumer niche. It is a continual investigation that involves the study of statistical, social, and psychological data and analysis of competitors and innovators in the apparel field. Environmental scanning is also an intuitive process that includes identifying trends and activities in ancillary fields.

Demographics are statistical data relating to an individual's age, education, family size, ethnicity, gender, income, marital status, occupation, religion, region, and spending habits (Keiser & Garner, 2008, p. 68). Designers can use this information to form a baseline understanding of a particular consumer group. The U.S. Census Bureau (www.census.gov) provides a large amount of demographic data gained from national censuses taken every ten years.

Figure 2.7

Rick Owens (a), Yohji Yamamoto, Comme de Garçons, and Jean Paul Gaultier garnered reactions ranging from mild surprise to shock when they featured men wearing skirts in their recent runway shows. However, skirt-like kilts do not raise an eyebrow in Scotland, where the traditional style is commonly seen in ceremonies, at formal occasions, and worn by Highland workers (b). *Courtesy of WWD/ Giovanni Glannoni (a)*
© *Dewitt Jones/Corbis (b)*

Consumers' activities, attitudes, lifestyles, opinions, personalities, reference groups, life cycles, and values can also be studied. Called **psychographics**, these social and psychological data can be difficult to measure because they are subjective (pp. 73–74), but they aid designers in further refining their styling direction for a particular market. Psychographic data can be gathered firsthand through observation and questioning members of the group, or it can be purchased from companies specializing in market research. Economic and political factors will also impact fashion design, as will technological advances and materials that are available to the designer.

inspiration from A to Z

Unlikely sources can spark innovation, and in today's global community, the key to environmental scanning is to be ever-vigilant in utilizing a variety of sources both inside and outside the field. A designer's milieu of reference should include everything from architecture to the zeitgeist.

Following each inspiration, make notes on how you could use that source for design. Also, sketch your raw ideas in your *DIN* so you can refer back to them later.

architecture

Look to architecture for structure and form and also materials used. Iconic structures, such as the Eiffel Tower, and iconic architectural styles, such as that of Frank Lloyd Wright or Frank Gehry, can be translated to apparel by means of seaming, pleating, and detailing. Metal, plastics, and other architectural materials can be incorporated into innovative art-to-wear. Fashion designers are even experimenting with the core principle of architecture as shelter, and creating garments that provide a structure of warmth, security, and cover.

_____

_____

_____

art

Art is a kindred spirit with fashion. Like fashion, art often reflects the time in which it is created and so offers insight into the culture of the period. Art is informative, expressive, and imaginative. Art can inspire. Largely because of the Internet, art exhibitions are seen worldwide, and they often influence fashion color and silhouette direction. Ideas can also emanate from the emotion of a ballet, the mood captured in a photograph, the intensity of a song, and the flowing lines of a poem.

_____

_____

_____

Inspiration can be derived from any concept on the A-Z list, but art has a special connection to fashion. Activity 2.3 invites you to explore the relationship between the two methods of expression.

continued on page 66

Figure 2.8
Designers in tune with the popular culture take cues from their environment. Movies, television shows, video games, and books have recently featured vampire-related themes. The theme has also found its way to the runway. This Jean Paul Gaultier design appears to be influenced by the genre. The skirt resembles the vampire cape, the points of the lapels are likened to fangs, and the red fingernails are the perfect haunting accessory. *Courtesy of WWD/Giovanni Giannoni*

Art and Fashion

Just as fashion is an expression of ideas and emotions, so is art. It is imagined that there are reciprocal forces between the two concepts: Art influences fashion; fashion influences art. Some contend that fashion is art. Regardless of this ongoing debate, fashion designers should become apprised of past art movements and remain curious concerning events in the contemporary world of art. This activity looks at the connections between art and fashion. Throughout history artists used many different styles to represent concepts, and fashion can relate to them all. The Internet makes these styles available to you.

Identify four styles or periods of art, or consider them from the following list, and find a contemporary fashion design that appears to be inspired by it.

Abstract	Cubism	Modern
Art Deco	Expressionism	Pop
Art Nouveau	Folk	Primitive
Art style originating in a specific country	Gothic	Realism
	Impressionism	Renaissance
Baroque	Medieval	Surrealism
Contemporary		

Art Style or Period	Designer
Example of Art	Fashion Design Inspired by the Artistic Piece

Art Style or Period	Designer
Example of Art	Fashion Design Inspired by the Artistic Piece

Art Style or Period	Designer
Example of Art	Fashion Design Inspired by the Artistic Piece

Art Style or Period	Designer
Example of Art	Fashion Design Inspired by the Artistic Piece

continued from page 63

cinema, television, and other media

The cinema has a long history of influencing fashion. Films set in past centuries, such as *Shakespeare in Love*, *Pride and Prejudice*, and *Dangerous Liaisons* romanticize certain historic periods, and they can prompt revivals of corsets, lace fabrications, and exaggerated detailing. In the 1970s, the film *Annie Hall* popularized vests, baggy pants, and ties for women. The fantasy of films such as *Barbarella*, *Road Warrior*, and *Blade Runner* has prompted fashion designers to explore futuristic styling.

Television, too, has its devotees. Shows as varied as *Star Trek* and *Gossip Girl* have influenced the runway. During its long run, the show *Sex and the City* popularized innumerable looks, including Manolo Blahnik shoes.

_____

_____

_____

current events

Events large and small can have an impact on fashion. A new presidency can be the impetus for fashion change. President Barak Obama, often found working in his shirtsleeves, has been noted as ushering in an informal culture to the White House (Stolberg, 2009) (Figure 2.9). The troubled economy of 2008 and 2009 greatly influenced the apparel field. *Women's Wear Daily* reported that the recession sparked a paradigm shift in fashion. Fundamental industry changes were prompted by consumers demanding value at low prices, companies having to do more with less, and a society that has linked brand awareness to social issues (Shifting Paradigm, 2009, pp. 8–10).

_____

_____

_____

design

The world of design can include everything from common household utensils to computer-generated graphics. Design is inherent in nearly every aspect of life, from the mundane to the sublime. Because of its ubiquitous nature though, it is often taken for granted. Good design is often thought to add pleasure and civility to living. Look to design for craftsmanship, composition, communication of ideas, decoration, embellishment, and beauty. Examine typography, computer interfaces, printmaking, products, visuals, and systems for their intrinsic design. Graphic design often captures the essence of a mood in quick, easy strokes and an economy of lines.

_____

_____

_____

Figure 2.9

First Lady Michelle Obama brings her own design aesthetic to the White House. Although she is known to wear pricier items from Narciso Rodriguez and Jimmy Choo and mix and match designer brands with lesser known names, she embraces affordable brands, such as Talbots, White House/Black Market, and J Crew (shown here). Her children, Sasha and Malia, are often seen in the J Crew kid's line, crewcuts. © *Jim Young/Reuters/Corbis*

international focus

The people of the world are connected by a world-wide network of ideas and products. The Internet has made it possible for information to be transmitted immediately and continuously. Geography no longer constrains where designers seek inspiration or where they will find a market for their products. The international focus opens up innumerable increased opportunities for designers, but they can also expect increased competition from international entities.

_____

_____

_____

nature and raw materials

Nature is a time-tested source of design inspiration, but with the renewed focus on protecting the environment, back-to-nature designing has taken on new relevance. With careful consideration, many natural resources are renewable and biodegradable, so their use may cause less pollution and less strain on landfills. Natural materials, such as stone, grasses, and wood, can add exciting touches via zipper pulls, buttons, and surface decoration and also interesting avenues for avant-garde wearable art and exploratory design. Manmade materials are equally conducive to experimentation. Plastics and metals can be molded to form the body. Chain mail, featured in various sizes, can cowl and drape as beautifully as some silks.

_____

_____

_____

popular culture

Popular culture contains the perspectives and attitudes of a group. It is highly influenced by media of all sorts, including music, film, advertising, sports, fashion, and a number of online forums and blogs. It can be fickle and unpredictable, however, and it changes constantly. Popular culture is unique in that it is a reflection of one particular place in time and a window into that period.

_____

_____

_____

print and online materials

A preponderance of fashion magazines and periodicals makes it possible to keep up with changes in style. The _Vogue_ series, _Elle_, _Women's Wear Daily_, _Details_, _GQ_, the _Collezioni_ series, and _InStyle_ are all resources that present timely fashions and trends. _Lucky_, a self-proclaimed magazine about shopping and style, offers information on updating wardrobes, the latest fashions, and beauty. Many of these periodicals offer online editions, too. Style.com is a comprehensive online website that offers up-to-the-minute information on designer runway shows and other fashion events.

Although all of these resources are invaluable to the fashion designer, you should also venture outside of the fashion world for media scanning. Publications highlighting lifestyle, fitness, music, and culture can offer fresh perspectives, and there are numerous magazines devoted to numerous specific niches. News weeklies, such as *Newsweek* and *Time*, newspapers, and online news services all seek out new and interesting information and report on it.

---

sports

College and professional sports team attire is a huge business. Many sports require players to wear a uniform, but in such sports as tennis and golf, players' attire is sponsored and planned well in advance of the sporting event. Some athletes are equally influential off the playing field. Soccer superstar David Beckham has endorsed Adidas and Armani clothing lines, and he has been featured on the cover of several fashion magazines, including *W*. Other sports stars use their celebrity to promote their own clothing brands. Venus Williams, a high-ranked tennis professional, promotes her EleVen line of affordable sportswear accessories and footwear.

---

subculture

Subcultures are groups that are brought together by a common bond. Members often use dress to show their affiliation with the group. Characteristics such as ethnicity and age can delineate groups, as can ideology. Preppy, glam, rave, emo, goth, punk, and grunge are all subcultures with their own style that can influence fashion.

---

technology

New technologies for fashion design are continually being introduced, and designers can find inspiration in technological developments in and out of the apparel field. Computerization of patternmaking, grading or sizing of patterns, and laser cutting has sped up the apparel production process. Progress has been made in the practical applications of fabrics by making them more fire resistant, eco-friendly, or absorbent. Anti-microbial fibers can eliminate odors and kill bacteria. Smart textiles have been created to react to a variety of environmental conditions. They attempt to mimic the role that skin plays in detecting and reacting to ambient conditions. Advances have also been made in recreational textiles. Garments can now be wired to work with any number of computer technologies, and conductive thread can be sewn in standard sewing machines and carry a current within a garment's fabrication. Chapter 3 presents these technological advances in further detail.

_____

_____

_____

_____

zeitgeist

This is not a conclusive list of design influences and inspiration. What's missing? Global events? The cyberworld? Politics? List your own favorite areas of inspiration, and also search out some new ones.

_____

_____

_____

_____

When using a variety of sources to scan a period, the designer begins to get a feel for the overall ambience of the time. A collective consciousness can be gleaned by investigating economic, political, cultural, sociological, and psychological, elements. All fashion designs respond in some way to the zeitgeist of a time.

change of environment

Your surroundings provide nearly limitless opportunities for insight and inspiration. It is easy to become complacent about your environs, though. Day-to-day routines can take the wonder out of everyday surroundings. It is then that you must begin to look at things in a new way or change your environment altogether. Within your home, school, and workplace, inspiration can be found by dissecting commonplace objects and concentrating on a part, rather than the whole. New ideas can be found in the petals of a flower, the pattern of a tile floor, or the inner workings of a clock. The design line of a teapot can translate into the curved seaming of a dress, or the back of a wooden chair can be interpreted into the panels of a jacket. The creativity-enhancing exercise SCAMPER offers new ways to look at objects and ideas. Complete Activity 2.4 to expand on how you look at the world.

continued on page 73

Creativity-Enhancing Exercise: SCAMPER

The current milieu, viewed in a different way, can inspire design. The creativity-enhancing exercise, SCAMPER, originated by Alex Osborn and refined into the mnemonic by Bob Eberle, suggests that new ideas can be generated by modifying something that already exists (Michalko, 2001, p. 95). In fashion, examples demonstrating this principle abound. In 1964, Rudi Gernreich created the innovative "monokini" or topless swimsuit when he modified the traditional one-piece swimsuit. In the 1980s, Norma Kamali modified women's standard shoulder lines by highlighting them with shoulder pads measuring one inch and more in thickness. In his book, *Cracking Creativity*, Michalko reminds us that "all ideas are in a state of flux" (p. 99). Designers recognize that there is no final, best design, but, rather, that all ideas build upon one another.

(left)
Rudi Gernreich "minimized" the swimsuit to such a degree that the top half disappeared altogether. © *The Metropolitan Museum of Art/Art Resource, NY*

(right)
In the exaggerated style of early Norma Kamali, the shoulder line of Lady Gaga's costumes is often "maximized" for dramatic effect. © *Ronald Wittek/ epa/Corbis*

The SCAMPER technique can be used to change an existing product into an innovative one (Michalko, 2001, pp. 95–99). Each letter in the word SCAMPER suggests an action to be performed. For this creativity-enhancing exercise, sketch one of your designs and then perform the suggested changes to transform the existing design into something new.

Substitute fabrication, trims, or style lines. *(Could a high-tech metallic be used instead of the wool twill?)*

Combine, mix, and integrate design ideas. *(Can evening wear and active wear be combined to make a multi-purpose garment?)*

Adapt, alter, or change the purpose of the garment. *(Could zippers be used to seam and hem a garment?)*

Modify, magnify, minify, or carry to a dramatic extreme. *(Can the little black dress be made in shocking chartreuse?)*

Put to another use: Determine other uses for the garment. *(Can the t-shirt zip up to form a carry-all?)*

Eliminate, subtract, simplify, or remove elements. *(Can the design be reduced to its core elements?)*

Reverse or rearrange the components. Turn the item inside out and upside down. *(Can the front of the jacket be put to the back?)*

Original Design	S

continued on page 72

continued from page 71

ACTIVITY 2.4

C	A
M	P
E	R

continued from page 69

Observant designers are able to find inspiration in their environment, but creative blocks inevitably arise, and everyday surroundings get stale. One way to try to break a creative block is to venture outside your comfort zone and explore a new setting. Creativity is often identified with change, but a change in scenery is not a magic formula for creativity. A change of surroundings is most productive when designers are intentional about what they want to get out of the change. "What this means is that unless one enters the situation with some deeply felt question and the symbolic skills necessary to answer it, nothing much is likely to happen" (Csikszent-mihalyi, 1996, p. 136). When designers with prepared minds open themselves to planned new experiences, these experiences then intermingle with old ones, and new, novel combinations become possible.

a global perspective

Designers travel to other countries and make connections with other cultures for a number of reasons. First, they work within an increasingly international marketplace. Understanding the diverse attitudes and behaviors of other cultures can enable you to conduct business in a respectful and productive manner. Learning about other cultures can also enrich life experiences. "For some, developing knowledge of a second language and culture is like expanding one's personality, acquiring options that are both enriching and liberating" (Language, 2009). As part of the designer's macroenvironment, these new perspectives can provide depth and insight into design. Activity 2.5 asks you to walk in the footsteps of someone from another culture and design a line honoring his or her traditions.

Most cultures have long-established traditions with customs represented by meaningful symbols and craftsmanship that took many, many years to develop. In search of novelty, designers sometimes use these indigenous icons to adorn everything from designer fashions to T-shirts and tote bags.

Find examples where designers have used cultural symbols in their creations. Discuss the use of cultural icons in fashion design. Cite the pros and cons and state your conclusion.

Place images of fashions that incorporate cultural symbols here.

pros

_____

_____

_____

cons

_____

_____

_____

conclusion

_____

_____

_____

ACTIVITY 2.5

Creative Connections: Cultural Traditions

Most cultures have developed and matured over time. Their practices have been time-tested for centuries. It would be difficult to obtain a full understanding of a culture through a cursory investigation. A first impression of a culture may prove inaccurate. It may be unfair, and even disrespectful, to a people to take away bits and pieces from a time-honored culture without a obtaining a full understanding of the symbols and meanings behind those artifacts. Any introduction to a new environment is bound to be enlightening, but designers should take care to respect the cultural traditions of other peoples. Most museums do a great job of presenting a balanced and thorough view of the cultures they highlight in their exhibits. Some of the aspects they consider include:

Traditional clothing has cultural significance. A Sami father and son are pictured here in customary dress at a wedding in Kautokeino, Northern Norway. *Bryan and Cherry Alexander/ Photo Researchers, Inc.*

- The terrain and geography of the region
- Natural resources available to the people
- Textiles and apparel items, including shoes and headdresses
- Handmade items, crafts, and artifacts
- Ethic identities
- Local cuisine
- Annual events and celebrations
- Religions and beliefs
- Architecture and housing
- Customs
- Technologies used

Identify an indigenous culture whose traditions are celebrated in a museum or exhibit. Investigate the traditions using at least three different sources. Compile *DIN* spreads and *Ideas* lists based on the bulleted points. Illustrate a collection of coordinated designs that honors the collective aspects of the culture.

Culture example	Research notes

Sketch

a change of mind

World travel is undeniably stimulating, but it is not always possible. A change of mental environment also inspires, and it can be accomplished in so many ways. A weekend in a new city, a museum visit, a thrift store shopping trip, or even a perusal of an unfamiliar magazine can jolt an individual out of customary habits and prompt unexpected connections (Figure 2.10). Exploring outside the apparel discipline can be especially conducive to making unusual connections. Architecture, art, history, and music are fields that offer rich possibilities, but also consider an investigative project in biology, chemistry, philosophy, or physics for making those unusual associations that can bring life into a line. These different mental surroundings can spark creativity and Activity 2.6 asks you to move out of your comfort zone by exploring an environment that is new to you.

environmentally friendly designing

Designers can take an active role in sustaining the creativity-friendly environment in which they live and work. Rich and varied surroundings are the lifeblood of designers, so they have a stake in supporting endeavors that maintain their wide-ranging sources of inspiration. **Sustainable fashion, eco-fashion,** and **eco-friendly design** are terms that refer to a holistic approach to fashion design and consider the social and environmental impact of a product. **Full-cycle sustainability** considers the life of a product to be circular in nature. The usefulness of a product does not end when the consumer no longer wants it. The product is cycled back into production and its components are used again. In an industry that advocates "out with the old and in with the new" each season, it may seem that sustainable fashion is an oxymoron and incompatible with practices that help preserve the environment. Historically, there have been many

Figure 2.10
You don't have to take a trip to a far away land to be exposed to new ideas. Inspiration is as near as the closest museum. This Tim Burton exhibit at the Museum of Modern Art, NY, blends aspects of filmmaking, drawing, painting, photography, concept art, puppetry, and costuming for a medley of pop culture expression. *Getty Images*

instances where this was indeed true. From the ground and water pollution resulting from fiber and fabric production to wasteful apparel production practices, the apparel industry has been guilty of grievous assaults on the environment. Although the industry has a long way to go to in aligning its practices with those that will sustain the environment, progress has been made at every step in the life cycle of an apparel product. Organic fiber production, low-impact dyeing and finishing, garment recycling, and other new eco-friendly practices are alternatives to traditional apparel production methods. Designers can embrace these environmentally friendly practices while also gaining new perspectives on design. Searching for ways to use and reuse current resources efficiently can provide fresh inspiration for creative design.

There is no single, correct approach to environmentally friendly design. Designers should try to find a method that works for them and their customers. The first step may be to become aware of the entire life cycle of the goods one produces to see where contributions to sustainability can be made. Inroads into sustainability are possible at each juncture, but by understanding the entire life of an apparel item, you can consider the entire impact of the garment. For example, bamboo is a fast-growing, renewable resource that requires little or no pesticides because it is naturally resistant to many bothersome pests. However, bamboo fabric is often finished using traditional, chemical-based dyeing and finishing processes that may contribute to water pollution. During their life, most apparel items pass through the following phases:

- Fiber production
- Textile production
- Apparel design
- Apparel manufacture
- Packaging and shipping
- Retail outlets
- Consumer
- Post consumer

Armed with the full knowledge of the life cycle of their products, designers can determine how to make the most impact on sustaining their environment.

fiber production

Growing crops for fiber production requires water and usually fertilizers and chemicals to control pests and weeds. Natural fibers like cotton, silk, linen, and wool require chemicals, if not in the growing, then in the treating of the fibers. Manufactured fibers generally require less water in the production process than natural fibers, but the amount of energy consumed and the use of nonrenewable resources is much greater. Organic and low-chemical crops can be grown under careful conditions to mitigate harm to local water supplies. Recycled fibers and renewable fibers, such as bamboo, lyocell, or PLA, which is made from corn (Figure 2.11) may be viable alternatives to more traditional fibers (Fletcher, 2008).

textile production

Converting raw fiber into finished fabric requires energy, water, and, most often, toxic chemicals, but the production process is constantly being improved to lessen the impact on the environment. Designers can consider fabrics made from natural,

Figure 2.11
Fashion fabrics made from corn offer promising avenues for eco-friendly design. Corn fiber is biodegradable, compostable, and annually renewable. The trim on this dress made of PLA corn fiber is a salute to the fabric's origin. The "beads" at the tie ends are actual kernels of corn. *Photographer: Eileen Molony. Courtesy of the author's collection*

A Change of Scenery

Move out of your comfort zone by exploring an environment that is new to you. Record the experience by entering information into your *DIN*. Suggestions include trying a new cuisine, visiting a museum exhibit with a dedicated theme, taking a city walk and exploring the local architecture, or taking an online trip to a discipline or topic you are unfamiliar with. Use the thumbnail templates below to create sketches inspired by your change of scenery experiences. Additional templates could be found in the Appendix.

Notes for Discussion

_____

_____

_____

_____

_____

_____

_____

_____

undyed fibers, such as wool or alpaca, instead of fabrics dyed in hues like red or black (Figure 2.12). More chemicals are required to create these deep colors. Also, interesting color and print patterns can be derived from experimenting with a variety of natural plant dyes ranging from madder and indigo to rhubarb root and walnut hulls. It should be noted, though, that even these dyes usually require polluting fixing agents to set the colors.

apparel design

Sustainable fashion design can sometimes prove challenging for small designers because textile production practices are not always transparent, and it may be difficult to uncover the environmental impact of some of the fabrics they use. Terms like "organic" and "natural" can be ambiguous and misleading. There is ample potential, however, for sustainable design in the apparel design stage. Opportunities range from recycling and no-waste designing to multi-use apparel and garment customization.

recycling

Any action that keeps materials out of the landfills can contribute to a cleaner environment. Designers can take advantage of the volume of clothing items made available by a disposable culture. Entrepreneurs are creating new designs by piecing together eclectic found and donated apparel items (Figure 2.13). Knitted sweaters can be unraveled and the yarn reused. The sheer abundance and limitless availability of denim jeans makes reworking denim apparel especially feasible.

Figure 2.12 (above) Natural hair and plant fibers, such as those in the undyed alpaca yarns shown here, are found in a variety of shades of beiges, tans, and grays. Traditional practices call for bleaching these fibers white and then dyeing them to the desired shade. By embracing the natural heathered hues of the fiber, pollution-causing processes can be eliminated in the textile production stage. *Courtesy of Cascade Yarns*

Figure 2.13 (left) This garment required no new resources. It was created completely from recycled materials. Thoughtful piecing makes an eclectic mix of fabrics viable in a single design composition. *Designer: Anna Chmel Photographer: Eileen Molony Courtesy of the author's collection*

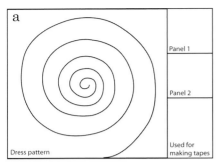

Figure 2.14
In no waste design, designers visualize not only how a garment will look on the consumer but also how the pattern pieces will layout in a marker. All pieces share cutting lines, leaving no fabric waste (a). This spiral dress design utilizes the entire yardage (b and c). Style does not have to be compromised in order to achieve good fabric utilization; however, considerable time is needed in the design process. *Designed and Illustrated: Hae Jin Gam Photographer: Jun Young Hur Model: Megan Jones Courtesy of the author's collection*

no-waste designing

Roughly 15 to 20 percent of the yardage of a typical garment can fall out as waste between the pattern pieces on a typical marker or pattern layout. This new fabric will be disposed of without ever being utilized. Enterprising designers can make use of these scraps by piecing or quilting them together in innovative ways. Or designers can work with their patternmakers to create designs that yield little or no waste. For knitted garments, the pattern can be planned so that only the exact pattern pieces are knitted and then sewn. In full-fashion knitting, needles are dropped to create an exact shape of the piece. Planned knitting and full-fashioning result in garments with no yarn waste.

Woven garments can also be made with no waste. Rectangular-shaped pieces are conducive to no-waste designing because they can fit together and interlock, jigsaw fashion. In the no-waste design in Figure 2.14, the entire yardage was utilized. By manipulating the size of the pleats and seam allowances and using elastic smocking for fit, the designer can create a range of sizes from a single full utilization marker.

multi-use apparel

The low cost and easy availability of today's fashions have helped to create a throwaway fashion culture wherein items are worn for one season and then discarded. This practice is detrimental to the environment because an overabundance of clothing is relegated to landfills. It takes hundreds of years for a polyester clothing item to decompose. One way to address this sustainability issue is to create coordinates that can be mixed and matched to create several outfits from varying combinations of a limited number of pieces. Another is to produce single garments that are versatile. Clothing that can be worn many different ways for many occasions can satisfy consumers' desire for variability without their having to purchase multiple items (Figure 2.15).

customization

Involving the consumer in the design process can also lead to more eco-friendly designing because consumers are more likely to keep and wear, and, hence, less likely to discard, pieces that they either had a hand in creating or that were designed just for them. This kind of designing capitalizes on the emotional attachment that can form between a user and a garment. Personalized and individualized garments can range from customizable jeans to digitally printed textiles. With digital printing, prints can be manipulated to individual tastes and personalized to have meaning to

Figure 2.15
The Butter dress by Nadia can be worn 12 different ways (front and back views shown). The versatile styling ranges from conservative daywear to alluring evening attire. Clever wrapping even allows for a variety of dress lengths, thus providing a multitude of wardrobe options within a single garment. Not only does this concept save natural resources, it is also economically prudent for the consumer. *Courtesy of Nadia Tarr of Butter by Nadia; images by Elizabeth Smolarz*

Figure 2.16
Digital printing offers
exciting new ways
to customize fashion
design. The garments
in this photo are
identical. They were
cut from the same
pattern and sewn the
same way. However,
the size and direction
of the stripes and the
size and placement
of the flowers were
manipulated on
the prototype on
the right to create
the illusion of a
smaller waist. *Print
designer: Susan Wu
Photographer:
Eileen Molony*

the wearer. The size of prints can be altered to better correspond to a person's stature or augmented to accent a person's figure. By strategically placing the digital graphic design on each individual pattern piece, designers are no longer constrained by the fixed textile designs of mass-produced piece goods, and no dye is wasted by printing fabric that will not be used. Designers can accentuate figure attributes and downplay problem areas (Jennings, 2007) (Figure 2.16).

apparel manufacturing

Often called the **cut-make-trim** stage, the manufacturing of apparel is a largely manual operation, focusing on social and worker concerns, rather than environmental issues (Fletcher, 2008). Manufacturing follows where the labor is least expensive. A lot of energy is used in the transport of fabric, cut garment pieces, and sewn garments. A single garment style could have components manufactured in several different countries (Figure 2.17). Manufacturing in the country where the clothing items are sold saves the energy required for shipping. Manufacturers can also consider how their product will be cleaned and cared for by the consumer. Garments that can be laundered in cold water and hung to dry have less environmental impact than garments that must be dry cleaned and professionally pressed.

Figure 2.17

Today's apparel industry is truly global. Textiles manufactured in different countries can be selected at a textile fair, such as the one in Shanghai (a), cut and sewn into clothing in another country (b), and sold at retail in a third country (c). The factory shown here is in Bolivia, where labor is cheaper for a U.S. manufacturer than it would be at home. Uniqlo, a Japanese company, exemplifies retailers whose business is international.
Getty Images (a);
AFP/Getty Images (b);
AFP/Getty Images (c)

apparel packaging and shipping

Packaging has undergone a lot of scrutiny in recent years. Although some packing materials are required to protect the product and keep it visually attractive, excessive and extraneous packaging has become harder to justify. Bagging and shipping multiple items together, instead of piece by piece, consumes less energy and also requires fewer packing materials. Shoes and handbags are often shipped with large amounts of packaging (Figure 2.18). This packaging is immediately discarded after it reaches the final consumer.

retail outlets

Efforts toward sustainable design do not have to stop after garments are shipped to retail outlets. Designers can establish relationships with retailers that will help continue their efforts toward sustainability (Figure 2.19). Retailers can act as a liaison between the designer/manufacturer and the consumer, passing along information about eco-friendly garment care and also product recycling. Retailers can also carefully consider their own sustainable practices. Packaging accompanies the sale of nearly every retail apparel item. This packaging, which often includes multiple layers of tissue paper, a folded box, and a bag, is most often discarded as soon as the customer arrives at home. Recycled and biodegradable bags and boxes can be used to reduce the impact that packaging makes on the environment. Some retail stores are reducing waste by encouraging customers to bring their own reusable bags when shopping.

consumer

Consumers support designers' efforts to become environmentally friendly. They want to purchase eco-friendly attire, but they just do not want to spend a lot of extra money on it or time researching the products (Leaner, 2009). Consumers are very wary of being **greenwashed**, wherein companies misrepresent their product's role in

sustainability (Still Green, 2008). Consumers are confused by the disparity of eco-terminology, and they need an environmental labeling system they can trust. With the goal of transparency, several companies are taking the lead in educating their customers in their sustainability efforts. Timberland has initiated a "green index" that investigates the climate impact, chemicals used, and resource consumption of their products. Patagonia's "Footprint Chronicles" is an interactive website that allows viewers to track the impact of some of their key products from design to delivery (Figure 2.20).

post consumer

Many may consider the consumer to be the end of the line for apparel items, but what consumers ultimately do with their clothing items can make a big impact on the environment. Will a garment be relegated to a landfill, or will it be recycled to extend its viable life? Patagonia sponsors the "Common Threads Garment Recycling Program," through which customers can return fleece, cotton t-shirts, and some

Figure 2.20
What does it mean when a retailer says it is "going green"? Timberland rates its products using a "green index." The lower the score, the smaller the environmental footprint associated with making the product (a). Patagonia provides a transparent production process. In the down sweater example shown here (b), the consumer is party to the company's sustainability efforts in (1) design, (2) the raising of geese for their down, (3) the down cleaning process, (4) the recycling of plastic bottles to make the polyester shell, (5) the manufacture of the articles in immaculate factories in China, and (6) the distribution process. *Courtesy of Timberland (a) and Patagonia (b)*

Figure 2.21

These Dacca Boots are made from post-consumer plastic bags. They are built by fusing several layers of plastic shopping bags together, resulting in a water resistant material, sturdy enough to mold. The original artwork of the bag remains, though, and contributes to the unique design. *Courtesy of Camila Labrá*

polyester and nylon products to the company. The environmentally focused company transforms the unusable garments into new clothing (Figure 2.21). Realizing the short lifecycle of today's fashions, other design entrepreneurs are designing garments for quick disassembly. **Upcycling** is a process whereby garments are returned to the manufacturer, taken apart, and recreated into new current styling. At the grass roots level, consumers are conducting **wardrobe surgery** workshops, where individuals swap and customize old clothing items.

At every stage in the garment production process there is opportunity for new avenues of eco-friendly design. At one time, the words "sustainable fashion" may have seemed contradictory, but, today, working towards full-cycle, environmentally friendly design is not only plausible, it is inspirational.

summary

Creativity can be fostered within both a designer's micro- and macroenvironment. Diverse, supportive, and exciting surroundings, where experimentation and flexibility thrive, are conducive to creativity. Stagnant and stressful environments that include excessive sanctions against mistakes derived from creative investigation, can inhibit creativity. Individuals can learn much about the world in which they design. Society abides by rules and laws that can constrain, but also focus and direct, a designer's vision. Designers develop their voices by opening themselves up to the boundless information and experiences available to them and refocusing them into exciting avenues for design inspiration.

KEY TERMS

creativogenic	lab	mannequin	sustainable fashion	cut-make-trim
congenial	studio	environmental scanning	eco-fashion	greenwashed
microenvironment	workroom	demographics	eco-friendly design	upcycling
macroenvironment	voice	psychographics	full-cycle sustainability	wardrobe surgery
mores	dress form			

DIN Challenge: Sustainable Design

Create a fashion design that uses environmentally friendly practices and no new or newly purchased materials. Use only found, owned, or borrowed materials. Consider deconstructing, reconstructing, overdyeing with natural dyes, embellishing with found natural resources, stripping, unraveling, folding, tying, and/or piecing the materials. Be sure to refer to what you have entered into your *DIN* for this chapter for inspiration. List *Ideas* that stem from all your entries, assemble *Themes*, and create *Connections* that will guide you in responding to the challenge.

Notes for Discussion

_____

_____

_____

_____

_____

_____

_____

3 creativity *and* cognition

"Creative people think a lot. They are thinking about the next step. They are thinking about the path they want to go on. They are thinking about what it is that they want to say in the end, what they will say visually at the end. There's a *lot* of thought involved." This statement by a fashion design instructor suggests that the fashion design process is more complex than it might appear. Popular media usually focus on the product and not on the process of fashion design, and the glamour, without all of the inherent hard work, is shown. In the shadows of the runway gowns are the concepts, connections, thoughts, and insights, or the **cognition**, behind those designs.

It is common to think of creativity in the affective realm. Emotional and motivational aspects of the concept are abundant. Creativity is thought to result from a combination of traits, however, and thought processes are also integral to an understanding of creativity. Remember that although these traits work in unison and interdependently, traits are singled out in these chapters in order to clarify certain concepts.

creativity-enhancing cognitive skills

Cognitive aspects of creativity revolve around making **connections**. Connections are made by associating information with, and in contrast to, other information. (Cropley, 2001, pp. 36–45.) Common associations can result in common connections. Unusual associations can result in unusual connections. A wide range of interests and a broad knowledge base that reaches across disciplines can foster the connection process. From a young age, individuals learn to place what they know into categories. This helps them make sense of the world, and it also allows for practical navigation through life's day-to-day events. For example, coffee filters are associated with making hot beverages. These practical associations can become an impediment to design, though, when they become fixed and prevent you from making new, more unusual associations. When filters are automatically placed into a category with

"Lightness and transparency, and various references to Pina Bausch, Lynn Chadwick and the 11th century's 'The Tale of Genji."
—Ralph Rucci, Chado Ralph Rucci

(opposite) Image of smoke that fashion designer Ralph Rucci used as inspiration for the Spring 2010 Ready to Wear (RTW) collection for New York Fashion Week. *Courtesy of WWD/ Graham Jeffrey*

OBJECTIVES

— To understand the role of cognition in apparel design

— To explore the design possibilities of divergent thinking

— To investigate the theory of multiple intelligences and discover its connections to creativity

— To survey the apparel industry's long history of technological advances

— To explore how technology can be used as a tool in contemporary fashion design

Figure 3.1
Hussein Chalayan is not limited by typical design constraints. In his *Afterwards* collection, he connects apparel design to furniture design. Chair covers transform into dresses and this telescoping skirt converts to a table when not being worn. *Courtesy of* WWD/*Giovanni Giannoni*

coffee, it keeps you from thinking that most filters are made from nonwoven textiles that could be utilized in interesting fashion design. In this way, common associations deter innovation. If one always categorizes a raincoat as double-breasted, tan, and belted, then opportunities for innovative raincoat design are limited. Creative designers will attempt to make unusual associations and build atypical categories so their designs are fresh and unexpected (Figure 3.1). You have a chance to practice making unusual connections in Activity 3.1.

divergent and convergent thinking

Cognition, as it refers to creativity, can be thought of as being divergent or convergent. **Divergent thinking** emphasizes multiple responses to open-ended situations. It is branching out. **Convergent thinking** is considered to be effective in situations that can be reasoned from existing information. It is focusing in. Both modes of thinking have applications in apparel design. Brainstorming strategies, for example, utilize both strategies. First, participants produce lots of ideas; then, to come up with a response to the challenge, they select relevant material from that list.

Divergent thinking, however, is more often associated with creativity because it is used as a way to generate novel ideas. It is free-flowing, transformative, and inspirational. Many fashion design classes make use of divergent thinking strategies. Challenges are often open ended, and students are encouraged to generate their own solutions to design problems, rather than repeat steps from a book or their instructor. Divergent thinking tactics include (Goff & Torrance, 2002):

* Fluency

* Originality

* Flexibility

* Elaboration

"**Fluency** is the ability to produce quantities of ideas which are relevant to the task. The creative person typically evidences the ability to generate multiple or alternative ideas and solutions, both verbally and figurally" (p. 26). Within a fashion design challenge, this tactic can relate to being able to design a large number of apparel items given one inspiration. Individuals working for mass market manufacturers need to be fluent designers. They are often required to create volumes of concepts based on a few new, hot trends. For example, an accessory designer may generate hundreds of ideas for gloves and hats each season.

"**Originality** is the ability to produce uncommon ideas or ideas that are totally new or unique. A creative person tends to produce such new ideas rather than follow the more common path" (p. 26). Whereas fluency considers the number of designs, originality—also known as *novelty*—looks at the uniqueness of those creations in relation to the other ideas presented. Original designs depart from the usual. They are surprising and exceptional. For example, a gored skirt might be a

Unusual Associations

Complete the chart to discover unusual associations that can be made with common concepts. The first column contains elements from the apparel field and other areas. In the second column, list traits commonly associated with those items. In the third column, list unconventional fashion approaches to the same item. Select the most interesting apparel associations and illustrate them in your *DIN*.

Concepts	Common Associations	Uncommon Associations
Beachwear	Sandals Swimsuit Floral sarong	As wedding attire Inspired by the business suit Using faux fur fabrication
Business suit		
Corset		
T-shirt		
Fusible interfacing		
Tape measure		
Gloves		
Screen mesh		
Bottle caps		
Macrame		

common response when a designer is challenged to use an umbrella as inspiration. A waterproof wearable cocoon might be an unusual response to the same design challenge because it refers more to the conceptual aspects of the umbrella, rather than the literal lines of the framework.

"**Flexibility** is the ability to process information or objects in different ways given the same stimulus. Flexible thinking is especially important when logical approaches fail to produce satisfactory results" (p. 26). Designs that result from flexible thinking fall into different categories. "Dresses," "blouses," and "skirts" can be said to be in the same category of women's apparel. "Lingerie" and "outerwear," however, are two different categories, and a designer who can create viable products in both can be said to be more flexible than the designer who is able to create within only one of the categories.

"**Elaboration** is the ability to embellish ideas with details. Rather than being restricted to the core idea, a creative person tends to provide such embellishment" (p. 26). When designers struggle with innovation, the core idea may not be the problem. Rather, a lack of novelty may be caused by a lack of complexity, amplification, and follow-through. Elaboration of design is a concerted dedication to the concept that brings together fabrication, styling, design detailing, and construction, and experienced designers do this with aplomb.

Designers can use divergent thinking tactics to gain inspiration from any number of concepts. Activity 3.2 asks you to consider architecture as your muse.

At first glance, convergent thinking appears to be the antithesis of creativity. It refers to narrowing, selecting, and following guidelines to arrive at an answer. This is not what most people think of when they consider fashion design. There is a place for convergent thinking in design, though. It is infinitely enjoyable to collect ideas and research history and other cultures in order to make novel connections. Perusing magazines and sketching in an inspiration notebook is play, not work, for most designers. There comes a time, though, when ideas and concepts must be realized in fabric. The broad network of ideas that a designer has gathered needs to be honed to a workable, viable, potent few. Convergent thinking, combined with evaluative or critical thinking, can be utilized effectively for this task. Designers use critical thinking skills when they reflect on the connections they have made and formulate a clear concept that will address the design challenge.

problem solving and problem finding

Creativity is often thought of as problem solving. **Problem solving** can simply refer to finding a solution to an existing condition. In fashion design and other forms of artistic expression this definition is incomplete. Many times, as in artistic endeavors, there is no problem that needs solving. The goal may be to communicate a concept or self-expression. So, to include these aesthetic aspects, the definition of problem solving is often expanded to include making progress toward some goal. However, there is a distinction between solving a design problem and actually envisaging the germane problem that needs to be solved. Creativity may actually be more dependent on recognizing and identifying the problem in the first place or **problem-finding** abilities (Runco, 2003). Beginners often look at the concrete, surface structure of a problem and try to solve it based on those superficial aspects. Experts, however, often look beyond the obvious problem to its underlying deep structure. This makes problem finding more arduous, but once the relevant problem has been identified, formulating a response to it may be surprisingly easy (Cropley, 2001, p. 48).

Inspiration with Divergent Thinking

Santiago Calatrava is a renowned painter, sculptor, and architect. His works are inspired by the repetitions and complexity found in nature. His architectural designs include the Puente del Alamillo (made for the Universal Exposition of Seville), the Milwaukee Art Museum, and the Olympics sports complex in Athens.

Refer to Calatrava's proposed Chicago Spire, or investigate any other of Calatrava's works, and practice the four divergent thinking techniques. Utilize the thumbnail templates from the Appendix to sketch the following:

- Apparel designs that remain relevant to the selected Calatrava work (fluency).

- Designs that are inherently unique and different from other designs you have sketched, but still remain relevant to the selected work (flexibility).

- Designs that are completely different from those by everyone else in the group (originality).

- Detailing; expand on your best designs to add richness, complexity, sophistication, and decoration (elaboration).

Illustrate your final design.

Final Illustration

The *Spire* by architect Santiago Calatrava.
Getty Images

In fashion design, for example, the solution to a particular design problem simply may be to put in a zipper that connects two components, but the question that the designer asked could have concerned the innate nature of a garment and how it could be used for multiple purposes.

> Creative people are constantly surprised. They don't assume that they understand what is happening around them, and they don't assume that anybody else does either. They question the obvious—not out of contrariness but because they see the shortcomings of accepted explanations before the rest of us do. . . . The reason we consider the artists of the Renaissance so creative is that they were able to express the emancipation of the human spirit from the shackles of religious tradition before the humanist scholars or anyone else did (Csikszentmihalyi, 1996, p. 363).

You can practice the skill of problem finding by (1) understanding what is personally important, (2) considering challenges from many viewpoints, (3) exploring the implications of the obstacle, and (4) keeping options open while attempting to reach the goal (pp. 364–366).

Language predisposes our minds to look at problems a certain way and locks us in to its inherent parameters. For example, we can only describe the beauty of a flower to the extent that our language enables us. The Creativity-Enhancing Exercise Mindmapping (Activity 3.3) can make our thoughts visible and open new avenues for expression. Renowned creativity thinkers have been known to use drawings, diagrams, pictures, lines, arrows, and other visual representations to help in problem finding and problem solving. Leonardo Da Vinci's notebooks reveal that he used illustrations to record his thoughts (Figure 3.2). His notes and language were secondary to the visual images. Albert Einstein, Martha Graham, Thomas A. Edison, and Charles Darwin all had the ability to represent their subjects visually by diagramming and mapping (Michalko, 2001, p. 53).

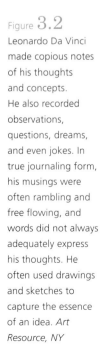

Figure 3.2
Leonardo Da Vinci made copious notes of his thoughts and concepts. He also recorded observations, questions, dreams, and even jokes. In true journaling form, his musings were often rambling and free flowing, and words did not always adequately express his thoughts. He often used drawings and sketches to capture the essence of an idea. *Art Resource, NY*

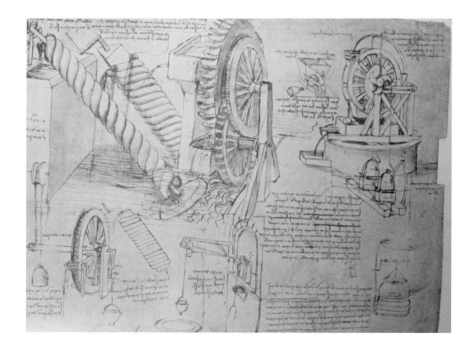

ACTIVITY 3.3

Creativity-Enhancing Exercise: Mindmapping

Mindmapping is a way to represent whatever is in your mind. The technique was introduced by British brain researcher Tony Buzan in the 1970s. It is a tool to help individuals break from the habit of thinking linearly and broaden the associations that lead to innovative connections and new inspiration. It encourages synthesizing concepts and making comparisons.

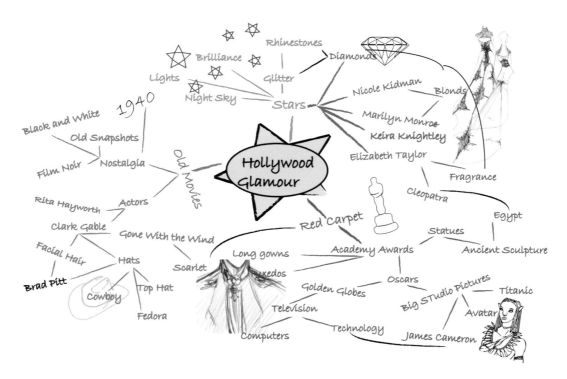

Mindmapping guidelines (Michalko, 2001, p. 58–60):

1. Place a design theme word or visual representation of the theme in the center of a large sheet of paper. Draw a circle around it.

2. Around the circle, print, as quickly as you can, pertinent key words that represent thoughts associated with the center theme. (It is said that printing makes more of a visual image in your mind, so the key words will be easier to remember.) Just a few key words are needed.

3. Consider each key word and jot down everything that comes to mind. When you run out of ideas on one key word, pick any other thought on the map and continue adding ideas.

4. Connect the key words with lines so you can visualize relationships.

5. Use graphics and colors. Color code ideas, highlight main points, use numbers, arrows, and symbols to help you visualize connections and concepts.

6. Organize clusters of ideas into themes and note new associations.

7. Choose a viable theme that you can expand on through fashion design.

continued on page 96

continued from page 95

Mindmapping

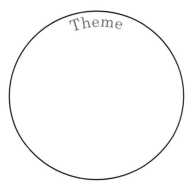

theory of multiple intelligences

In fashion design, students are encouraged to follow their own design path and develop their own voice. Designers, after all, are not all the same. Howard Gardner (1983) agrees and suggests that people possess a range of abilities. In his **theory of multiple intelligences**, he details how people can live and learn using the following eight forms of intelligence:

1. Linguistic intelligence

   - Comprehends written and spoken word

   - Enjoys debate

   - Enjoys reading

2. Logical-mathematical intelligence

   - Possesses problem-solving skills

   - Enjoys abstract ideas

   - Recognizes patterns

3. Musical intelligence

   - Enjoys singing and playing musical instruments

   - Thinks in patterns, rhythms, and sounds

   - Appreciates music

4. Visual and spatial intelligence

   - Uses visualization skills

   - Enjoys drawing, painting, and visual arts

   - Interprets images

5. Bodily kinesthetic intelligence

   - Enjoys dancing or sports

   - Possesses physical coordination and dexterity

   - Maintains strong physical control

6. Interpersonal intelligence

   - Understands and interacts with people

   - Assesses motivations of others

   - Enjoys groups and resolves conflicts

7. Intrapersonal intelligence

   - Is aware of emotional states, motivations, and feelings

   - Analyzes strengths and weaknesses

   - Is self-aware

8. Naturalistic intelligence (added in 1996)

   - Appreciates nature

   - Enjoys exploring and nurturing the environment

   - Hikes and gardens

Gardner states emphatically that these intelligences do not operate in isolation. Individuals possess varying degrees of each of the intelligences. So, the purpose is not to categorize individuals; it is to better understand them. This theory is often referenced in education, but it also has application in fashion design. Designers can come to understand their own strengths, and this can reinforce their personal design styles. Design challenges are often open-ended so designers, familiar with their intelligences, can cater to those tendencies and not have to struggle with actions that are contrary to their natural style. For example, a designer who favors a visual-spatial intelligence may prefer draping on a dress form to flat pattern making. Also, individuals wanting to make additional connections can expand their experience by attempting to design using intelligences that they normally do not prefer to use.

List the intelligences that best describe your thinking styles. Comment on why you included that intelligence.

Intelligence   Comment

1. _____

2. _____

3. _____

4. _____

5. _____

6. _____

7. _____

8. _____

The theory of multiple intelligences is also one more tool that designers can use to understand their customer base. Niche markets often develop around persons with a proclivity toward a particular intelligence. For example, imagine that North Face, a retail outlet specializing in active outdoor apparel, has developed its brand by catering to those with a naturalistic intelligence. When designers make connections to their customers' intelligences, customers repay them with loyalty to the designers' brand. Activity 3.4 asks you to think about the kind of apparel people with each intelligence like to wear.

technology

Like creativity, **technology** is a ubiquitous term that can have different meanings. It often arises out of cognitive thought processes that include reasoning and accuracy. In common parlance, the term is most often used to describe the newest advances in electrical and micro-engineering, but it is not all metal and machines. Random House (2009) defines technology as "the sum of the ways in which social groups provide themselves with the material objects of their civilization." This comprehensive definition is well suited to the apparel industry because the field has a long history of fiber, fabric, and design innovations that are both hand- and machine-produced.

Multiple Intelligences

Select eight blank pages in your DIN. Place a heading at the top of each page that corresponds to each of the intelligences. Search out designs that you think would appeal to persons with each intelligence, and enter them on the corresponding pages.

Choose a design theme (career, prom, garden party, and so on) and a style of clothing (suit, men's casual, club wear, and so on). Remain relevant to the theme and style of clothing, and sketch a design that would appeal to each of the intelligences. Enter the sketches into your *DIN*.

Design Theme _____

Style of Clothing _____

Notes for Discussion

_____

_____

_____

_____

_____

_____

_____

_____

Technology infuses nearly every aspect of the contemporary apparel industry. It can be found in the nanotechnology used to develop fibers with extraordinary properties and in the automated processes throughout the apparel production chain. Creativity and technology are the *yin and yang* that combine to form a single great product. Whereas creativity can be emotional, ambiguous, concept-oriented, and flexible, technology is often rational, procedural, detail-oriented, and beset with standards. Yet, they fuse seamlessly. It is possible to have creativity without technology, and it is possible to have technology without creativity, but when they are united, look for exciting results.

Origami is a traditional technology and an expression of creativity. It is also a reminder that technology can be handcrafted and does not always imply electronics, metals, and wires. Activity 3.5 invites you to experiment with this classic tradition and incorporate origami techniques in your next fashion design.

Origami-Inspired Design

Origami is the Japanese art of folding paper. It is popular, in part, because almost everyone can practice some form of the technique. Beginners can make beautiful representations of animals and flowers with only a few folds of paper. Advanced artists can devise mathematical formulas to assist in creating technical masterpieces. Traditional rules stipulate that only one sheet of paper may be used and no cuts can be made into that sheet.

Investigate the art of origami, and use it as inspiration for fashion design. Practice the technique first with paper; then select one of the paper pieces to be translated into fabric. Experiment folding and creasing different fabrics. Crisp fabrics, such as organza, poplin, and medium-weight denim, will make stiff folds and stand up when creased. Softer fabrics will not stand without being reinforced with interfacing. In general, fabrics made of thermoplastic fibers, such as nylon and polyester, can be heat set to hold in necessary creases.

Choose one of the following ways to honor the ancient origami tradition:

- Create an item of clothing by folding a single length of cloth. Use as few cuts into the fabric as possible.

- Use the art of folding to create surface interest on a portion of a garment, such as a yoke, pair of cuffs, or peplum.

© Sebastiao Moreira/epa/Corbis

Long before the advent of nanotechnology, inroads were being made in apparel craftsmanship. The short survey that follows highlights over 2,000 years of technological advances in Western civilization. Change does not fit so neatly in categories as the listing of periods might suggest, so our labeling of time periods is more for clarification than it is to identify definitive breaks in technological developments.

After each of the following sections, make notes on how the technology of that period can influence your designs today.

ancient world (3000 B.C. – A.D. 500)

In 3000 B.C. fiber technology was already well underway. Yarns from twisted fibers were made into ropes and ties. In the ancient Middle East, spinning and weaving techniques used to make linen cloth were well developed by as early as 2260 B.C. The Minoan people of that era were also thought to have perfected cloth making. Patterns found on Minoan art pieces suggest textiles that could have been created by intricate tapestry weaving, embroidery, or painting (Tortora & Eubanks, 2005, p. 45). Ancient Greeks, too, were thought to be skillful at creating fabrics with beautiful designs. They employed refined embroidery, beading, and pleating techniques (p. 49). Most early clothing items were draped and tied around the body using square or rectangular shapes of cloth. Unfinished edges may have been hemmed, but there was very little seaming or piecing of fabrics practiced during that time (p. 27).

_____

_____

_____

_____

the middle ages (500–1500)

Although finely woven linen and wool were predominant fabrics of the period, increased trade and travel spread knowledge of silk production from Chinese, Japanese, and Korean cultures. Silk was an esteemed fabric, and it drew high prices. It was intricately woven and often adorned with stones, embroidery, and appliqués (Tortora & Eubanks, 2005, p. 90). Cross-cultural contact also brought new fabrics, such as muslin, dimity, silk, and cotton into use (p. 101). Technological developments of the period include the spinning wheel and the horizontal loom, which allowed workers to sit and operate foot pedal controls. Textile production moved out of the homes to centers for cloth production, and guilds regulated fabric quality, worker compensation, and working conditions (p. 102). Military costume brought additional advances in textile technology. Soldiers needed protection. Armor was created from quilted fabric, hardened leather, large and small metal plates, or mail. The mail was made by interlocking metal rings. Clothing of the period evolved from the loose fitting, draped pieces seen in ancient times to more closely fitted garments with lacing closures. The detailed cut often signified that the wearer belonged to a leisure class. Fashion technology evolved slowly, and women may have kept certain apparel items their entire lives. However, nobility of the late middle ages appeared to have had lavish lifestyles that required elaborate costumes. Their fashions of rich silk brocades, velvets, and fur confirmed this. Both men and women sported parti-colored costume made from brightly pieced fabrics. Headgear displayed peacock feathers, flowers, and gold spangles (pp. 123–124).

_____

_____

_____

_____

the renaissance (1400–1600)

Although apparel technologies changed slowly during the Middle Ages, the nobility and their desire for elaborate costume helped to spur fashion changes. From that period forward, however, technological advances in all aspects of fashion and apparel came about at a rapid pace. The Renaissance is a period of renewed interest in Greek and Roman classical art, architecture, and philosophers' writings. It was a time for individualism and, regardless of the profession, people were encouraged to develop their full potential. Fine woolens, silks, brocades, satins, and velvets were created on improved looms. Hand knitting, used for stockings, was popularized during this period and the knitting machine was introduced. Surface decorations on fabrics were in style. Cutwork and embroidery were popular. Lacemaking, too, began during the Renaissance period. Lace differs from embroidery in that it is constructed entirely from threads and does not need any backing fabric. Garments required elaborate inner construction to support yards of fabric. Farthingales and bum roles were structures that gave shape to the costumes (Figure 3.3). Wide neckline ruffs were prevalent, and buttons were introduced.

_____

_____

_____

_____

Figure 3.3

Elaborate undergarments, technological wonders, were required to create the silhouettes of the late eighteenth century. The corset held in a woman's waist and the pannier held out her generous skirt. © V&A Images, Victoria and Albert Museum

baroque and rococo (1700–1800)

Baroque style was extravagant and excessive. Rococo style, too, was lavish, but it is characterized by curves, scrollwork, and a refinement that contrasts with the heavier themes of the Baroque period. Indian muslin, chintz, and calicos were popular. Changes in agriculture, manufacturing, and transportation profoundly affected nearly all aspects of life during this time. Largely influenced by textile industries, manual labor was being replaced by mechanization and the Industrial Revolution was on its way. "The Industrial Revolution in England began partly as a result of attempts to mechanize production of English cottons so that they would be more competitive with the cheaper imports from India, which were threatening English industry" (Tortora & Eubanks, 2005, p. 196). The **cotton gin**, patented in 1794, mechanized the very labor-intensive process of separating the cotton fibers from the seeds. Several advances in technology made spinning processes faster and faster. Fashion became an engine for growth and a motive for mass production. By the end of the eighteenth century, both steam and water power were being used to run textile machinery. The flying shuttle, which automatically carried yarn across the fabric, also sped up production.

---

the nineteenth century (1800–1900)

A factory system resulted from the Industrial Revolution. European and American manufacturers were able to replicate fabrics that they had previously imported. Womens' garments of the period still required considerable inner technologies to hold out full skirts and to hold in small waists. Bustles, hoop skirts, and corsets were prevalent. Trimmings included ruching or gathering, flounces, pleats, scallops, and cordings. Gloves and silk or cotton knitted stockings were worn.

In contrast, the gold rush in America created a need for durable trousers. Levi Strauss & Co. took advantage of the opportunity and created sturdy, blue denim pants that featured riveted pockets and double stitching. The first patents on the sewing machine were taken out in the 1840s, and the demand for uniforms for the civil war quickly revealed the usefulness of the machine. The Singer company was one of the first to manufacture appliances with interchangeable parts. Attachments to the sewing machines made braiding, tucking, and pleating quick and easy, hence, the use of trimmings increased (Tortora & Eubanks, 2005, pp. 306–307). Fashion in the nineteenth century was truly a product of technology. Low costs and increased availability made manufactured apparel items available to the masses (Figure 3.4).

Figure 3.4
With the invention of the sewing machine along came increased design and construction capabilities. Garments made with the double-thread sewing process were guaranteed not to rip. *The New-York Historical Society*

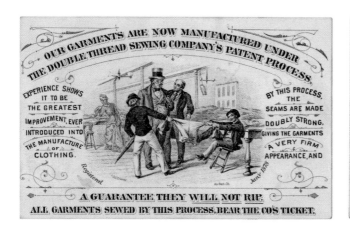

the twentieth century (1900–2000)

Automobiles and electricity ushered in the twentieth century, and factory production was in full force. The piecework concept made apparel manufacturing efficient and cost effective. By the early 1900s, every article of clothing could be bought in stores or by mail order.

Synthetic fabrics were introduced; rayon was first, followed by nylon. Polyester and innumerable other manufactured fibers became popular in the second half of the century. Microfibers, high performance fabrics, and fabrics engineered for specific purposes were prevalent by the end of the century. Special finishes, such as water proofing, further enhanced fabrics' properties, and zippers and hooks and eyes replaced the lacing closures seen in previous eras.

Movies, television, air travel, and computers were introduced during this century, and they each had a profound impact on the apparel industry. Technology was not only a means of producing of material objects; it was a system of gathering and disseminating information. Movie stars and fashion designers became household names and distant countries came within reach, if not in person via air travel, then virtually via the Internet.

----

the new millennium

Change is the one constant in technology. This is welcome news for the designer because a setting with ever-changing technologies provides innumerable avenues for fresh design inspiration. Creativity thrives when new connections are made. Consider synthetic fabrics. After the initial excitement upon their introduction, they lost popularity. They were often full of static and some did not allow the skin to breathe. Many synthetic fabrics today have enhanced qualities that not only mitigate those original objections but also have exciting new, specialized applications. At one time a designer may have considered synthetic fabrics to be inferior in quality and performance; today that same designer may decide to make new connections with synthetic fabrics and reconsider them for a collection.

Many of the technological advances seen in the apparel field today have to do with **smart textiles**. Textiles are labeled as smart if they can do something that a textile is not expected to do under normal circumstances. Much of the smart technology came out of the space field and the military and their need for high-performance materials. A thinner fiber generally offers more possibilities so the search was directed toward microfibers and nanotechnology. The definition of a **microfiber** is that it is 1/60th the thickness of human hair. Microfibers are lightweight, crease resistant, and strong. They have a good hand and are also easy to care for. These fibers can be made so thin that fabrics made from them can be waterproof, yet still breathable. **Nanotechnology** alters the properties of a material at the atom and molecule level. Finishes placed on fabrics at the nano level are extremely thin, so they can enhance the fabric without detriment to breathability or hand. **Micro-encapsulation** technology implants fibers with minuscule bubbles

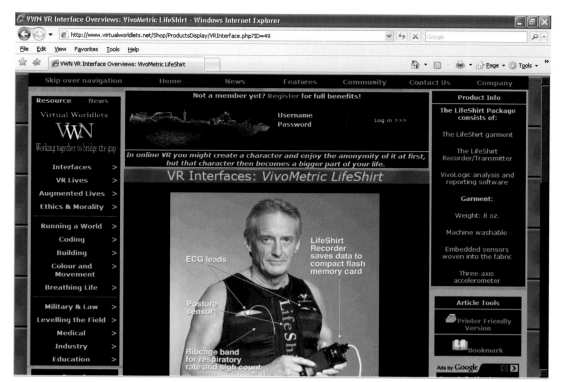

that can contain a range of products, including vitamins, insect repellents, perfumes, anti-bacterial substances, and medications. Normal wear or body heat causes the contents of the bubbles to be released. Smart textile technology has found applications in medicine, communications, and athletics.

medical field

In the healthcare field, traditional uses for textiles include sutures, components of plaster of Paris casts, and bandages. Contemporary bandages have evolved to enable the distribution of antibiotics and other drugs, and they are capable of monitoring the healing process. Textile's new promise in health care includes fiber-based materials that are being used in tissue engineering to promote cell growth and build bone structure. Developments in health-monitoring textiles can offer safety and comfort to users. Primarily focused on physiological measurements, they monitor body temperature, breathing, and other vital statistics. Wearable devices have even been developed to sense, and possibly prevent, repetitive stress injuries. VivoMetrics' Life Shirt System incorporates sensors in a lightweight, washable garment (Figure 3.5). The device can monitor patients' heart function, respiration, physical activity, and posture. The advantages of this type of shirt are that it is non-invasive, and it allows the patient full mobility. The shirt can also journal patients' daily activities and even garner clues to patients' mood (VivoMetrics).

athletics

Advances in textile technologies have made sports safer and athletes more competitive. Newer technologies utilize some of the same physiological monitoring devices used in medicine. Others allow for moisture management, wicking moisture away to the surface so it is not trapped within the garment. Some performance fabrics

are made from hollow-core fibers that provide good insulation. Technology in athletic wear is very specialized and directed at individual sports. There is debate on the ethical implications of using textile technology to enhance the performance of athletes. Some hold that with a new era comes new inherent technology, and this technology should be available to competitors. Others would like to keep the sport free of factors that have not been part of the sport over time. Numerous records in swimming were broken since the introduction of the all-in-one polyurethane-based swimsuit (Figure 3.6). Limits on competitive swim uniforms that took effect in 2010 now stipulate that racing suits must be made of a permeable material and also address how much of the swimmer's body can be covered.

communication

Individuals today are in nearly constant contact and the electronic devices that enable that communication are nearly always at their side. This has necessitated a mini revolution in the function of fashion. Garment pockets are now ubiquitous. To accommodate phones and other electronic accessories, pockets have become as mandatory as neck openings and armscyes (Figure 3.7). Even bridal gowns incorporate pockets for the in-touch bride. A blogger recently explained the situation by stating that he did not know anyone at his gym that did not listen to an MP3 player while working out. He lambasted exercise wear that did not provide the requisite pockets, and he extolled the convenience of wearable electronics that do away with fumbling with controls and head set wires. Exercise wear, jackets, hoodies, and even Levi's jeans can be found with integrated wiring and LCD displays. A number of washable input devices make wearable electronics possible. "Wearable computers are possible right now" (Thiry, 2009). GPS tracking devices can also be incorporated in clothing to aid hikers and campers. Parents, too, can follow their children's comings and goings with the *Blade Runner* tracker jacket (Crace, 2007). A GPS unit is placed in a specially designed jacket pocket and parents can follow the child's travels on the Internet.

Technologies in apparel applications are intended to help individuals better interact with the environment. They enhance and extend humans' capabilities. Future technology is looking to harness the energy in physical motion to power small electronic devices used by soldiers in the field, hikers, and others removed from power sources for a length of time. Wearable electronics can be cumbersome and unreliable, though. Even so, for some consumers, expanded capabilities and convenience outweigh the disadvantages of increased cost and specialized care requirements often inherent in wearable electronics.

virtual design

Long-established meanings of what it is to design and dress are being challenged by the virtual world. The term **virtual fashion** can be misleading. It can refer to fashion that is developed specifically for use in a virtual world like Second Life, or, as it is

Figure 3.6
Hi-tech polyurethane swimsuits reduce drag, muscle oscillation, and skin vibration, and allow swimmers to glide through water. Critics say that the suits can trap air and add to buoyancy, which is illegal in competitive swimming. *AFP/Getty Images*

You can do so much more with technology. It really opens up a totally different door. You definitely have more options. I think it helps creativity because it is faster and you can do more with it. — *Fashion Design Student*

Figure 3.7
Contemporary
apparel accom-
modates a variety
of electronic
devices. *Courtesy of
ScotteVest, Inc.*

referred to here, as an apparel development process using three-dimensional technologies for real world applications. Virtual applications are in place or are currently
being developed that can effectively eliminate the need for physical first design samples. With the help of three-dimensional body forms, or avatars, designers are able
to visualize their lines without creating physical products and, after either scanning
or entering in body measurements, consumers are able to "try on" those designs in
virtual fitting rooms before they buy. As virtual capabilities increase, they will surely
change how we define fashion. They have the potential to enrich avenues of design
because designers are not limited by the constraints of the physical world. But they
may also impersonalize the process. Designer Shenlei Winkler envisions designers
immersed in a virtual arena that encompasses nearly all aspects of their job descrip-
tion (Voice of Experience, p. 108).

With the help of technology, consumers are also getting into the design realm. As
online retailers make garment customization a reality, more and more individuals
are taking part in the design process. Bypassing the designer, consumers can at least
partially design their own t-shirts and sweatshirts on numerous online sites. Also,
several retailers, such as Nike and Lands' End, offer customers the opportunity to
customize certain aspects of their core products. Consumers are even acting as their
own fashion editors by pulling together looks and creating their own fashion spreads
on the online website Polyvore (www.polyvore.com).

There are challenges ahead for these new technologies. As lifelike as many of the
avatars are, they and the clothes they wear still look otherworldly, which makes it
hard for some designers to envision the end product, and for customers to equate
themselves with their avatar. It is also difficult to show how fabric drapes and moves,

continued on page 112

Shenlei Winkler CEO and founder of the Fashion Research Institute

Creativity is . . . defined through the words of your own experience. I think that people can be very creative in the way they go about organizing their life. Creativity is a way of looking at the world that is slightly askew from the way the rest of the world looks at it. I think that might be applicable across all disciplines and all industries and even across all people.

The apparel industry and design practices as a whole are undergoing a lot of paradigm changes right now. What I'm seeing is that people are really looking at the way that fashion is created. In the 1970s, there was a change in the way that people approached fashion design, and that was due to the rise of offshore production and mass manufacturing. What I'm seeing increasingly today is a sea change away from the idea of using these huge industrial complex factories. I see, at least in the younger designers, a much broader interest in having their own line, but not necessarily their own line in the way the major houses have, especially since we have seen so many of them fall into bankruptcy or reorganized in the last year. I've seen a lot of interest in slow design. Some hate that name, that we have fast fashion and slow design, but in the young people that I'm working with, I'm seeing a bigger interest in manufacturing at their home base, doing smaller runs, and doing more intimate pieces—intimate from the point of view that the designer is more involved with it and is more likely to actually connect with their end consumer.

I think I came out of the womb designing. It sounds like a traditional story. As soon as my legs were long enough to reach the sewing machine pedal, my mom started teaching me how to sew. I made my first blouse when I was eight. Over the years, I've really covered the gamut, from home product development to a very expensive couture line. Then, mass market. For a while I was very much into exploring corsets and corsetry and foundation garments. Believe it or not, the thing that I really enjoyed was my mass-market designing.

These days I'm developing new technology solutions for the apparel industry, particularly for some of these small to medium design firms that really want to be able to provide a quality product to the consumer. We do a lot of research at the Fashion Research Institute (FRI), hence the name. We have six research areas that we particularly focus on, which include immersive work spaces for the apparel industry. We have a new design solution that we will be launching in the next year or so, which is very exciting. It is a software services model where some of the smaller designers can actually come in and use the service. What it does is frees the designer from having to think about the technical design. It enables her to prototype her ideas quickly. The prototype is a 3-D model. It's a very low risk. When you get good at using the tools, it's very quick. Some of our initial results have shown that we have been able to cut off up to 75 percent of the design cycle. Recently, I had a dressmaker sample [developed that was typical of styles found at mass market retailers]. If I would have done exactly the same style using the old technique, with [Adobe] Illustrator and talking to the factory, it would have ended up costing about

> The best designers that I know are constantly educating themselves in many areas, which I think is a trait of most successful people.
>
> — Shenlei Winkler

$2,500 for the same sample that I had done for $50, which included the cost of a special custom textile. We were able to order our yardage and turn everything around within a month, including prototyping and testing the manufacturer who can handle the short run surface print. So it was incredibly fast, and in the process of creating that 3-D model, I generated a perfectly flawless, web-enabled, factory-ready technical specification with all of the requirements to get the thing produced in a mass market factory.

The benefit of starting from a 3-D model is that the designer can have exactly what she wants to scale, and she'll actually see how it's going to look in the avatar representation of the model. The nice thing about the system is that we take the technical design out of the hands of the line designers. That's actually really critically important because technical design is just not something that is commonly taught in fashion school. If you've gotten accurate quotes from the factory about each of the components that go into your product, you can end up with a really good estimate of how much it's going to cost to produce that garment in the factory. In the case of design, you can have your designer, your design director, you might have your project manager and your factory representative there, and you can have a conversation about that 3-D object. It goes very quickly. There's no cost for travel; there's no exposure to disease or safety considerations; everybody meets on the same platform; and you have your conversation about it. After that, if there's a problem with the sample, you can show the original model. It's very hard to argue with a 3-D model. You can argue with an Illustrator image because it's very difficult to express 3-D concepts with line.

Second Life is an interesting thing. It was in the virtual world that I first got exposure to the concept of world class, easy-to-use 3-D modeling tools. I got my start in 2005. I went back for another design degree, and I began developing avatar apparel at the same time. It was very much an escape from [the stresses of the degree program]. I realized that there was a really rich and deep possibility there. I went on to look at the way that people become educated, the way that people learn to immerse in virtual worlds. Our general consensus is that we're standing in 1993, so to speak. In 1993, the World Wide Web had three websites, and they weren't commonly visible or available for people to visit. By 1995, the Web had been commercialized, and by 1998, people were really building businesses on it. Now educators are dealing with the first generation of kids who have never known life without the Internet and the World Wide Web. It's interesting to look at it from that point of view. In Second Life these days, we have a research facility there and an entry portal for corporate and educational users, and we generate a lot of data through it. We get a chance to observe how new users come in, how they learn how to use the virtual world, and the process by which they learn to immerse themselves. And it's important, that immersion. People with avatar representation aren't really capable of getting into the business of doing real work and focusing on the work, as opposed to the technology, until they achieve what we call immersion. Immersion is the

Shenlei Winkler,
CEO, Fashion
Research Institute

continued on page 110

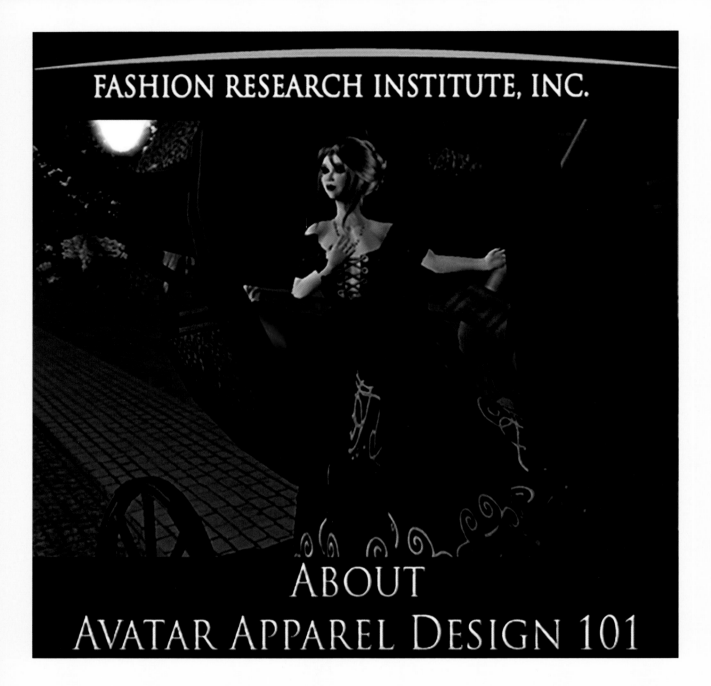

FASHION RESEARCH INSTITUTE, INC.

ABOUT
AVATAR APPAREL DESIGN 101

Avatar and virtual fashion design. *Fashion Research Institute's Virtual Campus in ScienceSim.*

point where the avatar-represented user stops thinking of the avatar as being doll or something that's unrelated to themselves, and they begin referring to their avatar as themselves.

It is rare to have unlimited materials and an unlimited budget. If you are developing within all of these production parameters—you have a very tightly defined market place and tightly defined materials that you can use—then it forces you to be very creative because you have to figure out a way to express your vision, do it within your parameters, and do it in a way that will sell. Fashion design is a weird marketplace. It's not enough to be creative because if the stuff doesn't sell, you're not going to be a successful designer, whatever price point you are going into, whether it is couture or mass market. If your stuff sits on a shelf, and your customer is not happy, you've got a problem. The market is voting with their pocketbook, and if the products stay on the shelf, you probably won't be invited back again next year. It's interesting to me to deal with people who think that the term creative is a license for rampant egotism and narcissism.

You won't successfully stay in this industry—we do have an incredible turn rate and an incredible burn-out rate—if you are not fast, disciplined, and focused. You also need to learn persistence. It's very important. You don't just design your one dress and stop there. You have to have a willingness to educate yourself. The best designers that I know are constantly educating themselves in many areas, which I think is a trait of most successful people. I think that you have to have discipline. We have an aggressive industry, and if you don't discipline yourself it will discipline you.

Something that I hammer on a lot with my students is humility and compassion. It's humility because your success or failure is determined not by any sort of innate talent that you may have or innate creativity but how your audience perceives what you give them. They are the ultimate arbiters. You can be as creative as you want to be, but if you are the only one that is valuing your work, then what good is it to be wildly creative? Fashion designers are designing for an audience that is expected to reach into their pockets and buy designs. I'm about as far removed from your mass-market shopper as you can imagine, so it would be very easy for me to be very arrogant towards my customer. There are not a lot of common points between myself and your average [mass-market] shopper, but if you lose compassion for your customer, you lose that human connection that enables you to develop solid designs that [prompt consumers to] actually want to reach into their pocketbook, take out their hard earned money, and buy. Have compassion for your customer from their point of view. Then, people have the ability to move audiences and change worlds with their design.

continued from page 107

and fabrics cannot be touched in the tactile sense. In spite of these set backs, virtual design has the potential to:

- Drive customer-generated design innovations. If preferences are tracked when consumers order customized goods, they can drive new product development. Designers home in on those desires, thus making their lines more relevant to their niche.

- Save money. Prototype development is often a large part of a product developer's budget, especially for those working in small to medium-size companies. With three-dimensional technology, materials, shipping, travel, and labor costs are substantially reduced or eliminated. Designers, and even those students participating in school-sponsored runway shows, can save money by producing a virtual fashion show, rather than a traditional runway exhibition which incurs costs for models, set design, and personnel to run the show.

- Save time. No shipping time is necessary to communicate concepts between the design house and production. In fact, meetings can take place instantaneously, from anywhere in the world.

- Conserve natural resources. Fewer resources, from materials utilized in first samples to fuel used in inter-continental travel, would be needed.

Although new applications are being developed every day, many questions remain for designers that want to expand into virtual applications. Those questions include:

- Will designers be able to immerse themselves in the virtual world to such a degree that they can concentrate on designing, rather than the technology?

- Will the applications bring designers closer to their niche consumer, or will the customer be relegated to the status of data and impersonalized?

- Will online customization technologies bring in more customers or just pull current customers from land-based stores?

form and function

It is easy to be mesmerized by technology and attracted to its shiny allure. You should never lose sight of the original objective of the design, though. Technology is only a tool; it is not the goal. Fashion design of the new millennium appreciates technology, but it does not revere it. It recognizes technology's potential contributions, but it does not compromise design to incorporate it. Yet, fashion design and technology are in collusion, and, if these concepts had animated features, it would be easy to visualize one giving the other a conspiratorial wink.

innovators

Today's designers are utilizing technology in exciting new ways. They are going beyond employing it as a design tactic and using it to change the very nature of what we know to be apparel. Three innovative designers are detailed here to exemplify the point.

hussein chalayan

Hussein Chalayan's work demonstrates a progressive attitude toward new technology. A retrospective of his designs at the Design Museum in early 2009 evidenced

Figure 3.8
Hussein Chalayan's fashion design materials are not limited to fabric and thread. He makes use of lights, crystals, wood, and even aircraft construction material (shown here) for his futuristic designs. *Courtesy of* WWD/*Giovanni Giannoni*

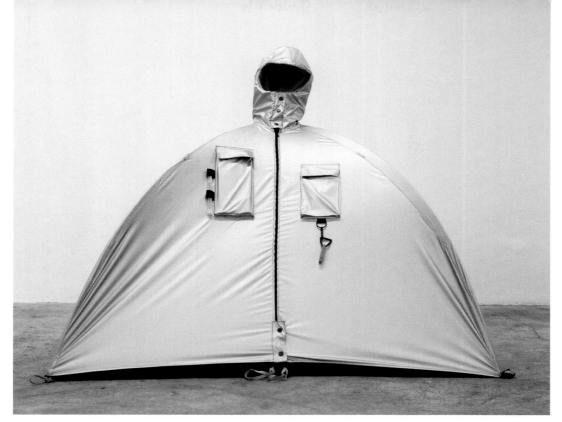

many technological themes. *Airborne* is an amalgamation of Swarovski crystals and over 15,000 flickering lights (Figure 3.8), and *Readings* utilizes over 200 moving lasers. *Before Minus Now* changes shape via remote control. The exhibit also included Chalayan's famous *Afterwords*, a design that explores wearable architecture as it transforms from garment to furniture and back again. Chalayan states that he would like the visitor to see "how different worlds relate to each other, how everything is interconnected. My work is a reaction to things that happen in the world—history, anthropology, science, technology—it represents a merging of all these worlds which is what makes the work unique" (Design Museum).

lucy orta

Lucy Orta expresses herself through art that combines both clothing and architecture. Her work questions the perception that clothing and environment need to be separate entities (Quinn, 2002, pp. 19–20).

> Orta's wearable shelters critique social and political issues and provide practical solutions to the problems of transitional living. . . . The inspiration behind her work is the human form, the body's need for protection against the elements and the social elements that fashion addresses—but her work explores issues like homelessness, the integrity of the individual, and society's awareness of its own needs.

The designer uses a variety of high-tech synthetic fabrics to create the multifunctional clothing environments. A system of zippers and pockets allows the pieces to be assembled and reassembled. *Refugee Wear* is a personal, portable habitat that can be transported quickly and easily (Figure 3.9). *Modular Architecture* allows individual modular pieces to be combined into a communal concept.

Figure 3.10
Issey Miyake's A-POC
concept challenges
conventional cut-
and-sew apparel
technology. Designs
are woven into a
tube of fabric with
the clothing outline
etched on. Wearers
cut out their own
garments, making
design decisions as
they go. With the
snip of a scissors,
a dress becomes a
top and long sleeves
become short.
© Siemoneit Ronald/
Corbis Sygma

issey miyake

Pleating has a long history dating back to ancient times. Issey Miyake borrows from these established pleating traditions in his contemporary collections. He is noted for transforming two-dimensional fabrics into sculptural forms (Braddock Clarke & Mahony, 2005, p. 120). Pleats Please Issey Miyake uses thermoplastic polyester jersey to heat-set pleats permanently into the soft, easy care fabric. Unlike traditional pleating, Miyake's garments are sewn first, then pleated.

Additional lines under the Miyake name also make use of high-technology fabrics. Miyake has developed a way to meld thread into clothing, thus eliminating the need for needles, threads, and seams. A-POC or A-Piece of Cloth begins with a tubular knitted length of cloth (Figure 3.10). Outlines of clothing items are imprinted and the customer frees the fashion from the fabric by cutting around the preplanned garment shapes. The result is an entire wardrobe that can be cut out of one single piece of cloth. While cutting, the customer makes design decisions on things such as lengths of sleeves and hems. There is no raveling, and no sewing is required. The A-POC concept questions the long-held belief that fabric needs to be cut into pieces, then sewn before it is worn.

home-grown technology

Just as Miyake's traditional and advanced pleating techniques exist in harmony, other designers find inspiration in mixing old world and new world ideas. There has been a renewed interest in traditional technologies in recent years. This is evidenced in the resurgence of hand crafts like knitting, shibori dyeing techniques, and fiber arts, and a rise in **slow fashion** (Figure 3.11). Slow fashion is a focus on artisanship and craftsmanship that is counter to the impersonal approach of mass production. Some posit that this trend is backlash to the irresponsible ways of many

Figure 3.11
The return to craftsmanship is seen as a reaction against fast fashion and churning out large quantities of inexpensive clothing under intense time pressure. Slow fashion values quality over quantity. This Rodarte dress features the homespun aesthetic that can be achieved by handcrafts such as piecing, crochet, knotting, and knitting. *Courtesy of WWD/Thomas Iannaccone*

corporations in recent years. Today's designers want to know and show that they are not only ethically, but also socially and environmentally responsible. Others believe renewed interest in artisanship is related to the fact that we no longer have the opportunity to see a product developed from inception to completion. It is a rarity if a garment is designed, cut, sewn, and sold in only one country, and this can cause one to feel disconnected from the design process. One do-it-yourself artist and journalist explained the return to traditional techniques as a reaction against our "hyper-fast culture, increasing reliance on digital technology, the proliferation of consumer culture, and even war. . . . Even though we all have frequent access to the Internet and are able to communicate with people through digital media, we are still sensual beings. We need to maintain a tactile relationship to the world" (Levine & Heimerl, 2008, p. 26). With home-grown technology and slow fashion, the creator and consumer are in control. They expect personalization and individualization. Websites like etsy.com have sprung up in large part because of designers' and consumers' craving for uniqueness. It is technology, but on the individual's terms.

summary

Cognition is the concepts, thoughts, and insights behind creativity. It is making connections. Useful connections are made by increasing the probability of unique associations. Cognition also involves problem solving, but creativity may be more concerned with problem-finding abilities that cause the designer to look beyond the surface structure to the underlying systems of a situation. Cognition can be described as divergent and convergent thinking. A designer may practice divergent thinking to foster quantities of novel ideas.

Not everyone thinks alike. Most people work with a range of cognitive intelligences. Discovering these abilities can help designers develop their own design styles, break out of their normal routines so they may make unusual associations, and consider their audiences' design intelligences.

The apparel industry has a long and esteemed history of technological advances. Over time textile production has been a major economic force in Europe and America. Creativity causes advances in technology, which then enables more creativity. Contemporary designers use technology as a tool to reach their design goals. Virtual fashion design has the potential to alter our current understanding of the design process, but the impact of those applications will remain unclear until the technologies are fully operational.

KEY TERMS

cognition	originality	theory of multiple intelligences	microfiber
connections	flexibility		nanotechnology
divergent thinking	elaboration	technology	micro-encapsulation
convergent thinking	problem solving	cotton gin	virtual fashion
fluency	problem finding	smart textiles	slow fashion

DIN Challenge: Rediscovering Artisanship

There has been a resurgence of hand-crafted technologies used in fashion design. Many times these skills require time and patience to execute, and these characteristics are contrary to some quick-turnaround mass-production processes. Slow fashion requires a concentration on artisanship.

Investigate a hand-crafted technology. Identify your own, or choose a technique from the list. Referring to the entries you have made in your *DIN* thus far, design a look based on a slow technology. You might consider blending craftsmanship from past eras with aspects of high technology today. Some techniques have a learning curve, but most of the techniques are welcoming of beginners. Choose one that suits the time available and your expertise.

Hand-Crafting Techniques

Applique	Felting	Macrame
Crochet	Foiling	Piecing
Devore	Hand-dyeing techniques, such as batik or block printing	Quilting
Embroidery		Slashing
Fabric painting	Knitting	Stitch and dissolve

Notes for Discussion

_____

_____

_____

_____

_____

_____

_____

_____

_____

4 creativity *and* character traits

Character traits influence creativity. Creativity influences character traits. Either statement may be true, and, in all likelihood, both statements are true. **Traits** are the identifiable characteristics that define a person, concept, or item. Individuals with certain character traits are attracted to specific disciplines, such as fashion design. Designers' affinity for their field enables them to do well and even stretch the boundaries within that field. In this way, their traits relate to the creativity they do in design. Confidence gained from successful creative endeavors, in turn, feeds additional exploration in design, and their creativity influences their traits. This chapter investigates character traits and those affective, expressive, and emotional aspects that can either enhance or inhibit creativity in fashion design. It also considers traits that can be represented through apparel. Fashion design can express emotion, affect self-esteem, and tell a story (Figure 4.1.).

character traits associated with creativity

Each person has a set of creativity-associated character traits that intermingle with environmental, cognitive, and motivational factors to create a unique individual. From the vast array of possible character trait combinations, it is not possible to derive a simple formula for those traits that lead to creativity. However, decades of research have identified character traits that are often present in creative individuals. These traits appear with consistency across people, disciplines, and time. (See Cropley, 2001, and Dacey & Lennon, 1998, for references to a number of these studies.) Humans are incredibly agile beings, though, and what one lacks in one area, one can compensate for with another. Rare, indeed, is the individual over whom all creative stars align in harmony. There is even evidence to suggest that creative individuals thrive on an imbalance in the distribution of creativity-enhancing traits, and they may become more motivated to work and create when they experience an

Black-and-white photograph by Deitmar Busse.

(opposite) Inspiration for fashion designer Doo-Ri for the Fall 2009 Doo Ri clothing collection. *Courtesy of WWD/Dietmar Busse*

OBJECTIVES

— To investigate character traits that enhance and inhibit creativity

— To recognize fear as a common cause of creator's block and to explore tactics that could lessen that fear

— To consider the affective aspects of fashion design

— To acknowledge meanings of dress

intermediate amount of tension and unpredictability in their lives (Gardner, 1993, p. 382). It appears that this marginality is so enticing that creative individuals actually seek out conditions where their talents are not entirely in sync with the world around them. If things are going too smoothly, they are likely to create their own "asynchrony" (p. 382).

The creativity-enhancing exercise in Activity 4.1 gives you practice in designing in conditions to which you are probably not accustomed. It asks you to create using all five senses.

Researchers (Dacey & Lennon, 1998, pp. 98–135; Cropley, 2001, p. 148; Jones, 2005, p. 9) have identified a number of personal qualities that characterize creative individuals. Several of them are detailed here:

- Tolerance for ambiguity

- Freedom

- Risk taking

- Preference for disorder

- Perseverance and delay of gratification

- Courage

- Self control

Creativity-Enhancing Exercise: The Five Senses

Concentrating on senses is another way to open new avenues of inspiration for fashion design. All five senses are associated with creativity:

- Sight

- Hearing

- Smell

- Taste

- Touch

Designers commonly utilize sight when they are selecting silhouettes and touch when they are selecting fabrics. The rustle of crisp fabrics can herald a person's arrival on the scene. This creativity exercise asks you to sketch a collection of five designs, each focusing exclusively on a single sense. Decide a major design theme and a focused set of materials, and keep it consistent throughout the exercise. For example, you might decide to create line of casual cotton shirts for the menswear market. Make notes and rough sketches of your thoughts. Complete the exercise by illustrating your sense-able collection in your *DIN*.

- Consider one of the five senses.

- Consider the essence or nature of the sense. List what you think of when you ponder it. List ways that the sense can be represented in apparel.

- Use the list to inspire a garment with a singular focus on that sense. Of course, other senses will be automatically involved, but they should play supporting and secondary roles in the overall composition.

Design Theme _____

Notes for Discussion

_____

_____

_____

_____

_____

_____

_____

_____

_____

You have to look deep inside to find a person's creativity. I don't think that there's any set list of personality traits that go with that. I'm a strong believer that **everyone is creative in their own way**. — *Fashion Design Student*

Figure 4.2
Exploring beyond the zipper's usual function enabled designer and artist Cat Chow to envision this *Red Zipper Dress.*
Courtesy of RISD Museum

tolerance for ambiguity

An ambiguous situation is one in which there is no predetermined way to respond to a challenge or problem. If there are rules, they are vague. If there are guidelines, they are amorphous. **Ambiguity** can leave you wondering which tactics to use, and when. Creative individuals are not intimidated by uncertainty, and they may even thrive in open-ended situations and unfamiliar circumstances. They find incongruity exciting. An ambiguous fashion design assignment would be one that is not restricted by styling directives. Most designers delight in the challenge of making sense of a situation on their own terms.

freedom

Designers should grant themselves the freedom to look at every new challenge with a sense of wonder. There is a human tendency to create artificial boundaries or rules that box in a challenge that is too open-ended. Creative individuals with **freedom** do not invent parameters where they do not exist. They do not close off avenues prematurely before they have been fully investigated. Actually, even if parameters do exist, they often skirt them in order to meet their goals. Creative people recognize that a lack of freedom is a threat to their creativity; many go to great lengths to break free of assumptions and those environments that perpetuate them. Some, like Henry David Thoreau, seclude themselves from outside influences for long periods of time. Others intentionally work in austere or unusual settings. A designer with freedom would not hold back a design idea for fear of being wrong, or someone else's possibly not liking it, or its being offensive, when there is no indication that this is the case.

freedom from fixed functions

The function of a button is to go through a buttonhole and secure a garment closed. Envisioning the button only as a device to close a garment is a typical response and an example of a lack of freedom. Freedom looks beyond common definitions and uses and finds novel applications for items and ideas (Figure 4.2). Creativity researcher John Dacey and his colleagues (1998) go so far as to suggest that education interferes with the ability to think freely. They state that the more education one has, the more fixed will be the perception of function. An item's "correct" function is reinforced over and over again through the years. Designers may want to remind themselves to look at the world with a child's eyes and sense of possibility. What might a child perceive that button to be before learning that its function is to secure clothing?

freedom from sex-role stereotyping

From a very young age, individuals learn the roles that are typically ascribed to gender. Common stereotypes suggest that women should not be aggressive and authoritative, and that men should not show their emotions. By adhering to these typecasts, however, a whole horizon of possible associations is eliminated, thus negating creative connections. It has been found that creative individuals do not limit themselves to typical gender roles. "Creative males need to have that stereotypically female characteristic—sensitivity to the feelings of others—in order to get in touch with their own creative urges. On the other hand, females need assertiveness, a stereotypically male attribute, in order to champion their ideas courageously in a critical world" (Dacey & Lennon, 1998, p. 109). Those free from gender-role stereotypes react in a manner appropriate to the situation, regardless of their gender.

preference for disorder

Creative people prefer disorder because it is more interesting than order. Order is linear, simple, and symmetrical, and, hence, expected. **Disorder**, however, is always surprising. Given order, creative individuals will disrupt it and strive to make it asymmetrical and complex. Given disorder, they will dive into the challenge with fervor and attempt to make sense of it. Fashion designers' studios often are piled high with a mix of media. The casual observer may have a hard time finding direction in the chaos, but designers can find inspiration in connections derived from the disarray.

perseverance and delay of gratification

Creativity takes time and effort, and, as mentioned in Chapter 1, establishing an underpinning of knowledge in the field takes dedication. Designs rarely come out as desired the first time. Students may need to sew up several muslin prototypes before their design is the way they envisioned it, and even established designers continue to make first samples before diving into production. Creative breakthroughs are the products of hard work, and designers may work for years before they are recognized. Successful designers have been heard to say that it took ten years for them to become overnight sensations. Honing a craft can take a decade or more of dedicated study. During that time, individuals may receive very little validation for their efforts. They must delay their gratification or satisfaction. This is contrary to the culture of instant gratification that often exists in contemporary society. Some suggest that access to easy credit, instantaneous information available on the Internet, and immediate and constant communication has contributed to a society that is unused to delaying gratification and persevering through tough times. Designers are often pitted against economic downturns, the whims of consumers, and the pressures of delivering new fashions several times a year. **Perseverance**, resolve, and determination can help a designer bridge those times of hardship (Figure 4.3). Delay of gratification and perseverance will enable those designers to stay focused on long term goals and the big picture.

risk taking

"Failing to take sensible risks may lead to a sense of security but not to creativity" (Dacey & Lennon, 1998, p. 105). Taking too few risks is safe, but it yields very little reward. Taking huge risks is unlikely to be successful. Creativity is associated with taking moderate risks. Some failure is inherent in **risk taking**. People who have not failed most likely have not pushed themselves enough and could be capable of making greater creative contributions.

Figure 4.3
Designer Alana Devine will spend many hours perfecting an aesthetically pleasing sequence of ribbons, feathers, lace, and netting as she gets her design ready for a national competition. *Courtesy of the author's collection*

courage

It takes courage to be creative. The essence of creativity suggests that a person is not working with commonplace ideas. This singles out the creator as being unconventional or even a nonconformist, and it takes courage to sustain a vision when it is contrary to what the crowd may be thinking. **Courage** is fighting for and following through on what you believe in, even if there is a minority of those that think as you do. It is also hard to defend that alternative position for a long period of time. Designers might come to decide that holding on to the creative vision is not worth the effort, or they may come to doubt their own abilities. Courage is needed to be able to communicate a creative design to others, too. This is opening up a designer to criticism and even rejection. You can begin by participating in classroom critiques and exhibiting your designs in university fashion shows. As you gain experience, you should consider entering your designs into the many national design competitions that are introduced each year. This practice gets you ready for your work as a designer in the industry, where you will have to present your ideas to buyers and others on a regular basis.

self control

Creative individuals need self control in order to use time effectively, work diligently, and have the perseverance to bring a product to its full fruition. Time management is often one of the greatest hurdles that a designer has to face. On the surface, creative individuals may sometimes seem unrestrained and impulsive, but a deeper look reveals that they most often have the discipline to tackle all that is entailed in an arduous and sometimes solitary endeavor. Simply put, **self control** enables people to do, or not do, what they want (Dacey & Lennon, 1998, p. 116). For example, designers may want to enter their garments into a design competition, but find they have limited funds and a busy life. The designers with self control will be in a better position to enter that competition because they will economize on expenses and devote the necessary time to the workmanship of the piece in order to make it happen for themselves.

other character traits of creative individuals

The list of creativity-facilitating traits is by no means comprehensive. A number of connected and interrelated traits add to the intricacy of the creativity concept. For example, adventurousness and independence are associated with freedom, and commitment is related to perseverance. It follows that a person with courage and self-control would also have ego-strength and self-acceptance. Related traits that have been found to characterize creativity include the following:

Adventurousness	Ego-strength	Leadership
Confidence	Humor	Openness
Commitment	Imagination	Positive attitude
Curiosity	Independence	Complexity
Decisiveness	Intuitiveness	Self-acceptance

polarities of traits

Creative individuals' personalities are complicated. This complexity enables them to understand and have empathy for the extremes of both sides of a concept without inner conflict. This does not imply that the person is indecisive. Rather, it indicates the ability to fluctuate flexibly from one extreme to the other as the situation dictates. Csikszentmihalyi (1996) suggests that individuals can develop this skill and strengthen their ability to utilize the weaker poles (pp. 58–76).

Listed here are ten opposing polarities. Mark where your traits lie by placing an X at that spot on the continuum. In the next days or weeks, focus on the weaker of the two characteristics in each pair by reacting and responding to situations using that trait. Take notes about the situations in which you tried to strengthen your weaker traits and the results of your efforts, and enter those thoughts in your *DIN*. Developing these unknown traits opens up new possibilities for making associations and connections.

Physical energy _____ Quiet, thoughtful

Smart _____ Naïve

Playful _____ Disciplined

Imaginative _____ Rooted in reality

Introvert _____ Extrovert

Humble _____ Proud

Gender reliant _____ Androgynous

Independent _____ Traditionalist

Passionate _____ Objective

Frustrated _____ Satisfied

fear

In general, all of the traits listed here are positive and are thought to facilitate creative production. One additional trait, however, is debilitating to creativity. That trait is **fear**. Cameron (2002) suggests that creator's block is really rooted in fear (p. 152). The fear could stem from fear of failure, fear of success, fear of critique, fear of embarrassment, and the list goes on. The fear is rational—there will be times you have to face criticism, rejection, and even failure—but if you want to communicate your work as a designer, you will have to learn to address that fear. Shenlei Winkler, a prolific fashion designer whose work has spanned couture, mass market, and virtual design suggests that fear is a normal aspect of creating that designers will have to come to terms with (personal communication, October, 2009):

> I think the only way to really get past fear is to become a very prolific designer. It's critically important, at least in the early phases of learning to design, to sketch a lot, to constantly have your sketch pad with you, to sketch out your ideas. Find a friendly audience, whether it's a friend, a teacher, or a mentor, show them your [designs], and ask for criticism. Nobody ever likes

it. It never gets better, but in order to be successful as a fashion designer, you have to learn to accept criticism. The more that you design, the less painful it gets because you've just done such a huge body of work. If somebody doesn't like one of your 800 designs, you can deal with it. And learn to face your fear. Why are you really afraid of being criticized? Learn to separate your work and your design from yourself. That may just be a process of [maturing]. Sometimes there are forces in the world that will elevate one of your designs that is not as strong as the others. Or, you may have a design that is well-executed, but it's just the wrong time. It's serendipity.

Strategies to overcome fear include:

• Setting realistic goals

• Visualizing success

• Improving performance

• Determining the causes of jealousy

• Building up a repertoire of successful experiences

• Letting go

setting realistic goals

Many of us want to be the next great couture designer and immortalized like Chanel, Dior, or Saint Laurent. Or students may want to be the next wunderkind, graduating from a fashion design program and quickly establishing a company like Zac Posen or Proenza Schouler. One reason that noted designers and lines resonate with so many people is that they are the ones we read about in magazines and see on the Internet. Most books about fashion designers do not commemorate those lesser-known designers who have found a niche and provide innovative styling that is comfortable and affordable. New designers will surely be intimidated and fearful if they expect each of their designs to be a masterpiece like those they have seen featured in various media. Although being the venerated designer of a generation may be your long-term goal, you should recognize that getting there will require small, sequential steps. Realistic goals are ones that can be attained in the short term and that you have a reasonable chance of completing successfully. They may include graduating from design school, taking a refresher course, learning a new technique, entering into design competitions, and presenting a small collection in a university or local charity runway exhibition.

visualizing success

What does success look like? Success does not look the same to everyone. Some design for personal pleasure; some design because they have an affinity for a particular niche market; and others want to express their feelings concerning contemporary issues. Visualizing success keeps the designer focused and lessens fear. Individuals are more willing to risk opening themselves to others if they know that through the exposure they will gain valuable feedback that will help them meet their goals. In

Fear can hold you back from being creative. — *Fashion Design Instructor*

addition, the visualization process helps designers home in on important aspects that make their designs more relevant to their niche and, hence, less susceptible to criticism.

improving performance

One way to reach goals is to improve performance. Many times, improved performance comes from repetition with increasingly challenging assignments. Consider the task of driving a car. The first outings are intimidating, and the driver is usually tense. However, after many varied experiences with driving, such as driving at night, then driving in the rain, then driving on ice, drivers slowly become quite confident that they can handle a variety of driving conditions, and their anxiety lessens. When confronted with the new experience of driving in fog, the driver might be apprehensive, but repeated experiences with the other conditions lessen the fear considerably. The goal is not to become rote and automatic; it is to increase ability incrementally. Continuing education or gaining new skills are ways to ensure that performance is growing toward a larger goal.

determining causes of jealousy

Artist and author Julia Cameron (2002) singles out jealousy as a cause of fear. She claims that jealousy stems from looking at what someone else has or has done and thinking that it should be one's own (pp. 123–124). When we sit back with jealousy instead of acting on the challenge, it is due to the fear that our capability is not competitive with those who are already successful. Cameron suggests that jealousy narrows our ability to see our own field in perspective. When designers are jealous, they think that the other person has already reached the goal, so then the challenge has been accomplished and the work is done. They fail to see that there is room for many and varied interpretations in their discipline. When designers join in, instead of hanging back with fear, they become part of the group of designers in their niche, and jealousy then changes to camaraderie, borne of the realization that they are all in the endeavor together.

building a repertoire of successes

Successful experiences are self-perpetuating. Maintaining a string of successes builds confidence, which in turn encourages more ambitious projects, and a cycle that inspires confidence is established. As we begin to see that creativity is really possible, fear subsides.

letting go

Designers create from the heart, so it is easy for them to become very attached to their designs. They sometimes forget that a design is simply one expression of their selves. It is not a representation of their selves. Identifying too strongly with a product can lead to fear because individuals can perceive that they are opening up themselves to criticism. After designers are prepared to let go of their work, apprehension immediately lessens, and they will not fear showing their fashions to others. If a garment is fairly judged to be lacking in some element, they can easily let it go and move on to more promising areas because it was only an articulation, not an actual component of their being.

passion for fashion

There is one character trait that makes all the others possible—**passion**. Without passion, design work becomes a chore to be gotten out of the way as quickly as possible. "No one ever sustained creativity without a passion for the field" (Piirto, 2004, p. 441). Creative people are passionate about what they do, and that passion can sustain them through arduous projects that sometimes yield little gratification. They will dive into projects that interest them, but they are also sensitive to boredom, and they are quick to free themselves of tedium. Do you want to enhance your personal creativity? Start doing more of what you are passionate about and do less of what you hate (Csikszentmihalyi, 1996, p. 357). Csikszentmihalyi suggests that individuals can maintain their passion and enhance creativity by learning to look at things differently, learning to think new thoughts, and learning to act in a new way that is compatible with creativity. "Thus it helps to consider how to apply what we learned about the personalities of creative individuals to the traits that may be useful in everyday life" (p. 359). He suggests that it is incumbent upon those who want to enhance their creativity to develop those areas that they are lacking.

affective dimensions of design

The ability to understand your feelings and motives can lead to a stronger design style. Collections that remain true to the designer's style are cohesive. They tell a continuing, but evolving story. Playwright Anton Chekhov aptly noted, "If you want to work on your art, work on your life." Design cannot be compartmentalized and separated from the individual. Experiences, emotions, feelings, and affective traits can make important contributions to a designer's style. Without them, collections can seem impersonal and uninspired. A design journal such as your *Dynamic Inspiration Notebook* can help you articulate your style. Over time, themes will evolve. Recurring themes that continue to resonate give you clues to your budding design style. They give strong indications as to where your passions lie. In addition, focusing on your passion makes designing infinitely enjoyable.

Take stock of the entries in your *DIN*. Review your *Ideas* and *Themes*, and list those concepts that keep popping up over and over again. Articulate your design style by writing it out in sentence form. Note that this style will be continually evolving. Keep yourself open to new influences and revisit this statement often.

My style is _____

_____

_____

_____

_____

_____

dimensions of personality

There are a number of tests that can identify character traits and personality profiles. Some of these tests are used by employers to recognize job applicants who will be a good fit in their company. Many times, such tests are used to help individuals decide their majors in school and career paths. However, these tests can also help individuals learn more about their own personal motives and traits. The Myers-Briggs Type Indicator (MBTI) is one such measure. It is important to note that with the MBTI and similar devices, there is no preference for one type over another. There is no "best" personality type. The results are informative, not diagnostic. "All types are equal. The goal of knowing about personality type is to understand and appreciate differences between people" (Myers-Briggs). The Meyers-Briggs type indicator asks individuals to note their preference concerning four dichotomies:

- Extraversion or introversion

- Sensing or intuition

- Thinking or feeling

- Judging or perceiving

Insight into different personality types, derived from interaction among the dichotomies, can be of value in fine tuning a personal style and identifying the origins of a design voice. Equally important, by identifying their own traits, those who want to venture out of their usual style and explore areas that they might not have otherwise can develop a visible path.

emotions and feelings as inspiration

Inspiration for design can come from travel, art, architecture, and any number of other tangible sources that you can see, feel, and physically experience. When viewing a work of art, consider the colors, materials, and techniques employed.

continued on page 132

Figure 4.4
Intangible concepts, such as the melancholy associated with a midnight rain (a) or the charged excitement of an electrical storm (b) are potent muses for fashion designers. *Photographer: Miriam Carlson*

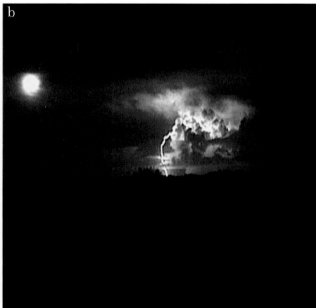

Takara Fashion and Jewelry Designer

Photographer:
Abel Berumen

Creativity is . . . not about art. It's how you live your life. Creativity is there, but you have to be open to it. A lot of people believe that they are not creative, but actually it's a natural part of being. I wake up, and each day is an opportunity to be creative. It could be in anything. It could be in how I dress that day; it could be in the accessories I wear; it can be in the food that I choose or the route I take home. It is not something intangible. It is a real part of who you are.

I started designing accessories when I was about 19 years old, maybe even younger than that. I designed and manufactured for a lot of department stores: Marshall Fields (now Macy's), Lord and Taylor, Nordstrom, Spiegel catalog. It was a long list. Once, I made 40,000 pairs of earrings for Sears. We had boxes and piles of earrings. It was phenomenal. It was a great experience. The thing is, I went into [the Sears accessory agreement] without knowing how to do such a large mass-production order. You learn along the way, and you never let on that you don't know what you're doing. You just make sure that [the buyers] are confident that you know what you are doing. When I left the meeting, I thought, "Oh my God, what am I doing!" But, everything worked out OK. I ended up serving all of the Sears stores, and when I went into the stores and saw my product on the rounders, it was exciting. I also designed for a few films. I did Spike Lee movies, a lot of photo work for ads, and won a lot of awards. I stopped making mass production jewelry design about ten years ago.

Now I sell my fashion design line and specialty jewelry out of my boutique. How did I get from mass production jewelry to [where I am now]? I never took a sewing class. It was all intuitive. I taught myself how to sew. I stayed up one night and taught myself. It wasn't the type of workmanship that could be put in a store, but the sewing was good enough to make the samples that I took to the contractor. I started, and people just loved the clothes that I was wearing. They were literally stopping me on the street, and I thought, "I made this this morning on my bed!" I remember my mattress was all cut up because I didn't have a cutting table. My mattress was my cutting table. That's how I started. I made coats, tops, skirts, everything. I took the scraps and made hats and gloves. I did everything that I didn't know I wasn't supposed to do.

From there, it evolved into what it is now. And I still don't know how to do that sort of artistic drawing that they do in school. Mine almost look like stick people. I wear the pieces that I design. I love wrapped styles. A lot of my designs are based on wraps. They are really very complementary to women who have hips. I love long skirts. I wear long skirts every day. They elongate the body. I add on little specialty pieces to make the outfits pop. I specialize in doing after-five [evening wear] as well. I've done many weddings. It has been an amazing career. Now my line is focused in my Takara store and a few other boutiques in the city. Recently, I've been doing a lot of special orders, too.

I do all of my production locally. I want to have access to my manufacturers. I want to go and talk to them and change things up. It's really hard for me to send my things out of the state or overseas, but that always depends on the quantity of garments that are manufactured.

My pieces are different. When you walk into a room [wearing one of my designs], you will stand out. My pieces are like soft architecture. I have a knack for covering the body and making it look smaller than it is. I can camouflage [problem areas on] the body in ways that are really amazing. I'm an impulse designer. Whatever I pick up, that's what I use to design. You cannot have a tidy studio to do it this way. Sometimes it happens so fast that I get behind and have to catch up to my ideas. It's really an interesting process. I remember one night I didn't have thread with me, so I had to use Stitch Witchery [fusible webbing]—the entire outfit was made with Stitch Witchery. If I didn't do it right away, I would have forgotten it.

It's all based on emotion. Just feel it. You have to think out of the box. It's nice to look at magazines for ideas, not necessarily to copy, but to be open to the ideas. I don't take in a lot of influence from other designers. I think that can be disrupting to your psyche because without realizing it, you start emulating what they are doing. I design from a place that is very deep. Sometimes I can design from a place of joy. One thing that I've learned from my career is that I never design from anger. If I'm really angry, I just stay away from my studio.

In my jewelry designing, I design with only natural things, and I really feel the energy of the materials. Sometimes I find a random bead on the floor. I see that it looks great, pick it off the floor, put it in the jewelry design, and keep going. I love architecture, and I get a lot of my fashion design ideas from it. I love shapes and angles. I love wrapping. I love movement. My pieces are like soft sculptures. My designs are so impulsive, I gather things and have them ready for when the mood strikes me. Recently, I used some materials that I had for 25 years! It just depends on when it is time for that piece to come out and make its presentation.

I don't follow a diagram. I receive whatever the universe decides to give me. It takes a lot out of you, though. The design process is sort of like being in a trance, and when I come out of it, it's like "Whew!" Once it's finished, I feel disconnected from the process. It's like I'm looking at the design for the first time. Some of the older pieces are priceless now, and I don't have any of them. Once I'm finished [with a design], I move on. Just recently, I made some interesting designs, and they sold out in four days. Now, I wish I would have photographed them first though!

> # It's all based on emotion. Just feel it. You have to think out of the box.

Figure 4.5
Fashion designs can make powerful artistic statements. Li Xiaofeng creates contemporary wearable art born of the shards of ancient traditions. *Beijing Memory* is made entirely of blue and white porcelain from the Ming and Qing dynasties. *AP/Wide World Photos*

continued from page 129

But art elicits feelings and emotions, too. Just as designers can derive inspiration from the concrete aspects of the art, they can also use abstract and intangible traits as their muse (Figure 4.4). Art, music, poetry, dance, and theater can all bring out feelings that can inspire design, as can a storm; a quarrel; a pounding tide; and raw emotions, such as love and hatred. What does happiness look like? How might a fashion designer portray rage? Emotions are always unique to the individual, so they can be powerful inspirations for innovative design. Activity 4.2 lists a variety of human emotions. Be sure to add those emotions that portray your feelings on the list.

Activities 4.2 and 4.3 invite you to conceptualize some of these emotions into fashion designs. For these activities, make artistic articulation paramount (Figure 4.5). Usual questions, such as "Who would wear that?" can be placed on hold to ensure that expression is not stifled by practicality. This is an opportunity to create wearable art pieces, fiber and textile art work, and concept designs.

expressing concepts

Designers also do the introspective work of identifying their personal style because they are very often called upon to express these traits visually and verbally. Every fashion design is created through a combination of self-expression and inspiration, and these concepts need to be communicated to others. A **mood board** is a designer's concept statement that is made visual by the use of pictures, fabric swatches, sketches, and colors (Figure 4.6). Mood boards are great tools because they can quickly and concisely relay information about a collection. They are often affixed to the design studio wall and used as a reference by everyone working on the line, so that the line remains cohesive and true to the original concept.

The articulated statement is just as important as the visual statement. This **design statement** is a verbalization of the mood board. Designers should be able to convey background information, inspiration, fabric story, color story, and unique characteristics of the collection in a manner that is concise and understandable. The clearer and more defined the concept and designer's voice, the better able the designer is to formulate the words to get that concept across to others. Designers may be asked to articulate their vision to their design team, to partners or shareholders, or to buyers. See the Design Statement on page 136 for an example of the statement that pertains to the design in Figure 4.6b.

expressing traits through fashion design

Traits can be expressed through fashion design. For example, some design styling, such as frilly ruffles, has built-in connotations. Designers can identify these intrinsic traits and use them to make informed decisions about their fashion designs. Styling that is contrary to these common attributes may be new and exciting, or it may confuse the audience. Individual cultures view traits differently. What is accepted and common in one culture may be offensive or nonsensical in another. Also, some meanings change over time. Historically, ruffles were not always considered to be uniquely feminine design details. They were commonly worn by both men and women. You should consider your audience when utilizing styling, fabrics, and colors with intrinsic meanings.

continued on page 138

Figure 4.6
This mood board captures the overt and covert symbols of the Victorian era (a). The resulting fashion design incorporates both opulence and structure to realize the inspiration (b).
Photographer:
Eileen Molony

Expressing Emotions

Select several emotions from the list that resonate with you. Enter into the chart below your thoughts and ideas when you consider each aspect. Find pictures of both apparel and nonapparel items that help you represent the concept.

Emotion	Item Suggesting the Emotion	Design Inspired by Emotion

List of Human Emotions

Acceptance	Disgust	Isolation
Affection	Distraction	Jealousy
Aggression	Doubtfulness	Joy
Anticipation	Eagerness	Jubilation
Anxiety	Ecstasy	Passion
Apprehension	Elation	Peace
Bewilderment	Enthusiasm	Pleasure
Boredom	Exasperation	Rage
Boldness	Excitability	Relaxation
Bravery	Euphoria	Relief
Calm	Fascination	Sadness
Capability	Fear	Shock
Caution	Frustration	Surprise
Charm	Grief	Terror
Cheerfulness	Guilt	Worry
Competitiveness	Happiness	Add additional emotions here
Concern	Hope	
Confidence	Hostility	_____
Confusion	Impatience	
Depression	Insecurity	_____
Determination	Inspiration	
		_____

Emotion	Item Suggesting the Emotion	Design Inspired by Emotion

With All the Trimmings

This two-piece design draws its inspiration from the opulent dress of the Victorian upper class. The Victorian period was a time of propriety and rigid social conventions. Corsets and crinolines, hallmarks of the era, mimicked the confining social structure. However, close investigation of the period reveals that there was unrest against the inflexible social restrictions, and surreptitious romantic liaisons were commonplace. This design acknowledges the significance of corsets and crinolines to the period, but the restrictive structures are brought to the outside of the piece to bring the hidden Victorian actions into the daylight and question hypocrisy.

The bodice is made of 100 percent silk dupioni, and 15 different kinds of coordinating red, gold, and metallic trims are used to represent the wealth and status of the women who wore the lavish Victorian style. Boning, placed under each row of trim, gives the shell its form and the piece its foundation. Soft chiffon is used for the underskirt. It denotes a more compliant form of human nature coming through.

ACTIVITY 4.3

Music and Poetry as Muses

Autumn

The morns are meeker than they were,

The nuts are getting brown;

The berry's cheek is plumper,

The rose is out of town.

The maple wears a gayer scarf,

The field is scarlet brown.

Lest I should be old-fashioned,

I'll put a trinket on.

The poem is by Emily Dickinson and the autumn season inspired her words. As designers, we are used to getting inspiration from what we see, but we can also derive inspiration from intangible concepts, such as feelings stirred by a new season. Music and poetry can evoke powerful emotional responses. Listen to a favorite song or consider a meaningful poem, and use it as the inspiration for a fashion design. Or, use the Dickinson poem as inspiration, and imagine what the trinket she describes looks like. Start with a series of thumbnail sketches; then select the idea that best brings out your feelings as you experience the artwork. Illustrate it in color. Write the name of the inspiring poem or song on your illustration, and be prepared to discuss how the design expresses your reaction to the work that inspired it.

Inspiring Poem or Song _____

Notes for Discussion

_____

_____

_____

_____

_____

_____

Illustration

continued from page 132

styling

There has been over 5,000 years of costume. Over this long period of time, certain styling has come to be associated with certain traits, and these connotations can give clothes their personality. The sailor pant, for example, is inextricably associated with the military. The collars worn during the Victorian era are so representative of the period that the high, lace style of collar came to be named after that era. Designers' challenges lie in how to employ these established notions in their collections. They may want to use the association to help build a strong story, or they may want to design contrary to these connotations to add an element of surprise or interest to their lines. For example, a designer building a story around a military and naval theme may decide to include wide and tied "sailor" collars and button placket "sailor" pants in the collection. This styling is so compatible with the sailor theme that the collection becomes immediately understandable to the audience. However, if the designer also decides to add full and banded-cuff "harem" pants, this would be incongruous to the naval theme. A clever designer can make this unusual association work, and some consumers may be drawn to the bizarre juxtaposition. Designs should stand on their own merit, though, and not need additional explanations in order to be understood. If the design does not make sense to the audience, it will be rejected. Activity 4.4 offers examples of common styling with built in connotations. What do you think of when you visualize these items?

fabrics

Fabrics, too, have traits that lend themselves to various uses. Satin's luster makes it a good choice for dressy, evening attire, and satin and lace are very often used in bridal gowns. Denim and chino are common fabrics for trousers. Seersucker, calico, and cotton broadcloth are all popular fabrics used in children's wear. Over the years, fabrics have gained reputations for certain uses. Usually practicality prevails, and the fabric best suited for the purpose is selected. In the interest of creative design, though, designers may choose to use alternative fabrics for select purposes and alternative purposes for select fabrics. Recently, trends in children's wear have included fabrics that are normally reserved for adults. Boys' jackets were made of leather and girls' dresses were made of damask, and both boys and girls were seen sporting metallic touches borrowed from collections for more mature wearers. Providing the fabric will stand up to the demands of the new utilization, using fabrics in unexpected applications can offer fresh avenues for design.

color's multiple personalities

Color is complex. Entire courses and even industries are devoted to the topic. Pantone, described as a color think tank on its website, has developed a standard language for accurate color communication, and associations such as Color Association (www. colorassociation.com) have formed to investigate the innumerable nuances of color. This chapter touches on the subject of color as it pertains to traits. Just as individuals, styles, and fabrics have specific traits, so do colors. Colors, or hues, seem to have their own personalities, and they can instigate emotions. Most people are very sensitive to color. They can tell the difference between fuchsia, pink, coral, raspberry and shell, and they can visualize apple, chartreuse, emerald, green, ivy, jade, kelly, lime, moss, olive, pea, and pine as having distinct properties. Colors are especially imbued with cultural connotations. They do not inherently elicit emotional responses. These responses are learned, so an attribute that is significant for one culture may not be relevant

continued on page 141

Style Associations

The following is a list of common styling. Sketch or find a picture of each item. Write what you think of when you visualize the term. Avoid describing the item. Instead, list what emotions, feelings, and design concepts the term evokes.

Example: Smoking jacket	Cape

© John Springer Collection/Corbis

Common Association: *Affluence; leisure class; stuffy organizations; Hugh Hefner; smelly cigars*

Cardigan sweater	Nehru jacket

continued on page 140

continued from page 139

ACTIVITY 4.4

Trench coat	Peasant blouse
Safari shirt	Western-cut shirt
Tie blouse	Jodhpurs

continued from page 138

for another. Interestingly, those learned responses may be counter to true biological responses. "In spite of physical evidence to the contrary, most people continue to equate red tones with excitement and activity and blue tones with passivity and tranquility in color-mood association research" (Fehrman & Fehrman, 2004, p. 108). Hue changes with variations in saturation, interactions with the light source, and the color of the objects that it is viewed with. And color preferences can change over time. Still, one associates red with stop lights, blue with the sky, and yellow with the sun, and learned color associations are ingrained enough to guide designers in creating themes for their collections. A sampling of common colors and their sometimes characteristics are presented in the following sections.

black

In fashion, black is associated with formal attire worn for lavish events. It is *the* classic, timeless color that is never out of fashion. It has been suggested that every woman should have a *little black dress* in her closet because it is appropriate for nearly every occasion. Each season, a new color is proclaimed to have the status of black, as in, "Red is the new black." Black lends a slimming quality to a garment, and a slim black skirt is thought to be flattering on most women's figures.

The emotional response to black is that it can convey power and sophistication. In modern Western culture, black is also associated with death and mourning (Figure 4.7), as well as menace. Villains, such as the fictional Dracula, are often clothed in black.

white

In fashion in the West, white is the favored choice for bridal attire. In the United States, it is considered taboo, if only tongue in cheek, to wear white after Labor Day.

Figure 4.7
In Western cultures, dark, somber colors are often worn during periods of mourning. The lack of flamboyance is thought to be respectful of the deceased. © *Mary Evans Picture Library/ The Image Works*

Textile items that used to be available only in white are now available in an array of colors. The term "white sale" was derived from the time that bed linens were nearly always white. At one time, doctors' and nurses' uniforms were also white. Today, you can find this apparel in a variety of colors and even prints, but white is still linked with cleanliness and sterile hospital environments. White and black, when contrasted, are used to represent good and evil as in white knights and cowboys with black hats. White is often associated with innocence and purity, as suggested by the phrase "pure as the driven snow." However, as it is the color of the flag used in surrender, white also can be associated with defeat (Figure 4.8).

red

In fashion, the red carpet is rolled out for only the most important dignitaries or the most flamboyant of events. Actors attending the Academy Awards ceremony walk the red carpet as they enter the auditorium. Red clothing draws attention to the wearer, and Bill Blass eloquently summed up the power of the color red when he stated, "When in doubt, wear red."

Red is thought to represent passion and love. It is the color of fire; hence, it represents intensity, heat, and blood, as well as fertility and a vital life source, which is why it is the traditional color of bridal dresses for Chinese and Indian brides (Figure 4.9). Red is also associated with danger, and it is the color of stop lights and fire engines. Nathaniel Hawthorne utilizes many of the connotations associated with the color red in his novel *The Scarlet Letter* when he relates sin, pride, and passion to the scarlet-colored letter his heroine, Hestor Prynne, is forced to wear.

blue

Uniforms and denim are often blue. Blue-collar workers are so described because of the blue work shirts they have been known to wear at their physical labor jobs. Blue denim is so ubiquitous that it is considered a neutral, on par with gray, brown, or black. The popular color *navy blue* was derived from the color of naval uniforms (Figure 4.10). The color blue is seldom found growing in nature, so, in apparel, it can have connotations of synthetic materials. Even so, blue is many people's favorite color.

Blue is the color of sky, and water as it reflects the sky, so it is often associated with coolness, even coldness. As do deep water and a clear sky, blue also evokes feelings of serenity, peacefulness, and calmness. In some cultures, it also represents spirituality.

green

Green symbolizes nature, and it can be a preferred color in apparel lines that emphasize environmental concerns.

As the color of nature and freshness, green is often thought to represent life and fertility (Figure 4.11). It is the color of new growth, so it sometimes represents inexperience or naïveté. Inferences from the color green can be contradictory. It is thought to be calming, so guests on television or on a theater stage wait in *green rooms*, but it also is the color used to symbolize the intense feelings of jealousy and envy.

yellow

The color yellow is inextricably associated with the sun; therefore, yellow seems more harmonious with warmer climates. Children gravitate towards bright colors, so yellow is a popular hue for children's wear. In general, however, yellow is one of the least favorite colors chosen by people (Fehrman & Fehrman, 2004, p. 69). It is considered a trendy fashion color that goes in and out of style very quickly.

The color yellow can represent a real dichotomy of emotions. Its association with the sun brings feelings of warmth and optimism. Yet, the very bright hue attracts one's eye, so it also is the color of caution and hazardous situations. It can represent hope, as when a yellow ribbon is tied to a tree to encourage a loved one's safe return, but also cowardice (Figure 4.12).

meanings of dress

Styling, fabric, and color have traits and they are part of the concept of dress. Actually, *dress* is a comprehensive term that refers to much more than those three aspects. **Dress** is defined as "an assemblage of modifications of the body and/or supplements to the body," and this includes things such as jewelry, accessories, coiffed hair, and pierced ears (Roach-Higgins & Eicher, 1992, pp. 1–8). Tattooing is a form of body modification that is practiced all over the world, in an array of

Figure 4.12
In Thai tradition, a color is assigned to each day of the week. For example, yellow is associated with Monday. King Bhumibol Adulyadej was born on Monday, so the nation celebrates his birthday by wearing the bright hue. *Bloomberg/Getty Images*

Figure 4.13
These Muslim women are wearing moderate and extreme attire affiliated with their culture. *AFP/Getty Images*

different cultures. Activity 4.5 asks you to take a closer look at meanings behind this form of artistic self-expression and derive styling from the art form.

Dress is imbued with meaning. Even those who pay no attention to the world of fashion and design, make a statement with their dress. Dress is a way for individuals to establish and support their personal identities, and it can be given context according to social situation, person characteristics, such as age and gender, and the sound, movement, or fit of materials. Dress can also be viewed through culture (Figure 4.13), group association, and self-esteem. Examples of each are given included in the following sections (Kaiser, 1997).

culture

Culture is defined as the "accumulation of shared meanings, rituals, norms, and traditions among members of an organization or society" (Solomon & Rabolt, 2004, p. 37). Our relationships with cultures are complex. They are fraught with symbolism and emotion. Individuals connect with a culture because of its social structure,

continued on page 148

Tattoo Art as Design Inspiration

Tattoos are found everywhere in today's society. They can represent spirituality, religious and cultural affiliation, rebellion, and identity. Tattooing has a deep and broad history, and contemporary tattoo art results from a variety of influences. For example, the Japanese style of tattooing is realistic in detail and full of striking color. Both fashion design and tattooing are outlets for articulating feelings, emotions, ideas, and commentary. Their ultimate goals are the same, even if the media that convey the message differ.

Tattoo-inspired textile design. *Photographer: Eileen Molony*

Motif Example

Research a style of tattoo art and sketch a print design inspired by the history and artistry. You might decide to create an all-over print by repeating a pattern or design a simple motif for a shirt front or sleeve. Determine how you would place the print design on an article of clothing and illustrate the design. Title your creation. Be prepared to discuss the inspiration, meaning, and connections behind your tattoo-inspired print and garment design.

Sketch motifs inspired by your research. Manipulate these images as desired using computer graphic design software, such as Adobe Illustrator, by tracing them and creating templates for hand stamping, or by repeating the motif to create all-over print designs. Heat transfer paper is available in most craft and sewing stores. A small print design, created either on the computer or hand illustrated and then scanned into the computer, can be printed using your home printer. The pattern can then be heat set onto a textile when you are ready to make up your design in fabric.

Style of Tattoo Art _____

Origin _____

Research _____

_____

_____

_____

Title

Print Design	Garment Illustration

continued from page 145

adaptation to the immediate environment, and ideology, or common views (p. 42). *Material culture*, quite often in the form of apparel, is frequently used to represent the *nonmaterial culture*. Nonmaterial culture includes patterns of thought, feelings, and behaviors of a group.

Cultural ideals change over time. Miller-Spillman (2005) illustrates this concept with her activity concerning Western cultural standards of pregnancy through time (pp. 25–27). Readers are asked to consider the evolution of a standard that once required women to seclude themselves when they were "in the family way." Accompanying images contrast a fully covered bride from the fifteenth century who is dressed to appear pregnant, Princess Diana's conservative maternity attire, and Demi Moore's nude and pregnant appearance on the cover of *Vanity Fair*.

group association

A culture of a society is made up of many groups. Subcultures can be formed around religious beliefs, ethnicity, history, families, group affiliation, age, gender, and other aspects that unite people. People who share common characteristics identify with particular groups, and clothing is an integral way for members to show their affiliation with their group.

subculture

Subculture groups are many and varied. Goth, grunge, and hip hop are just a few of the ways that people can identify themselves. For example, even though inner-city teens represent only 8 percent of all people in that age group, they exert a great deal of influence on young people's fashion and musical tastes (Solomon & Rabolt, 2004, p. 78). The hip hop movement originated in the 1970s was an expression of the urban black experience. Many in the mainstream now want to associate themselves with this culture even though they have little or no connection to its original roots. They want to connect symbolically to the rogue elements that the culture represents (Figure 4.14). These associations are reinforced by the media and deliberate machinations of designers and marketers (pp. 81–82). Because of this phenomenon, the vast array of fashion choices in today's marketplace is not really available to those who identify with the hip hop culture. They would not wear something that did not maintain their connection to it. Actually, through the process of *cultural selection*, all consumers filter choices through gatekeepers, such as their peer groups, and winnow out those items that do not reinforce the ideals of the culture (p. 82).

ethnicity / race

Ethnic and racial origins make up an important part of a person's identity. Different ethnic groups look for different features in clothing. Some also require different sizing structures. It is essential that designers learn the apparel desires and needs of their ethnic customers. However, it is also paramount that designers do not stereotype their customers and place them into neatly divided categories. Today, many people identify with several groups, and there is an increasing number of people with multiethnic backgrounds.

self esteem

Self esteem is connected to body image, appearance, and clothing. When people feel good about themselves, they pay attention to their appearance. Apparel and

Figure 4.14
The hip-hop
subculture is removed
from its inner city
roots. Other groups
adopted the fashions
associated with the
urban expression,
and meanings of
dress evolved in
the process. © Jon
Burbank/The Image
Works

appearance management can act as the symbols that expresses your self esteem
(Solomon & Rabolt, 2004, p. 143). Self esteem is influenced by comparing an
attribute of your actual self to some ideal of how you would like to be. Ideals are
culturally defined and molded by media, advertising, fashion designers, heroes, and
mentors. Those ideals may not be rooted in realism. For example, even though a
majority of people are not tall and thin, clothing is most often displayed on models
who are tall and thin. Movie stars and media reinforce this image. Some individuals attempt to address their perceived flaws through reconstructive surgery, whereas
others use clothing to highlight assets and hide their less than favorable figure traits.
Miller-Spillman (2005) suggests that perspective can be gained by looking to other
cultures for definitions of beauty (p. 23). She notes that, in general, all humans are
alike in that they are not satisfied with the characteristics they were born with.
Historically, most cultures have practiced some form of figure enhancement or
alteration. The theme is the same, only the body zone changes. While one culture
focuses on the bustline, another concentrates on the derrière. In one culture thin is
in, but in another, pleasingly plump is admired.

Some of the focus is now shifting away from the uniform idea of the ideal self.
Many individuals realize that they are frustratingly working toward an unattainable goal. Slogans such as "big and beautiful" are resonating with consumers who
do not fit the standard mold. In the book *The End of Fashion*, journalist Teri Agins
(1999) offers evidence that consumers are becoming more independent-minded.
They are no longer willing to follow the old order of fashion. She states that the
traditional roles of the fashion designer and the consumer have reversed. It is the
consumers who now have the power to determine what they want to wear, and they

are exerting that power by purchasing clothing that is on terms with their personal identity and lifestyle. Fashion designers will have to decide whether they want to perpetuate artificial standards of beauty, or if they want to be relevant and important to their audience.

summary

Designers use their character traits to express creativity and use their creativity to express their traits. Traits such as courage, risk-taking, and a tolerance for ambiguity are thought to enhance creativity, but fear can cause creator's block. Fashion can both express and elicit emotion. The affective aspect of fashion design cannot be neglected. If it were, design would be uninteresting and uninspired, and both designers and wearers of fashion would lose a conduit for self-expression and self-esteem. Some dress has built-in meaning, and other dress has meaning conferred upon it by cultures, groups, and individuals.

KEY TERMS

traits	delay of gratification	self-control	design statement
ambiguity	perseverance	fear	dress
freedom	risk taking	passion	culture
disorder	courage	mood board	self-esteem

DIN Challenge: Designing with Feeling

Fashion design can both elicit and express emotion. Refer to the affective aspects of apparel design, the list of emotions in Activity 4.2, and the entries you have made in your *DIN* thus far to design a series of looks based on the emotions, traits, and/or meanings of dress that resonate with you. List *Ideas* that stem from all your entries, assemble *Themes*, and create *Connections* that will guide you in responding to the challenge.

Notes for Discussion

_____

_____

_____

_____

_____

_____

_____

_____

_____

_____

_____

_____

_____

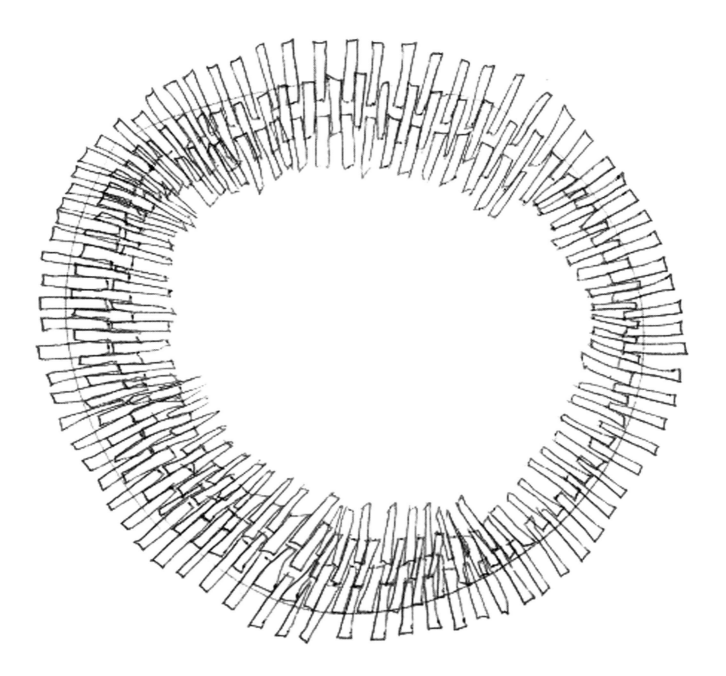

5 creativity *and* motivation

There is no template that describes all creative designers. Each brings a unique set of characteristics to creativity and fashion design. They do have one aspect in common, however. That is motivation. Fashion designers are just plain motivated! Anecdotes abound detailing how designers live on shoestring budgets, eat little, and go out even less so they can pursue their dream to design. Many individuals know from a young age that they want to be fashion designers. They tell of making paper doll clothes cut from magazine advertisements, coercing siblings into acting as mannequins for their patchwork creations, and attacking sewing projects well beyond their expertise. They are driven by passion and an inner force. No external source, peers, money, or the promise of fame, for example, can instill in them a desire to create equal to that which they already possess.

intrinsic and extrinsic motivation

Designing has been described in this book as a task that requires long hours and dedication. Why would someone commit to such a demanding field? It is most likely because of being intrinsically motivated to design. **Intrinsic motivation** is described as doing an activity simply for the interest or enjoyment of doing it. It is most often positive, and it enhances a person's self concept. On the contrary, **extrinsic motivation** is derived from external forces that sometimes offer superficial or untenable rewards. They could include grades, money, power, or fame. Both intrinsic and extrinsic motivation can influence creativity.

intrinsic motivation
Intrinsic motivation involves drive, energy, passion, and direction. It is conducive to creativity because it gives one the determination to complete tasks that are complex

Design by Henrik Vibskov

(opposite) Image of the inspiration for the Spring 2010 Ready-to-Wear (RTW) menswear line from Henrik Vibskov. *Courtesy of WWD*

OBJECTIVES

— To identify the components of intrinsic and extrinsic motivation

— To acknowledge alternative niches for design.

— To explore the relationship between imagination, play, flow, and reflection and creativity

— To understand that designers and consumers have various motivations to act

— To consider community involvement as motivation for design

and lengthy. When these traits originate from within the person, they are easier to sustain. For example, long hours and practice are often required in order to pursue a hobby. Even so, many people knit, hike, ride horses, scuba dive, rock climb, and quilt (Figure 5.1). Figuring out the patterns for a quilt can be complicated. Quilting requires a lot of precise sewing and color coordination skills. In addition, because blankets and comforters are readily and inexpensively available in retail stores, it is rarely necessary for individuals to assemble their own quilts in order to stay warm. Yet, quilters work hard at making their complex creations. Quilters and other hobbyists usually are not motivated by money or fame; they rarely show their work outside of their immediate circle of acquaintances. Most designers, like hobbyists, are intrinsically motivated.

Think back to childhood experiences of natural inquisitiveness and curiosity (Figure 5.2). Youth is a time to draw enjoyment and fulfillment through exploration, but these tendencies can be arrested at an early age by rules, structure at school, and the idea that there is just one best way to address a challenge. Designers should nurture their wonder at the world and be on the lookout for conditions that undermine it. Threats to internal motivation can include deadlines, excessive directives, and

Figure 5.1
Hobbyists can be described as intrinsically motivated because they work for the pleasure inherent in the challenge rather than for money or fame. © Mark Karrass/Corbis

pressured evaluations, because all take the locus of control away from the individual
and make it external to the person (Ryan & Deci, 2000).

promoting intrinsic motivation

Several factors can be said to promote intrinsic motivation. These motivational
aspects can be thought of as putting the "C" in creativity. The Cs of intrinsic motivation are (adapted from Malone & Lepper, 1987):

- Castles in the sky
- Challenge
- Competition
- Control
- Cooperation
- Credit
- Curiosity

castles in the sky

Some limitations are conducive to creativity. They allow designers to focus in on challenges and eliminate extraneous distractions. However, individuals should be free to use fantasy and imagination. Visualizing what might be and building castles in the sky maintains one's interest while producing fresh, original ideas. Too many constraints rein in possibilities.

challenge

Individuals are most motivated if design tasks are commensurate with their abilities. Assignments that are too easy soon become boring. Assignments that are too difficult are frustrating. Either way, designers may be tempted to quit those projects. Design activities with intermediate levels of difficulty and probable, but uncertain outcomes can have a positive effect on individuals' self-esteem because they allow designers to stretch their abilities while successfully reaching their goals.

competition

Actually, competition can, depending on the circumstances, foster or inhibit creativity. When a designer's work compares favorably to another's work, it is validation and an impetus to move forward. Competition can encourage designers to do their best work, and it can inspire camaraderie. Competition can be detrimental to motivation and creativity, however, if it prompts jealousy, pitting one designer against another, or if one relinquishes self-esteem from losing.

control

People want to be in control of what they do. If designers are able to choose what they design and the process by which they design it, it is easier for them to see the cause-and-effect relationship of their products. It is said that one of the consequences of a modern society is that many workers do not have the opportunity to see the fruition of their labors. They become a cog in the wheel of production, and they have no voice in or vision of the final outcome of the product. Intrinsic motivation can fade in this type of atmosphere. However, if designers have control over what they produce and feel as though they are an integral part of the process, they are much more likely to take a vested interest in its outcome.

cooperation

Designers do not work in isolation. They normally work with a team of professionals who are all working toward the same goals. When people work together, they are able to reach goals that they are not able to obtain on their own.

credit

Although intrinsically motivated people do not work for fame and adulation, it is still encouraging to receive credit and be recognized for one's accomplishments.

I think it's definitely something within me. I have gone through so many classes that were just standard, and I just had a need to do something that wasn't just papers and tests. So, I think it's something within me. — *Fashion Design Student*

People feel satisfaction when their work is appreciated, and they soon feel manipulated when their hard work is taken for granted.

curiosity

Individuals differ in how they perceive the world and in what arouses their curiosity. If designers are able to tap into their natural curiosity, projects become more interesting. When designers are interested, they are better able to become and remain engrossed in their work.

The Cs of intrinsic motivation are especially applicable in the design classroom. Many components of a typical college experience focus on extrinsic factors. Grades are important to those students hoping to go on to graduate school or keep their scholarships. Many students also have the challenge of paying their way through school. This can center students' focus on their part-time jobs and on making the next payment. Also, deadlines and other stresses of school rob students of their natural curiosity. Sometimes they just need to get a project done so they can move on to the next assignment. Classroom atmospheres and assignments that can reinforce the Cs of intrinsic motivation can help to focus students' attention on design work and away from external demotivators.

extrinsic motivation

Past the ages of early childhood, it becomes obvious that people cannot do only that which they are intrinsically motivated to do. There may be subjects in school that do not relate to one's inner curiosity. There may be chores at home that people find to be tedious, but they do them anyway. If individuals see value in the activity, feel competent to do it, and have a reasonable chance of succeeding, these chores do not necessarily inhibit motivation (Ryan & Deci, 2000). These extrinsic motivators do not inhibit creativity because they are recognized to be part of a larger goal of getting an education or wanting to be a productive member of a family.

Extrinsic motivation can be harmful to creativity, though, if the focus shifts from the problem at hand to something external to the project. Concern over grades, for example, can cause one to fixate on how to get the best score instead of on the best way to solve the problem or express an idea. A fashion design student hoping for a positive evaluation may opt to use a tried and safe technique, rather than an experimental approach, because the experimental approach might not be successful. This would inhibit creativity. Money, the search for praise or approval, and even the avoidance of punishment can motivate a person to take action, but creativity is more likely to result from focusing on the work and not the reward.

Examine your motivations to design and list them here. Identify whether the item is an intrinsic or extrinsic motivator by labeling it with either an "I" or an "E."

_____

_____

_____

_____

Consider the Cs of intrinsic motivation. List the ones that would help you enhance your intrinsic motivation.

_____

_____

_____

_____

_____

_____

_____

_____

_____

motivations to explore

Regardless of whether designers are in school or working in the industry, there are always going to be external forces that rob them of the focus they need to create. Constant deadlines and practical issues can divert one's attention from the more imaginative aspects of designing. Designers' time and energy can easily be usurped by these issues, but if designers allow that to happen, it leaves little room for the imagination that inspires creative design.

imagination

"Imagination is everything," Albert Einstein declared. He asserted that imagination was more important than knowledge because knowledge is limited to all one can know and understand. Imagination, however, embraces the entire world and all that will ever be known and understood. **Imagination** is fantasy, perception, art, memories, and plans. It is thinking outside the confines of the reality of the concrete world. It is what might be. **Imagery** is the ability to mentally represent what is imagined. One can see, hear, smell, feel, and taste using imagery. Fashion designers employ imagination and imagery in order to come up with designs that are fresh and new. Without imagination, styling would remain constant, and fashion would be just clothing.

Imagery is often used in competitive sports. Visualization exercises can prepare players for a number of dilemmas that they will face in their game. They imagine scenarios where they outwit their opponent and are ultimately victorious. Marathon runners often navigate imaginary obstacles as they mentally run through every turn of the long course. Designers, too, can use imagery to visualize how a garment will look when various elements are assembled. Fashion instructors often advise their students to imagine their garments on the runway. Students envision the overall presentation, how the fabric moves, how the model walks when wearing it, and even crowd reaction. After the visualization exercise, students are able to make changes to their designs, so they will better match what they imagined them to be. The creativity-enhancing exercise Vivid Imagination in Activity 5.1 can also help you practice expanding your imagination.

Creativity-Enhancing Exercise: Vivid Imagination

Imagine a creature living on a distant planet with a different atmosphere. What kind of being did you imagine? Most people visualize creatures that emulate life as we understand it, even though they are free to imagine anything (Michalko, 2001, p. 163). The creatures may have legs, arms, eyes, and noses, just as we do here on Earth, but there is no reason why space creatures, living in an atmosphere different from our own, would have those features. Even when we are trying to use our imagination, we are likely to structure ideas in highly predictable ways according to existing concepts, categories, and stereotypes (p. 164). This creativity-enhancing exercise is designed to draw out your vivid imagination.

- Identify a design challenge. (Design a bridal gown for a tropical destination wedding, for example.)
- Take 10 minutes to write down everything that you can think of that relates to that challenge. (You might think of sand, water, sun, etc.)
- Referring to those notes and using the thumbnail templates on page 160 and in the Appendix to enable you to quickly illustrate your ideas, take another 10 minutes to sketch several concepts that respond to the design challenge.
- Now, discard your ideas! None of the ideas that you wrote down or sketched are allowed! Reach deeper into your imagination for fresh ideas and design an original garment that responds to your challenge without using any of the concepts that you first listed.

Design Challenge

_____

Ideas

_____

_____

_____

_____

Reaching Deeper

_____

_____

_____

_____

_____

continued on page 160

continued from page 159

ACTIVITY 5.1

Ideas

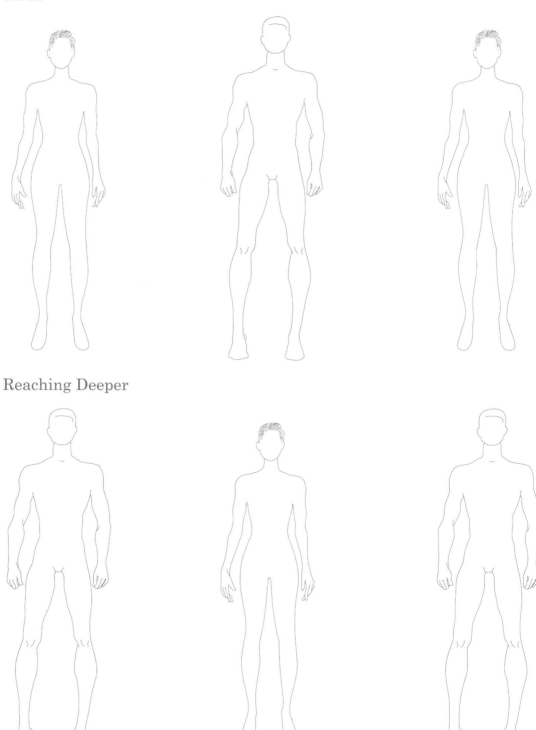

Reaching Deeper

play

Imagination allows us to engage in resourceful play. When we are young, we often spend large amounts of time imagining and playing. As we get older and as life's responsibilities creep in, we play less and less. As adults, we are taught to devote our attention to serious matters, and play is often thought to be frivolous and a waste of time. Some work environments discourage all forms of play. If a concrete, documented outcome is not possible, the activity is discouraged. Some managers and executives do recognize the organic nature of innovation, though. They install company game rooms, for example, that allow employees to remove themselves from the stresses and tedium of day-to-day responsibilities, so that one's imagination can thrive and ideas can germinate. Play is the wellspring of new ideas. Like child's play, inspired **play** is unstructured and free form. It is an intentional way to allow the imagination to flourish. Play is not about setting rules and following guidelines, but certain constraints are helpful in play. Too many possibilities can make the exercise frustrating because focus is diffused among multiple elements. To avoid confusion, for example, a fashion design play exercise might limit the number of materials used (Figure 5.3). Play could exhibit the following characteristics:

- Pleasurable

- Spontaneous

- Free from the constraints of reality

- Liberating

- Unordinary

- Free from pressure to perform

- Free from pressure to conform

- Free from rules

Figure 5.3
Make time for unstructured play. Gather assorted supplies and a dress form and see what materializes. Note your ideas in your *DIN*. *Courtesy of the author's collection*

continued on page 164

Nick Cave | Artist and Educator

There needs to be a level of commitment that is only driven by passion.

Creativity is . . . truth and freedom of expression. I think you have to be fearless in order to indulge in the pure essence of that.

I studied fiber art, art, and dance in school. I had a retail store for 10 years with another artist. We created one-of-a-kind garments, limited editions, and a lot of screen-printed fabrics. That was really the emphasis of the store, to create a body of work through the textiles. At the same time, I was doing performance-based work. Today, I no longer have the store, but I have private clients and do events. I work full time as an artist on my sculptural works, and I'm also the chair of the Fashion Department at the School of the Art Institute of Chicago.

I look at my pieces two ways: I look at them as sculptural objects that are figurative and static. The second part, sound suits, are the performative side of my work. I look at the sculptural as well as the performative, with a strong emphasis on embellishment and the building of surfaces.

My design philosophy stems from bridging the history of textiles with the history of art. I find myself on top of the fence. I look at my work as an intersection between art and design. That provides a balance for me. [The interdisciplinary aspect] is important. I think about how I want my work to function in the global world. Do I want it in a gallery setting, or is there a bigger purpose that I can connect to? That is more interesting to me. I look at my work as a vehicle for change. What that means is, I want to be able to intersect institution, corporate [philosophy], academia, and community to bring this experience full circle. I want to use my work as a sort of tool. I want to make these sculptural objects that become performative. In order for the performance aspect of it to happen, I need a body of people, and that body of people is the community. I'm doing these performance labs around the country. I bring in 40 sound suits, and the community builds the performances. If you go to You Tube, you can see a lot of them.

[My art is faceless.] The work is not gender based, nor race, nor class, nor any of that. That's what important to me. I want you to have this encounter with this

new hybrid. There's nothing about the work that you can make associations with. You can't categorize it with anything, so you are forced to go to a different type of accepting process. That curiosity really opens you up. How do I respond to it? How do I see this thing? How am I connecting to it? It touches on a lot of the things that I am interested in—humanity.

I spend a great deal of time traveling the world. I spend an enormous amount of time in flea markets and thrift stores. That becomes my surplus arena. That's where I get my inspiration. That's where I generate new ideas. I'm known for going to flea markets and literally creating new works on the spot. The world really is my canvas. It's the huge availability of resources, the abundance of materials, and visual sensation that is extraordinary for me. I'm not one who sketches. I work from impulse, intuition, and as response to something. I don't want to have the answer. I want my work to always have a question at the end. I want to always keep the door open, so I can pass through and move on in the next direction. I look at it as a form of exercising. It's exercising my way of thinking and approach to my work.

People ask me how I came to know that this is what I am going to do with my life. One day I woke up and said, "Now or never." I've done amazing things in my life, but I've always known that I needed art. It's like me as an African-American male. I can't change the color of my skin. That's how intense it is for me. I can't change what I am supposed to be doing with my life. The amazing thing is that I know what that is.

I don't think you should just look at fashion for inspiration. Inspiration is all around you. You must have a point of view, and you must attack your work in a fearless way. The competition is extreme. The questions always brought to me in graduate school were "What makes you stand out over the next person?" and "Why would I be more interested in your work instead of the next person's?" Those are questions you must maintain as part of your foundation.

The road has changed drastically with this recession and economy, and it's never going to be the same. I really don't think it's ever going to be the same. But the thing that's interesting is it brings me back to this Bohemian way of thinking. How do you restructure? I work the same way that corporations work. Corporations are all downsizing. You have to multitask in a corporation, and that's how artists are working now. We are no longer just painters. We are no longer just sculptors. We are no longer just performance artists. We are working within this transient and interdisciplinary arena. We are self promoting. We're turning our living rooms into galleries and showrooms. We're doing whatever we need to do in order to sustain our creativity. I think that's the way of the world today. When your gallery closes, what do you do? You think of new ways to position yourself in the world.

The only way you can foster creativity is by indulging yourself in it. In order to get better, you have to practice. You have to practice to be successful. Open a business or do any type of adventure. There needs to be a level of commitment that is only driven by passion. And that's really what it's going to take.

Courtesy of James Prinz

continued from page 161

One of the hardest concepts for adults to accept about play is that there does not have to be a product or final outcome after the exercise. The goal is to not set goals. One plays for the experience of freeing one's mind from pressures and duties and to unleash imagination. In play, there is no stigma in "bad" ideas or mistakes because nothing has been risked. Even though there are no explicit goals with play, the exercises do yield results. It is hoped that novel ideas are formed when concepts produced during play connect with existing ideas during periods of reflection and incubation. Activity 5.2 invites you to set your inhibitions aside and play as you did when you were younger.

ACTIVITY 5.2

Play

For this exercise, you use play to encourage imagination. It can be done alone or in a group setting. Play should be exciting and fun. A lively exchange of ideas and supportive comments is encouraged. Set aside a time every week to play.

- Schedule one-and-a-half hours for this exercise. Be sure that you will not be interrupted during this time.
- Clear the room as best you can of distractions. Use your favorite music to set the mood.
- Clear your mind from deadlines and assignments.
- Assemble a wide assortment of materials. Include dress forms, pencils, paper, and fabric, of course, but also unusual or unlikely materials. Consider wire screen, metals, craft mirrors, tapes, ribbons, beads, magazines, paper, tubes, wood slats, paints, tulle, etc.
- Utilize 1 hour imagining and playing with the materials.
- Utilize the last half hour entering your imagined ideas into your *DIN*.

Notes for Discussion

_____

_____

_____

_____

_____

_____

_____

_____

_____

reflection

There are numerous ways to think, reflect, and meditate on your ideas, but basically your **reflection** can be focused, indirect, or unconscious (Aspelund, 2010). *Focused reflection* is actively attending to a task. It is searching through materials and experimenting with alternatives to find a solution to a problem or challenge. Focused attention is very productive unless one becomes stuck or stalled on a task. When working on a problem, people have a tendency to become fixed on ideas, but this fixity does not bring one closer to an original solution. For example, a designer may plan on using the color red in a design. Red then becomes a fixed component of the garment. If elements of the design are not working together, a change of color is not considered as a solution to the problem because red is the only color the designer associates with that design. Focusing on issues other than the problem at hand can allow time for alternative ideas to enter the mind. While working on a separate project, with a blue and green color story, the designer might suddenly see that a blue and green combination could solve the aesthetic problem of the first garment. By simply going about the day-to-day activities of being a designer, one can break fixed thought patterns and allow alternative ideas to enter the mind. This is *indirect reflection*. Designers recognize that inspiration and solutions can spring from any number of sources so they keep their minds open to all possibilities. Indirect reflection is a stockpiling of ideas. While working on your *DIN*, you have been practicing both focused and indirect reflection.

When you are at a creative impasse, but you find that it is hard to take your mind away from a problem, it may be time to take an **excursion**, or a type of intentional indirect reflection. This creativity-enhancing technique suggests that taking a journey away, either figuratively or literally, is a way to break stubborn thought patterns and allow fresh, new ideas to enter. Generate ideas that are irrelevant to the challenge at hand by describing a favorite trip, exploring unknown disciplines, such as gardening or astronomy, or take a break with a round of charades or physical aerobic activity.

incubation

Have you ever finished a garment design right before a deadline? You might have been happy with it at that time, but when you returned to that piece days later, did you wish that you had time to make some changes? Ideas need time to formulate. If that time is not available, as is often the case in contemporary times, individuals will make simple and readily available connections when responding to a design challenge. However, if ideas have time to percolate, many more connections between ideas can be made, and there are increased chances for novel associations. **Incubation** can be described as allowing the mind the time for reflection.

the unconscious mind

Many consider that the **unconscious** plays a great role in creativity and that ideas are constantly churning in the subconscious mind. It is thought that even while a person is concentrating on unrelated tasks, the mind is at work on a problem. Dreaming demonstrates the point. While dreaming, the mind is active even though one is not intentionally attending to it. Those dreams can be wildly imaginative and productive. There have been many stories of people waking from a dream with a suddenly lucid plan for a solution that has evaded them for long time.

Nowadays, with electronics, everything is instant. Creativity takes time.

— Fashion Design Instructor

taking time

Contemporary life is incredibly scheduled and busy, and electronic devices allow people to remain in constant contact. Deadlines, pressures to compete in a tough economy, and organizational structures that cannot quantify the value of time spent in contemplation make it difficult to allocate time for imagination, play, and reflection. These activities that foster creativity are often counter to contemporary lifestyles because they require time that is quiet and removed from the bustle of daily life. Individuals have strong attachments to their electronic devices, and it is unclear whether they actually want to turn them off for a while and spend this rejuvenating downtime. Forced reflection is not productive, though. One has to realize the value of time spent in play, imagination, and reflection, or the exercises will quickly lead to boredom and frustration.

Carthusian monks live their lives in near silence so they are better able to pray, study, and write without distraction. They go about their days in quiet meditation so their thoughts are given the time and attention they need to coalesce. Do you want to optimize your capacity for creative thought? Activity 5.3 advocates occasionally shutting out the bustle of daily life and spending time in quiet contemplation.

intuition

Some designers are thought to have a sixth sense about which designs will resonate with their audience. They are perceptive and intuitive. Designers with intuition often "feel" how to respond to a challenge, rather than strategically devise it. **Intuition** comes from a combination of experience in the field and being in sync with and extraordinarily aware of one's surroundings. Although it sometimes seems that intuition just pops into one's head, it is actually the result of play, reflection, perception, and a broad and deep knowledge of the discipline and contemporary culture.

flow

Designers who are intrinsically motivated enjoy both the play and the hard work that goes into creating clothes. Many have said that they would design even if they were not paid, and, in fact, many do. Designers who fully devote themselves to difficult yet enjoyable tasks are said to be *in the zone* or experiencing flow. **Flow is** an effortless and highly focused state of consciousness, and it involves novelty and discovery (Csikszentmihalyi, 1996, p. 110). Drugs, alcohol, or spending cannot enable one to artificially replicate the feelings of being in the creative zone because, in flow, one is personally accomplishing a tough challenge. The flow experience has been described by persons in any number of disciplines and also across cultures (pp. 110–111). Several elements can lead you to the flow experience (pp. 111–113):

- There are clear goals. You feel confident that you know what needs to be done. You are not undecided on how to proceed.

- Action and awareness are merged. This simply means that you are able to think about the design. This seems obvious, but it may actually contrast what

Taking Time

Have you ever sat in complete silence for any length of time? Today, we rarely allow ourselves that down-time just to ponder. Spending time in silence may even make us feel uncomfortable. However, constant noise and activity may not allow our mind to do what it does best—concentrate and make innumerable connections that may lead to original ideas.

- Schedule one hour for this exercise.
- Turn off all electronic devices. Eliminate all distractions.
- Sit in a quiet room in absolute silence. No talking or listening to music.
- Spend time with your thoughts for half an hour. Do nothing during this time. Do not sketch.
- Continue the second half hour in silence, but go ahead and put your ideas to paper in your *DIN*.
- Schedule frequent times for quiet meditation.

Reflection

happens in everyday life where people's attentions are divided among so many conflicting forces.

- Self-consciousness disappears. When engrossed, you do not think about what others are thinking. After the task is complete, you often emerge from it with greater self-esteem because you have met a difficult challenge.

- The sense of time becomes distorted. With enjoyment, time passes quickly. Hours can seem like minutes.

- The activity becomes an end in itself. Most things in life are done in order to work towards some goal. In flow, the reason for doing a task is the pleasure inherent in the experience.

Flow cannot be forced. All you can do is remove obstacles that stand in its way and be attentive to those elements that are inherent in nearly all flow experiences.

aha moment

What better feeling than that "**aha" moment**! It is that sudden insight when all elements merge to form an elegant solution. It often appears when it is least expected, when you are in the shower or driving, perhaps. The aha moment seems mysterious, almost magical. When asked to reflect on that moment, however, designers invariably acknowledge they have been working on those challenges for a long time. It is likely that the designer's mind has been attentive to the problem all along. Rather than springing from nowhere, the aha moment is a consequence of hard work, play, knowledgeable insight, and a busy unconscious mind.

human motivations

Designers are motivated to create for a number of reasons. Some of those reasons may be surprising because the media often presents a one-dimensional view of the field. Fame and glamour are wonderful byproducts of a successful design career, but often an individual's motivation to design stems from connecting to a meaningful niche or to the community.

gestalt theory

People have a drive to make sense of the world. Gestalt theorists Wertheimer, Koffka, and Kohler explain the need to understand and create order out of disorder by suggesting that individuals perceive their environment and experiences as wholes or **gestalts**, rather than a compilation of assorted parts. When confronted with gaps in gestalts, or inconsistencies and missing components in what is known, people reorganize what they know in order to fill in those gaps and make sense of things. There are several tactics that people use to close incomplete gestalts:

- *Proximity*: Elements that are close to each other tend to be grouped together. For example, the four buttons on a double-breasted jacket will be perceived as a square, and they project lines vertically and horizontally when worn. This aspect can contribute to how flattering a garment is on the body.

- *Similarity*: Elements that are similar in nature tend to be grouped together. For example, the button, buckle, and chain detail on a garment will be grouped together as "embellishment." If these aspects are not cohesive in design, the effect will be disconcerting.

- *Closure*: If an element is perceived as incomplete, people will attempt to complete it. For example, people have the tendency to perceive arrow shapes when they see converging angled seams, even if those seams do not actually meet. This can cause unwanted effects if the seams point to figure problems, but seaming can also be used to draw attention to the face or other favorable areas.

- *Continuity*: People will form mental bridges to span implied gaps in elements. For example, even though a jacket and skirt are separate items, a design line begun in the jacket will be perceived as continuing to the skirt.

- *Simplicity*: Elements will be organized into simple structures. For example, people will extract simple shapes and lines from clothing silhouettes.

- *Membership*: Even if nothing intrinsic connects the elements, they are grouped together if they are seen in the same context. For example, all clothing found in a budget store may be perceived to be of low quality, even though that is not actually the case.

These factors are known as the *laws of organization*, and they allow us to make order out of a chaotic world. It is efficient and even automatic to close gaps by absorbing the missing elements into already existing, simple, and predictable gestalts. As the examples suggest, consumers use these tactics all the time, both consciously and unconsciously. In design, however, creativity results from delaying these reflexive responses and reorganizing gaps or inconsistencies into new, surprising gestalts. Fashion designers aware of gestalt principles should avoid filling gaps automatically. They can intentionally "ungroup" elements and regroup them in novel configurations. And they can be alert to offering predictable responses made by closing gaps in the easiest and quickest possible way. For example, when students are working with their designs on the dress form, at the sewing machine, or at the computer, those garments are within arm's reach. It is all close work, and the "whole" that students recognize is limited to what they see at close range. If a designer is too close, however, the lower half of a design might not be seen in relation to the upper half, or the size and shape of the pocket might not be seen in relation to the size and shape of the lapel, and decisions are made to close existing inconsistencies using too narrow of a focus. Standing back 20 or 30 feet from a garment can introduce a new whole. The garment itself is seen as a whole, and it is also seen in the context of a room with other components. This exercise can encourage the creation of varied and more complex gestalts.

maslow's hierarchy

All humans have basic needs that motivate their actions. They include the desire for power, knowledge, independence, social standing, companionship, vengeance, honor, justice, physical exercise, romance, family, order, sustenance, acceptance, tranquility, and frugality (Reiss, 2004.) Maslow (1954) arranged some of those

The students will spend hours and hours because **they're just involved with their work.** They want to see it through. — *Fashion Design Instructor*

human needs into a **hierarchy** (see Figure 5.4). He suggests that lower-level needs must be met before one can progress to higher-level needs. When people lack the basics of food and shelter, they will focus on meeting those needs before they concern themselves with self-actualization. Self-actualization, at the highest level of the hierarchy, describes the process of fulfilling one's potential, self-enrichment, and being all that one is capable of being. Creativity is also thought to be in this highest level.

Human interactions can satisfy many needs, such as love and friendship, but products can also be employed to address necessities. Activity 5.4 asks you to consider how clothing can meet basic human needs at each level of the hierarchy.

Today, this early framework appears somewhat simplistic; it does not account for many of the complexities of human behavior, and some find the hierarchy to be representative only of Western cultures. Even so, it can inform those looking to enhance their creativity, if for no other reason than to illustrate that the desire for creativity is in competition with a wide array of other needs. If not cognizant of these competing needs, individuals can easily lose sight of their ultimate goals.

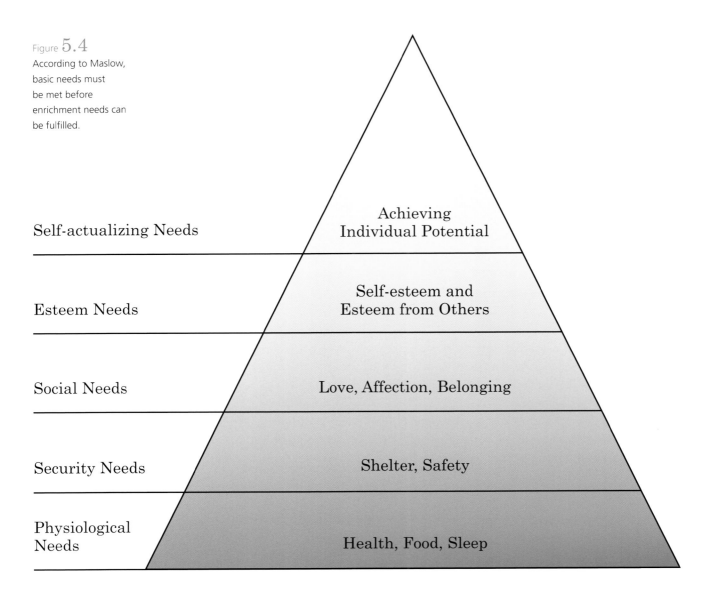

Figure 5.4
According to Maslow, basic needs must be met before enrichment needs can be fulfilled.

Self-actualizing Needs — Achieving Individual Potential

Esteem Needs — Self-esteem and Esteem from Others

Social Needs — Love, Affection, Belonging

Security Needs — Shelter, Safety

Physiological Needs — Health, Food, Sleep

Clothing Used to Meet Needs

Using the framework for Maslow's needs, fill in each corresponding area with clothing products that are relevant for that level.

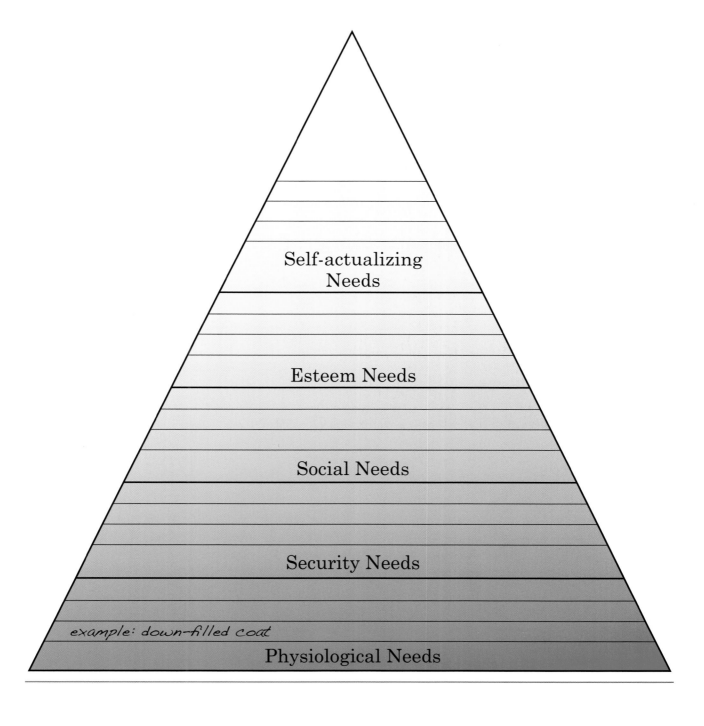

Self-actualizing
Needs

Esteem Needs

Social Needs

Security Needs

example: down-filled coat

Physiological Needs

fea consumer needs model

Some needs that prompt people to wear and buy clothes are straightforward. Simply, a warm coat is needed to survive long months in a cold climate. Most often, however, clothing is used to satisfy more esoteric desires. Clothing meets expressive and aesthetic needs, as well as functional ones. The **FEA Consumer Needs model** is presented as a general framework that can apply to all types of apparel design regardless of consumers' special needs (Lamb & Kallal, 1992) (Figure 5.5). At the core of the model is the target consumer. Designers build a profile of the customer using demographic and psychographic information, physical characteristics, activities, and preferences. All behavior takes place within a cultural context so, on the model, culture encircles the consumer. Then, user needs and wants provide the means for establishing design criteria. These considerations are (pp. 42–47):

- *Functional*: These relate to a product's utility. Protection, mobility, and thermal comfort are examples of functional requirements.

- *Expressive*: These relate to a product's communicative or symbolic aspects. Garments that communicate messages about the wearer—values, status, self-esteem, and roles—to others are examples of expressive requirements. For example, a policeman's uniform is functional, of course, but it also expresses authority.

- *Aesthetic*: These relate to the human desire for beauty and artistic elements. Items that follow the elements and principles of design are thought to be aesthetically pleasing.

This model is presented under the assumption that consumers want all three aspects—function, expression, and beauty—in the garments they wear. The considerations are interrelated, though, and they will relate in different ways for different target customers. The FEA model has been subsequently revised to incorporate concerns from the retail customer who may have constraints on the types of products they can sell (Kallal & Lamb, 1994).

motivations to design

Understanding human motivations can help designers meet the needs of their customers. It can also give them clues into their own motivations to create and be part of the web of ideas, clothing, and fashion that is the apparel industry today.

niche markets

There are a number of ways to differentiate target customers. In the women's apparel category, styling is often delineated as: couture, designer, bridge, better, contemporary, moderate, and budget. Apparel also can be allocated into markets such as lingerie, menswear, and maternity. Table 5.1 lists several apparel categories. Today, many designers focus on smaller, more specific niches. A **niche** market is a small, specific subset of a larger category. It has specialized needs that are generally not met by larger, mainstream businesses. Internet retailing and marketing allow designers to reach a large enough audience to maintain their livelihood while they concentrate on a small, well-defined niche. For example, nearly every sport has defined uniform requirements. Ice skating costumes worn in junior competitions comprise a comparatively narrow niche. Selling these items at local retailers might not produce enough

Figure 5.5

The FEA Consumer Needs model incorporates functional, expressive, and aesthetic considerations in fashion design. *Adapted from Lamb & Kallal, 1992*

TABLE 5.1

Apparel Categories

Age	Children's wear, Infant, Junior, Mature, Premie, Toddler, Teen, Tweens
Price	Better, Bridge, Budget, Designer, Discount, Luxury, Moderate
Market	Bridal/bridal party, Career wear, Contemporary, Couture, Evening/special occasion, Formal, Lingerie/ shapewear, Maternity and nursing, Menswear (and all corresponding subcategories, such as casual, suits, etc.), Outerwear, Sleepwear/loungewear, Sportswear, Tailored coats and suits
Function	Anti-allergy, Healthcare (scrubs, technician coats, etc.), Industrial (clean suits, etc.), Protective (Kevlar vests, etc.), Uniforms (and all corresponding subcategories, such as restaurant, airline, etc.), Work wear (laborer)
Activity/Event	Active wear, Art installation, Club wear, Costume (Halloween, etc.), Exercise wear (yoga, etc.), Holiday-inspired, Religious, Sports apparel (golf, tennis, ski wear, etc.), Swim wear and beach attire, Theatrical, Wearable art
Attributes	Big and tall, Half size, Husky, Petite, Plus size, Tall, Women's
Specialty	Accessories, Costume (cultural-inspired), Crossdressing, Custom tailored, Doll related, Environmentally-friendly/organic, Ethnic-inspired, Hand-crafted, Location-inspired (Western wear, urban, tropical, etc.), Modest apparel (to adhere to religious and cultural traditions), Pet related, Special needs (and all corresponding subcategories of adaptive clothing), Subculture (gothic, rave, motorcycle, etc.)

sales to support a design house. Retailing these items on the Internet allows niche designers to market their products nationally, and even internationally. Whereas competition is great in some of the well-established mainstream apparel markets (such as the contemporary junior category), designers just starting out may be able to get a foothold in the industry by identifying a small niche market that has a need.

attire for special needs

When discussing fashion design, we often refer to those highly publicized couture designers and forget that individuals design for a variety of reasons and for a variety of audiences. There are also those designers who create theatrical costumes; uniforms for flight attendants, firefighters, and law enforcement; affordable clothes for mass retailers; and clothing for consumers with special needs. It is for these specialized areas that the varied aspects of creativity are particularly needed. If the finest materials, best production facilities, and unlimited amounts of time are available, a designer can create unbridled. However, it is harder to achieve novelty with practical and functional restrictions, and it is a testament to designers' creativity when they are able to design within these constraints (Figure 5.6).

Creativity is needed for these specialized garments because the functional element takes on special importance, but the consumer does not want this functional aspect to appear that it is taking precedence over expressive and aesthetic aspects. Consumers with special needs and disabilities do not want to be stigmatized by their apparel. They want contemporary and flattering designs that conform to their contours, motions, and actions without being overtly utilitarian (Lamb & Kallal, 1992, p. 42). Persons with disabilities require a wide range of adaptive clothing that is functional, yet fashionable. Designers might consider creating adaptive clothing for the following people:

- With joint pain, arthritis, and limited mobility
- With paralysis
- In wheelchairs
- With amputated limbs
- Of shorter stature
- Of taller stature
- With crutches
- With a much larger physique
- Who are bedridden
- Who are sight-impaired

Each of these areas presents inherent guidelines for clothing design, yet often the special needs consumer cannot find apparel with these adaptations. When creating adaptive apparel, there are several things to consider.

- Is the garment easy to put on and take off. Will the wearer be able to dress independently?
- Will the wearer be able to open and close the garment? Should buttons be replaced with Velcro or large snap closures? Is the zipper pull easy to grasp?
- Is it comfortable? Surface design features, such as embroidery, pleating, and smocking, can enhance the attractiveness of a garment, but they may be uncomfortable to sit or lie on. Are seams smooth and flat? Are tags and labels nonirritating? Does the fabric breathe?
- Is the garment flattering? Does it draw attention to the wearer's face and away from more functional aspects of the design?
- Is it easy to care for? Is it durable, absorbent, and wrinkle-free?
- Will the item stay in place, or will it have a tendency to bunch up with use?
- Are the materials flame retardant or flame resistant?

These questions are general in nature. Additional questions, specific to the disability, have to be asked to ensure that garments are meeting the needs of the customer. Activity 5.5 allows you the opportunity to investigate and understand the challenges faced by the differently-abled.

Figure 5.6
Who would suspect that this dress was designed especially for nursing mothers? Slits under the flounces allow the mother to feed her infant without opening or lifting the top of the dress. *Courtesy of Mayreau Maternity & Nursing Clothing*

Designing for the Differently-abled

Those with special needs want functional clothes that are also fashionable. However, without careful consideration, the functional aspects of the clothing can overshadow the aesthetic ones, creating a utilitarian look. Create a fashionable article of clothing designed for a consumer with special needs.

• Identify a group with specialized clothing needs. You might decide to focus on those with a particular type of permanent disability. Or consider devising a design solution for those persons going through a phase or developmental stage. For example, young children who are learning to dress themselves but have not developed the dexterity to button small buttons and pregnant women in search of active sportswear also have unique and specialized needs in apparel.

• Research the needs of persons in that group. Interviews, focus groups, and surveys are good ways to obtain primary information about consumers. Or make a trip to the library to investigate printed materials and databases devoted to the subject. Also, organizations formed to support those with exceptional needs often create literature that is helpful in understanding the unique requirements of their members.

• Dedicate several pages of your *DIN* to your research. Include information that demonstrates your understanding of the topic and also your inspirations for the functional, aesthetic, and expressive aspects of the piece.

• Utilize *Ideas*, *Themes*, and *Combinations* to arrive at your design solution.

Specialized Need

_____

Research

_____

_____

_____

_____

_____

_____

_____

_____

_____

_____

_____

_____

_____

_____

Figure 5.7

Kate Moss wore the dress on the left to a gallery opening in 1995. In 2007, she brought back the vintage design for the debut of the Kate Moss for Topshop collection (center). The Forever 21 dress (right) appears to be a knockoff of the Topshop knockoff. Because neither manufacturer is trying to misrepresent copyrighted material, both knockoffs are most likely legal. However, looking to vintage designs for ideas is generally a more accepted practice than copying from a direct competitor. *Left: © Mitchell Gerber/ Corbis. Center: Gareth Cattermole/Getty Images*

fast fashion

In many situations, individuals have a personal association with niches that makes designing for them pleasurable and rewarding. For example, a designer with young children might take special delight in the challenge of creating children's wear. Individuals with the intrinsic motivation to design are especially fortunate. They have found a niche that has meaning to them so their vocation can also be their avocation. They have found a way to make a living, but they do not let that extrinsic motivator take precedence over more enjoyable aspects of designing. Today, fashion is big business and there are product developers who place making money above all else, pirating designs and counterfeiting goods to do it. The concept of fast fashion has brought out the best and the worst of the apparel industry. **Fast fashion** represents processes that streamline production and serve the consumer to a great degree. Computer-aided systems allow designers to communicate easily with overseas production facilities, and factories can be notified in real time as clothing items are sold in stores, thus aligning production very closely with demand. Fast fashion has also come to mean that knockoff garments are in the stores at nearly the same time as the original designer garments. Runway photos of designer lines are available almost immediately, and retailers such as Forever 21, Zara, and H & M, can have their adapted designer look in stores in as few as two to six weeks after the designer garments are introduced (Figure 5.7). **Knockoffs** are reproductions of garments made by other design houses. This practice is generally legal in the United States, assuming that the copy does not infringe on elements that can be copyrighted, such as print designs, or trademarked, such as logos. This is contrasted with **counterfeiting** which is illegal and includes blatantly copying the intellectual property of another (Figure 5.8). Trademarks, which include the "name, logo, image, or symbol that designates the source of a product," may not be copied (Jimenez, 2010, p. 26). Fashion law is a complicated issue and much more complex that can be presented here. Nonetheless, designers should become apprised of intellectual property rights to protect themselves and their creative designs and to avoid serious litigation.

Historically, the knockoff practice has been tolerated, if not accepted, by designers. The main reason that clothing is not protected under intellectual property law is that it serves functional, rather than aesthetic purposes. In the past, designer lines were copied and then retailed at lower price points. The copies became available to mass market consumers in a later season, after the original designers had moved on to other concepts. In this system, the copy could be thought of as a tribute to those designer lines that started the trends. Today, there are three overlapping trends that are changing the industry's laissez-faire attitude toward copying (Sanchez, 2007):

1. The Internet, flexible supply chains, and just-in-time inventory have greatly shortened the time it takes to produce knockoff products. Fast production allows copies to appear in stores at nearly the same time as their high-end inspirations.

2. Retailers, such as Target and Kohl's, are blurring the distinction between high-end and mass-market retailing by employing traditionally high-end designers for their mass-market lines. Engaging in **masstige** (a combination of mass market and prestige), designers who once sold their lines to an exclusive, limited clientele are launching lines at multiple price points (Figure 5.9).

3. "High-low" aesthetics have become popular. Historically, consumers clustered their purchases in one market tier. Today, clearly delineated market tiers are blurring as consumers choose high-end accessories to accent their middle-tier purchases, and traditionally high-end consumers also shop at mass-market

Figure 5.8

It is illegal to copy the intellectual property of another. The manufacturer of this counterfeited belt is really trying to maximize illicit profits. The buckle swivels to the brand of choice, "Hugo Boss" or "Nikey." The blatancy of the counterfeit suggests that the incorrect spelling of "Nike" is more likely due to ignorance rather than any attempt to differentiate the buckle from the copyrighted version.
Photographer: Eileen Molony

Coat
$149.00

Karl Lagerfeld
for
H&M

Launches November 12th in select H&M stores
www.hm.com

retailers. Where once the knockoff buyer was not considered to be the designer label customer, designers are beginning to view copies as direct competition.

These trends have prompted the Council of Fashion Designers of America to lobby for the **Design Piracy Prohibition Act**. This act calls for a special, limited three-year copyright in fashion designs (CFDA). The Council asserts that copies of original designs devalue the originals and challenge the growth of the field. Dissenters assert that there is a fine line between inspiration and copying, and pursuing copyright infringement in such a fast-paced field would bog the industry down in litigation and ambiguous disputes. Most styles have an historical precedent, and, when challenged, fast fashion firms may simply comb fashion archives until they have found the precedent for a look. The debate is ongoing. Table 5.2 highlights points on each side of the issue.

TABLE 5.2

Knockoffs in the Design Industry: The Debate

Those in favor of design piracy laws assert	Those against legislation stopping design piracy assert
Original designs are like paintings, music, books, and movies and they should be protected in the same way.	Creativity cannot be owned outright. It thrives on connections and associations. All designs are amalgamations of what came before.
Advances in technology have accelerated the process by which copiers can profit from stolen designs.	Bootleg copies of music or software are near perfect adaptations of the original. Knockoff fashion designs usually differ in fabric and quality.
Copying threatens creativity because it discourages individuals to do original work.	Much innovation in fashion is drawn from amateurs on the street and their ideas are not protected by law.
Design piracy is the same as counterfeiting, and there is protection against counterfeiting.	Intellectual property laws concerning clothing are just newer versions of Elizabethan sumptuary laws in which class boundaries were kept distinct by who wore which items.
The pirate does not have to assume any of the cost or risk of original design development.	Copying may harm individuals, but it is good for the industry because it popularizes and burns out trends quickly, thus speeding up the fashion cycle and creating demand for new trends.
Couture customers will flee those labels that have goods seen at other price points.	It is capitalism and competition at work.
Most garments are not strictly utilitarian. They are embodiments of design statements, expressions, and art.	Consumers love the choices and availability that fast fashion offers.
The laws would align with those already in existence in other countries. Works are protected against pirating in Europe.	There is no current data that shows harm has been done. Luxury fashion and fast fashion are currently coexisting.
European countries which allow copyright show no evidence of monopolies or shortages.	Monopolies in the apparel industry will be created. A finite number of garment designs will be controlled by a select group of designers.
Fast fashion and the quest for cheaper products promote exploitation of labor in underdeveloped countries.	There is currently little enthusiasm in enforcing the laws, and there is no easy way to file a suit. The time and cost will outweigh any benefit gained. By the time a suit is addressed, three or four seasons will have passed.
Creators of original designs are not being paid for their work. Pirates are not paying for the design portion of product development.	Too much control will diminish fashion's vitality. It will become sterile and predictable.
It is demoralizing to see one's hard work reduced to fast fashion.	With the masstige trend, designers already introduce their ideas at all market tiers, thus beating the pirates at their own game.
Young and new designers could benefit from having others license their work.	Designers could not, or would not, use others' work as inspiration for fear of violating laws. This would hinder a new designer wanting to enter the field.

Sanchez, J. (2007, September 14). Thou shalt not knock off. *The American*. http://american.com.

CFDA. Council of Fashion Designers of America. www.cfda.com.

Bollier, D. & Racine, L. (2003, September 9). Control of creativity: Fashion's secret. *Christian Science Monitor*, www.csmonitor.com.

What are your thoughts on the controversy? Which side presents the more convincing argument? State your conclusion here.

_____

_____

_____

_____

_____

community involvement

Designers create collections for a number of reasons, among them are expressing ideas and earning a living. Most likely, the motivation to design results from a complex interplay of causes. Designers may want express ideas and also give back to their community. They may want to make a living but use that livelihood to enable them to make a difference in the world. The following sections reflect three examples of designers' involvement in their local and global communities. Criticism of altruistic practices that are less than transparent is also noted.

corporate social responsibility

An article in *Women's Wear Daily* (2003) noted that today's fashion companies are about more than design. They are being associated with larger purposes. Consumers are more globally aware than ever before. They also have more choice than ever before, and they exercise that choice by associating themselves with brands that align with their social sensibilities. "Properly integrated and fully funded corporate social responsibility programs are becoming a requirement of doing business. . . ." (Tucker, 2009, p. 10.) The article singled out Kenneth Cole as having successfully combined business with social cause. In his book *Footnotes*, Cole (2003, p. 19) relates how he wants his company to be about something meaningful. He states:

> From the time I started our company, I've looked for ways to make what we do about something more than what we wear. And like most people, I was also searching for something to make my life more meaningful. . . . So I started doing something that I thought might help the company truly help others. I began an advertising campaign that had more to do with raising awareness about social issues than it did about raising awareness of personal style.

Over the years, Cole's advertising campaigns have been directed at raising awareness for AIDS, the homeless, gun control, women's equality, and voting.

the (red) campaign

The (RED) campaign is an example of companies joining together to create global community awareness. It was formed with the idea that the collective power of consumers can help those in need. (RED) emphasizes that it is not a charity. It is a business model designed to create awareness and a sustainable flow of money from the private sector into the Global Fund, to help eliminate AIDS in Africa (Red Campaign). Emporio Armani, Gap, Converse, Apple, Dell, Hallmark, American Express,

Figure 5.10
A percentage of the profit made on the sale of (RED) products is donated to The Global Fund, which is established to fight disease in Africa. *Photographer: Avital Aronowitz*

Starbucks, Bugaboo, and Windows are among the well-known brands that contribute to the cause. They create (RED) products that are said to be at no extra cost to the consumer (Figure 5.10) and then donate up to 50 percent of the profits from those products to an established fund. Money received provides access to education, nutrition, counseling, and medical services (Red Campaign).

fair trade

Fair trade is described as an economic partnership based on dialogue, transparency, and respect. It is a way to bring producers in developing countries into productive and profitable international trade relationships. It is also a way to infuse those relations with goals to end hunger, ensure education, create gender equality, and save lives (DeCarlo, 2007, pp. 3–16). Fair trade differs from conventional trade in several ways: (1) Fair trade places concern for people and the planet into the same top category as making a profit. Profit is often the central motive in conventional trade. (2) With conventional trade, payment is typically received within 30 to 90 days of delivery. In fair trade, assistance is given to disadvantaged groups by advancing credit during slow seasons and during production. (3) Fair trade provides technical assistance and training; attempts to build up the local community; and gives disadvantaged groups, such as women and minorities, opportunities to partner in the fair trade supply network. Socially responsible business practices are paramount. Conventional trade does not operate under a single method, but often the quest for inexpensive labor and materials is placed above concern for people and community (p. 20). The Fair Trade Federation has established criteria that define the values of the fair trade movement (Fair Trade Federation). They are:

- Creating opportunities for economically and socially marginalized producers
- Developing transparent and accountable relationships
- Building capacity
- Promoting fair trade
- Paying promptly and fairly

- Supporting safe and empowering working conditions

- Ensuring the rights of children

- Cultivating environmental stewardship

- Respecting cultural identity

Designers wanting to incorporate fair trade fibers, fabrics, beads, and other materials into their products can seek out those members of the Fair Trade Federation (Figure 5.11). They need to be flexible, however; currently many fair trade suppliers cannot provide continuity of product for reorders and subsequent seasons, and lots are smaller than what one would expect from a large traditional manufacturer. This negative can also be considered a positive because it ensures that designers' lines will be fresh and new each season.

the critics of corporate social action

Critics suggest that fair trade does not address the underlying problems in under-developed countries, and that the extra aid that artisans receive creates an artificial market that cannot be sustained in the free trade arena. Others suggest that fair trade helps too few people, and this tactic cannot make the impact that is required to raise living conditions for the poor.

There are also critics opposed to fashion design houses affiliating with social causes. They suggest that companies that connect themselves with charitable causes are using those in need to advance their own agendas. After all, the companies are profiting from advertising and promoting the cause. Kenneth Cole (2003, p. 22) agrees that it may appear that way:

> This is a real conflict for me. I am sometimes reluctant to admit that involving ourselves in social causes is actually good for business. Profit, should it come, happens to be a fringe benefit, and while it's not why we do it, it *is* the reason we can keep on doing it. But in saying that, we are in danger of appearing insincere, or worse, trivializing the issues.

The (RED) campaign states that through its initiative "desire and virtue are together at last" (Red Campaign). Some disagree with this kind of social intervention. They suggest that when companies promote a cause, they are detracting attention from legitimate charities that have better records of helping and more money going to the cause instead of administrative costs.

What role should corporations play in social issues?

_____

_____

_____

_____

_____

_____

Figure 5.11
Fair trade is a holistic approach to trade and development aimed at creating sustainable economic opportunities for socially marginalized producers in developing countries. *Courtesy of Global Mamas*

Motivations for design are numerous. Designers who explore their motives and their audiences' motives can readily determine whether their actions relate to their established goals. Not every social cause needs to be a global and expansive undertaking. Designers can also give back by becoming involved in their local communities.

summary

Motivation is related to creativity because it gives a person the desire and dedication necessary to complete a difficult, challenging task. Intrinsic motivation is described as doing an activity simply for the interest or enjoyment of doing it. Extrinsic motivation is derived from external forces such as praise, grades, and money. Creative work is more likely to result from people who love what they are doing and who focus on the work and not the reward.

In busy, contemporary society, there is rarely time for quiet reflection and unstructured play. Individuals' lives are scheduled and electronic devices are ubiquitous. Creativity requires time for imagination, contemplation, and incubation; however, this downtime cannot be forced upon a person. Designers wanting to enhance their creativity will consider allowing time for reflective activities.

Designers and consumers alike are motivated to act by a number of forces. They may be driven by a need for clothing and shelter, expression and esteem, or to satisfy aesthetic considerations. Designers often want to be contributing and participating members of their local and global community. Those wanting to associate their designs with larger causes should explore their motivations to ensure that their actions align with the goals that they have established for their brand.

KEY TERMS

intrinsic motivation	excursion	gestalts	knockoffs
extrinsic motivation	incubation	Maslow's hierarchy	counterfeiting
imagination	unconscious mind	FEA Consumer Needs model	masstige
imagery	intuition	niche	Design Piracy Prohibition Act
play	flow	fast fashion	fair trade
reflection	aha moment		

DIN Challenge: Connecting Design with the Community

Most designers want to be participating and contributing members of their community, but critics caution against using a cause to further goals that are profit-driven rather than altruistic. Refer to your *DIN* to identify ideas that are important to you. Identifying those concepts that have personal meaning helps to substantiate that your motives are based in genuine concern. Develop a series of sketches, or a collection, that match your interests with the needs of the broader community, and determine a way that your collection could benefit a particular cause. For example, designers with an interest in helping the mentally challenged might decide to incorporate beads or handiwork into their fashions that were made by handicapped persons. Or, designers concerned with cruelty to animals might design clothing that can be considered as alternatives to leather or fur.

Notes for Discussion

_____

_____

_____

_____

_____

_____

_____

_____

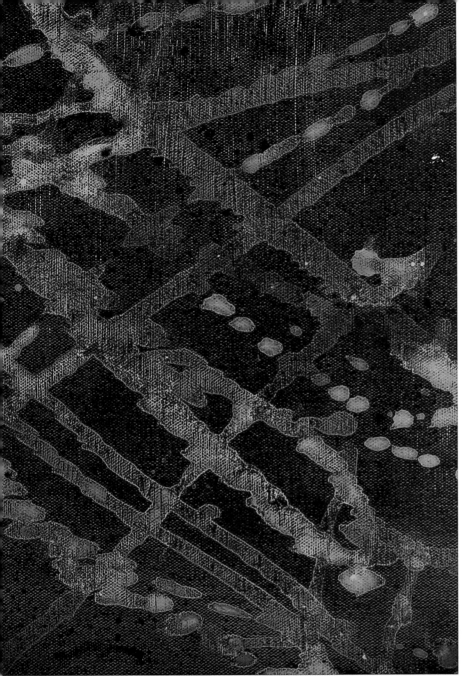

 +  +  +  = FALL COLLECTION

WISHBONE JEWELRY   PATCHWORK   LEATHER   LEGWEAR

6 creativity *and* the design process

When we see a beautiful design, we are considering the final **product**. We look at its color, fabric, and aesthetic components as they relate to one another. We rarely contemplate all the corresponding work, time, and thoughts that went into creating the piece. Even fashion designers seldom consciously ponder the **process** by which they create (Figure 6.1). However, when called upon to discuss how they design, they often are very cognizant of their processes (Lawson, 2006). Although the structure of the process is unique to the individual, and most likely unique in some way to each individual design, there are stages that most designers inevitably go through. Rather than examine the product, this chapter considers designers and their design processes. There are many approaches to the design process. Even within a single discipline, such as apparel design, design process models are often devised and expanded upon. (See LaBat & Sokolowski, 1999, pp. 11–20 for an overview of design process models used in several fields.) Three different approaches to the design process are investigated here: (1) the holistic approach, (2) the phase approach, and (3) the creative problem solving approach.

why a design process?

Certain actions have to happen in order for a designer to be able to claim to have created a fashion design. The design and designer may have gone through stages. Designers may have times of intense involvement and other times when they sit back and contemplate what is to be done and what they have already done. Lawson (2006, p. 31) humorously noted that those stages begin with enthusiasm, move through disillusionment, and progress into panic, and at some point designers probably do experience a number of interesting phases in the path to reaching their goal. A look into these stages can give you insight into your own processes, confirming what works and highlighting what might be tried. When all is going smoothly and inspiration is flowing, design processes are often working seamlessly in the background. However, when creator's block makes it difficult to design, an

Inspirational swatches.

(opposite, top) James Long's inspiration for Fall 2010 collection. *Courtesy of* WWD

Elements of an equation.

(opposite, bottom) Inspiration for fashion designer Cynthia Rowley for the Fall 2009 clothing collection. *Courtesy of* WWD

OBJECTIVES

— To acknowledge that there are several approaches to designing fashion

— To differentiate design products from design processes

— To explore the benefits of establishing a design process

— To investigate design as problem finding and problem solving

Figure 6.1
The design process
is not evident in this
complex McQueen
gown, but something
this intricate
undoubtedly was
a problem-solving
process that went
through many stages.
Courtesy of WWD/
Giovanni Giannoni

understanding of your own and others' design processes can give you insight into the problem. Knowledge of processes:

- Can serve as a frame of reference. When encountering a new challenge, it can give direction on how to proceed.

- Can be called upon to help identify what is going wrong. When you continually encounter problems that are similar in nature, you can go back to the basics to get back on track.

- Is helpful in teaching and learning situations. Design and creativity can be amorphous concepts, so identifying a stage can help instructors and students focus on content and problems.

- Can help break creator's block. It can suggest alternative phases or paths.

- Can empower you as a designer. It places control in your hands rather than in fate or circumstance.

a design process is not . . .

Individuals can look to design processes for insight into areas in which they are having some difficulty. They can look to experienced designers to see how they approach their craft. Lawson (2006) helps clarify what a design process is and what it is not.

a design process is not endless

If the designer allows, the design process can be endless. Researching and investigating is always interesting. There is always something new and exciting to explore (Figure 6.2). Also, there will always be a way to improve upon what you have done. Additional feedback can prompt an individual to rework an idea. New materials can improve performance. Most often, deadlines and economics tell a designer when it is time to complete the design process. These external conditions can cause frustration because designers may have to stop before they think their work is satisfactory. Familiarity with design processes can inform you when additional work on a design will not yield a corresponding level of benefit.

a design process is not right or wrong

There is no definitive process. Everyone tackles design problems with slightly different approaches. Understanding a process does not mean altering your own to conform to the new process. Rather, it suggests you should learn to be flexible in your practices, and learn to modify your process to meet the challenge of the design. "Controlling and varying the design process [are] the most important skills a designer must develop" (p. 124).

a design process is . . .

People use a variety of tools to accomplish the task of designing. They may analyze one day, synthesize the next, and evaluate yet another. Wallas (1926) introduced the phase model of creative production. He distinguished four stages: (1) Information—familiarizing oneself with the content, (2) Incubation—reflecting on the information, (3) Illumination—solution becomes evident, and (4) Verification—testing the solution. Since that time, many models have been introduced to explain how one goes about meeting the challenges and solving the problems of design.

the design process is meeting challenges and solving problems

There are many ways to solve a problem. Viewing it in a singular way and using tired, worn-out responses will probably solve the problem, but the solution will not be a creative one. Creative approaches to problem solving include examining information from many different points of view. This means that flexibility is key, and a variety of approaches with sensitivity to the context may be preferred over a single, best response.

the design process is finding challenges and problems

Finding the right challenge is as important as meeting a design challenge. Creativity is needed most in problem finding and discovering those situations that will have an impact on the future. This is envisioning, rather than reacting. The newer air permeable textiles offer an example of problem finding. The age-old problem was that when products were made to be waterproof, they did not let the skin breathe. This caused perspiration to build up inside items made to be waterproof.

Figure 6.2

There will always be more research that can be done or new materials could become available that would further enhance the design. For the design shown here, new jacquard trims could be found to better show the concept. Familiarity with a design process tells the experienced designer when it is time to rework a design and when additional research and experimentation will not yield additional benefit. *Photographer: Eileen Molony*

I try to make sure that I'm pushing them toward their creative process. Some [students] have different processes from mine, the way they create. **I try to work with whatever their process is.** I don't want them to feel that I'm trying to make them me or make them like the establishment or anything else. — *Fashion Design Instructor*

Figure 6.3
With ingenious problem finding and problem solving, air permeable products are made to be waterproof while still allowing vapor to escape. *Courtesy of Mountain Hardwear/REI*

Problem-solving methods looked at ways to add grommeted circulation holes to allow inside air to escape. Problem-finding methods discovered that textiles could be produced in such a way that air molecules could escape, but water molecules could not pass through. Searching for the root of that problem has led to a whole array of air-permeable products (Figure 6.3).

your design process

Neither new nor experienced designers are always attentive to their design processes. It takes practice to become cognizant both of what works and what does not work. Activity 6.1 asks you to journal your design process as you complete a design challenge.

Refer to the design you created in Activity 6.1 or think of a time when you created something unique and successful. What was your design process? How did you get your idea? How did you solve problems that arose? What did you go through to get to your final project?

Recreate the steps you took to arrive at your goal. Rather than list the steps, sketch the organic path from beginning inspiration to final product. (The design process path is rarely linear. Your design path may meander and double back upon itself.)

Getting Inspiration

Final Product

continued on page 193

Engineered Stripes

This is a basic design challenge: Take a cut of striped material and engineer the stripes in such a way that the stripe placement becomes central to the design. In other words, you may not place the stripes at random; they must be strategically placed to create a design feature on the garment. For example, one-inch wide black and white stripes can be pleated in such a way to eliminate the white in certain areas and the black in other areas. Or the stripes can be seamed and angled to create optical illusions. The goal of this challenge is, of course, to create a unique design, but it is also to document your design process.

- Select a striped material. Bold, wide stripes work best.
- Select an article of clothing to be designed—a shirt or skirt, for example.
- Use draping or flat pattern techniques to engineer the stripes and place them strategically on the body.
- Create the piece.
- Document your process every step of the way. Be sure to write down what you are thinking and doing as you go through the steps of making the engineered stripe design. Don't forget to note how you decided on your design idea, what changes were necessary and when, and how you feel about the finished product. Record all design steps here.

Steps

_____

_____

_____

_____

_____

_____

_____

_____

_____

_____

_____

_____

continued on page 192

continued from page 191

ACTIVITY 6.1

Swatch

Sketch

continued from page 190

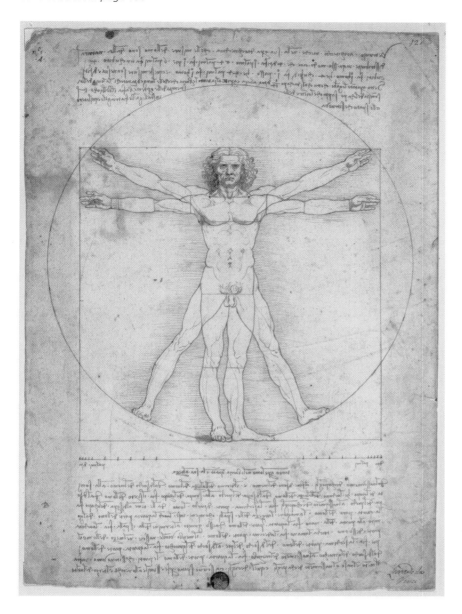

Figure 6.4
Leonardo Da Vinci's *Vitruvian Man* blends his interest in art and science. The illustration has come to represent a holistic view of mankind and nature. © *Scala/ Art Resource, NY*

the holistic approach: seven da vincian principles

One way to consider the design process is to examine those of a master creator. Leonardo da Vinci may be considered the ultimate Renaissance man. The Renaissance was a time of rebirth in the arts, sciences, and classical ideals after several centuries of limited exploration, and a Renaissance man is thought to be one who is proficient in a wide variety of areas including both the arts and sciences. Da Vinci was an artist, architect, sculptor, inventor, military engineer, and scientist. His life, notes, sketches, and journals offer insight into his **holistic approach** to life and his creative processes (Figure 6.4). Author and innovator Michael Gelb (2004) identified seven principles exemplified by da Vinci and Renaissance creators. Out of homage to his inspiration, Gelb named them in da Vinci's native Italian. Here, they are interpreted and placed into the context of this book.

continued on page 197

Agga B. Raya

> We wanted to create good air circulation. We are fashion designers. We all do fashion, but we don't want to limit ourselves to that form of art.

Creativity is . . . to create. I take it literally, which means building and making something out of your imagination and collaboration with other people. It's about bringing more to the world and helping other people by ideas. It is very organic. It is being open minded and full of ideas.

My background is in fashion design and fashion styling. I've been designing for six years and styling for more than that. I do high-end women's ready-to-wear. My clients are 30 years old and up. My line has a bit of European flair. It's elegant and well-tailored, with wonderful fabrics. Four fashion designers (Agga B. Raya, Anna Fong, Melissa Serpico, and Lidia Wachowska) have been collaborating with Toyota Concept Cars for a year and a half right now. We are all independent designers. We are independent companies, but, we share a design space called the Creative Lounge.

The whole concept [for the Creative Lounge] came from Toyota Conceptual Cars. In 2008, a few engineers came from Japan to become familiar with the fashion program here. Fashion week was just around the corner and Toyota Conceptual Cars decided to be a part of it. [They sponsored] a competition for designers to design fashion pieces inspired by the conceptual cars, which are cars that we may never see on the street, but they are an inspiration and future direction for the company. Four designers' designs were chosen, and at that time we didn't know at all where the whole thing was going. The award was a trip to Japan. We thought it would be a nice vacation, but we were handed a schedule, and from 7:00 am to 7:00 pm we had meeting after meeting after meeting at the Toyota headquarters. The competition evolved into a very busy collaboration between us fashion designers and the car designers in Japan. We tried to think of what would be the best way for all of us to work together, and that turned out to be the Creative Lounge. It's an unbelievable experience and a surprise that came out of nowhere. It was something that none of us, even Toyota, expected. The first meeting was like, "So, what do you guys want to do?" "How do you want to connect with other people?" That was how it started. But right now, what is really amazing, is the fact that there actually are other locations appearing, and people from Spain and other places are coming to see our space to get an idea and taste of what we are doing.

Chicago is the pilot location, but there are new locations in Bilbao [Spain] and Bangkok [Thailand] being planned. Another location is Tokyo [Japan]. The plan is pretty ambitious. It is supposed to be this net around the world with Lounges dedicated to creative people, ideas, and interactions among all kinds of people. Right now, we are the very first step in building this network. This whole thing started as a single conversation when we were in Japan, and it evolved into this space. It is supposed to be a really technologically-advanced network, so we can exchange ideas and build something together. We are all going to be connected by different projections and computer systems, but it is still at a beginner level.

Each of the four fashion designers is free to do whatever he or she wants with the space. [The Creative Lounge] is about a 7,000 square foot space. I'm the person who

Photographer:
Agga B. Raya

plans the art events. I am a fashion stylist, too, and I'm pretty involved in the whole fashion scene. We have this space 30 or 31 days a month, and we do fashion and art here every day. We have so many people working. We felt that we could reach more people by not limiting ourselves to fashion but by opening up to fiber design, to interior, to architecture. We wanted to create good air circulation. We are fashion designers. We all do fashion, but we don't want to limit ourselves to that form of art.

We're bringing artists to the space every day. We're bringing painters, musicians, architects, any kind of designer, dancers. We're bringing many different talents, and we're highlighting an event that happens on the first of every month. It's called "The First." The First features an artist that the Lounge chooses, and it follows a certain topic. Conceptual Cars is based on philosophies, which come from human relations, nature, peace of mind, and so forth. The theme of each month connects a little bit to the philosophy of the conceptual cars. So, for example, this month we have the theme "Flux." The event has been so popular. We're getting a great turn out, and the artists are so amazing. When Toyota heard how great the thing was going, they flew in to see the whole event. We're going to pick one artist with art that can be shown in Japan, Spain, and Thailand. The eventual goal is to start rotating artwork around the world—artwork that has a meaning.

Toyota Conceptual Cars is a creative team like every company has. They want to discover the new direction, the new thought. Do people really need four-wheel cars? Will they need them in ten years? The company reached the point where they wanted to do some market research. Maybe we inspired them a little bit. We don't get much direction

continued on page 196

from them; we don't get any specifications. It is mostly talking about ideas. We are all just seeds, and we'll see where it is all going to grow. We've had people from Thailand visiting, from Spain, and we've already had some small rotations starting. We're still developing the right procedure for this kind of thing. It is kind of a big project.

My life lately is like this huge bubble gum machine that holds all of these bubble gum balls. You know, you put a quarter in, and each time you get a different color, but you don't know which color you'll get. It is like that every day, with so many different artists. It's dealing with many students, and older people, too, and teachers, and amazing, inspiring personalities. I love it. It is never ending circulation and energy. We try to make it very, very exciting and never limit ourselves to one form of art. We go for sculpture. We go for multimedia projections. We go for painting, photography, and scientific art. So, it's a big mixture of many different minds and thoughts. And it's very interesting how people from all of the different areas can express the same theme in so many different ways. One month the theme was "vice," and one month it was "dimension."

So that is how I design, too. I always have this theme or idea behind my collection, and there are so many ways you can go about it. Working with so many artists, seeing so many different angles, it is definitely very inspiring, and it makes you very flexible and very open-minded. And less critical. I start with the inspiration that is in the air in the Lounge and the mixture of different minds and thoughts. My designs evolve organically from that.

Event at the Creative Lounge.
Photographer: Agga B. Raya

continued from page 193

curiosity

"Curiosità—An insatiably curious approach to life and an unrelenting quest for continuous learning" (p. 48). This inquisitiveness is not only directed at one's studies; it is a natural part of daily life and a desire to understand the world. Gelb suggests that curious people ask lots of questions. They want to know who, what, when, where, why, and how (pp. 48–75). Designers can spark their curiosity by asking questions such as, Who does this affect?, What does this relate to?, When is this a problem?, Why is it done this way?, and How else can it be done?

demonstration

"Dimostrazione—A commitment to test knowledge through experience, persistence, and a willingness to learn from mistakes" (p. 76). Da Vinci delved into his experiences with originality and independence of thought. In addition to da Vinci's considerable successes are his notable mistakes. Gelb tells of Leonardo's failed attempts at diverting the flow of the Arno River and at serving a banquet with sculpted miniature and edible dinner courses. With experimentation, mistakes are inevitable. The key is to continue to learn from them (pp. 76–93).

the senses

"Sensazione—The continual refinement of the senses, especially sight, as the means to enliven experience" (p. 94). Leonardo noted that the average human "looks without seeing." What is the color of the hallway floor outside of your design classroom? Can you describe a scene from a movie in vivid detail? The responses to these questions require a heightened awareness of certain senses. This attentiveness can nourish creative inspiration and design (pp. 94–141).

ambiguity, paradox, and uncertainty

"Sfumato—A willingness to embrace ambiguity, paradox, and uncertainty" (p. 142). Art critics use the term to describe the hazy and mysterious quality of da Vinci's paintings. Uncertainty is disconcerting, but, today, change is happening rapidly and ambiguity is increasing. Gelb suggests that poise in the face of paradox is the key to effectiveness and sanity in a rapidly changing world (pp. 142–163). Fashion designers always face uncertainty. Their products are oriented toward the future so they are not sure what their clients' reactions will be. If designs are rooted in current times, then they are more likely to be expected. Unexpected and creative designs contain an inherent risk. The designer's challenge is to embrace this uncertainty as excitement and anticipation rather than fear and anxiety.

art/science

"Arte/Scienza—The development of the balance between science and art, logic and imagination" (p. 164). This balance suggests a need for whole-brain thinking. The left side of the brain is responsible for logical and critical thinking. The right side of the brain is associated with imaginative and divergent thought. Creativity requires the development of both aspects and a well-rounded approach to design (pp. 164–191).

health and well-being

"Corporalita—The cultivation of grace, ambidexterity, fitness, and poise" (p. 192). This aspect exemplifies da Vinci's holistic philosophy toward creating. He thought that individuals are responsible for their own health and fitness. Physical states can affect mental health, and mental attitudes can affect physical aspects (pp. 192–219). Creative processes are dependent on the comprehensive well-being of the individual.

connections

"Connessione—A recognition of and appreciation for the interconnectedness of all things and phenomena" (p. 220). This is systems thinking. Leonardo was known for making connections. He studied the anatomy of many living creatures and combined them in his paintings and depictions of fantasy creatures. All things are interconnected, but also, all things can be connected, sometimes with very interesting results (pp. 220–257).

holistic process summarized

Da Vinci's process is embodied in depictions of the Renaissance man. It is a holistic process that considers the body and mind, the arts and sciences. In a time of increasing specialization, attaining balance may require extra initiative. Gelb (2004, p. 19) suggests that modern Renaissance men and women will need to possess the following:

- A good knowledge of classical liberal arts
- Technical knowledge
- Creative thinking skills
- A global awareness and appreciation for other cultures

the phase approach: the design process

The word *process* as it is commonly understood suggests a linear path from one component to the other. Start at Point A and end at Point B. Designing, of course, is not linear. It is organic. It is free form. A **fashion design process** can be investigated as stages, but it is not defined as sequential stages. In addition, there is no clear evidence that these stages of design are separate and autonomous. Most likely many overlap and/or occur simultaneously. The caution against illustrating design processes is that the illustration may represent one designer's path but not that of many others. Out of practicality, phases of the design process are listed here in a sequential order, but in actuality they are practiced in a less linear manner (Figure 6.5).

Aspelund (2010) identified a seven stage design process:

1. Inspiration
2. Identification
3. Conceptualization
4. Exploration/Refinement
5. Definition/Modeling
6. Communication
7. Production

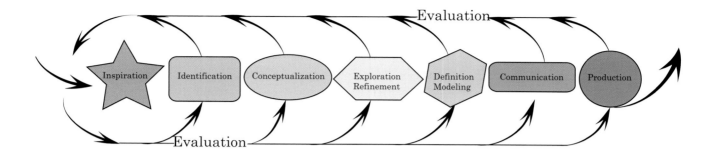

inspiration

Creativity in Fashion Design focuses on this aspect of the design process. For design to happen, designers must be inspired. The best designers are proactive about finding inspiration. They research. They experience. They seek it out. Inspiration sometimes seems like it strikes with no preparation, but it is more likely that inspiration culminates from the hard work of exposing oneself to a variety of influences. Keeping a design inspiration journal encourages inspiration in several ways. First, sparks of ideas are recorded so they are not lost or forgotten. Second, by combining ideas and themes, connections are easily made. Lastly, a design journal makes the inspiration part of the design process intentional. It removes inspiration from the mysterious and the happenstance and places it within the power of the designer.

identification

A concise inspiration will get a design project off to a good start. The identification stage is focusing on the inspiration as it relates to the project or challenge. This often includes identifying design constraints. Every design has constraints. External constraints are those imposed upon the designer. In fashion design, the wearer must be able to put on and take off the garment, and the item must function as intended. External constraints can also be imposed by available material resources, available production resources, budgetary concerns, societal expectations, or deadlines. Internal constraints are those within a designer's control. The function of the garment might be established, but the individual can choose how to design the garment so it functions properly. Internal constraints include limitations that designers impose on themselves. These constraints are easier for a designer to cope with. Designers may, for example, decide to use only sustainable materials. This certainly limits the options for the designers, but they are happy to work within these confines because they reinforce the designers' personal stance. As suggested in Chapter 2, constraints are not necessarily negative. They allow a designer to focus on a problem or challenge, and they exclude extraneous and superfluous information.

conceptualization

After the problem or challenge has been identified and the constraints have been examined, it is time to formulate a vision for a solution. Preliminary ideas formed through play or found within a design journal are just that—ideas. They are not necessarily well-formed enough to sustain an entire design project. Rarely does just one idea lead to an inspiration or one inspiration lead to a concept. Usually concepts that are strong enough to sustain a collection are the result of a number of connections.

Figure 6.5
Although the design process is presented in stages, it is usually not a linear process. Evaluation takes place at every stage.

Assembling a mood board or themes in a *DIN* can solidify a concept because it deliberately makes these connections visual and easy to read.

exploration/refinement

Concepts are sketched and tried out in the exploration/refinement stage. It is a time for experimentation, so no idea is too weird or unlikely. This is the stage of divergent thought production mentioned in Chapter 3. Aim for fluency, originality, and flexibility. Do not count any idea out just yet. Sketch ideas or drape them on the dress form. When you have a number of possibilities, elaborate on the design schemes. Add details and depth.

Reflection and incubation are important components of all design process stages, but they are especially necessary in the conceptualization and exploration stages. It is never a good idea to rush an idea through; ideas need time to simmer. Reworking ideas at later stages often costs more time and expense than if the extra time was taken at the outset.

definition/modeling

The conceptual and exploration stages are great enjoyment, but eventually the designer has to focus on the chosen design concept and define and model its design. This is funneling, focusing, deciding, and convergent thinking. In design class, students illustrate their ideas, pattern and sew them in muslin, or they simulate them using a computer-aided design program. After the prototype is made, it is time to stand back and take a critical look at the design. Flexibility is important at this stage. Be open to suggestions and alternative responses to the challenge. If design improvements can be made, now is the time to make those changes. Very little cost and risk has been expended so far, but soon it will be too late to change the course of the design.

communication

A garment, set of sketches, or collection is communicated to others in different ways at different stages of the process. If it is a student project, ideas, rough sketches, detailed illustrations, muslin prototypes are all communicated to others in the classroom and to the instructor. Most likely, the designs have undergone individual and class critiques. In the field, designers must also represent their ideas at several stages of their process. They may speak in conceptual terms, with the help of mood boards, to other members of their team who already understand this abbreviated design speak. On the contrary, they may have to prepare formal and professional presentations to clients. The clients' needs are paramount when considering how to present a concept. Some clients are proficient with computers and prefer three-dimensional representations of the garments. Other clients are quite savvy at visualizing designs and two-dimensional flats will suffice.

production

All the planning has come to fruition, and the garment or collection is ready for production. Good design should lead to smooth production, but inevitably problems will occur. Planned materials may no longer be available, or the overseas manufacturer may be unable to take the lot after all. These unexpected setbacks are part of the overall process. Designers should take them in stride and use their best creative thinking skills to solve the problems. Thinking of these problems as challenges rather than failures can help keep frustration at bay. Inherent in the production phase is delivery of goods to the ultimate client. The client will validate the product and assess its effectiveness.

design process summarized

After examining each stage, it becomes apparent that the phases in the design process are cohesive, but intertwined and overlapping events. One can certainly imagine that the inspiration, identification, and conceptualization stages often coincide. It is likely that good designers access feedback during the entire design process, and incubation can occur at any point before final production. So, what can a new designer make of the stages? They are reminders that designing is a comprehensive undertaking. If a design is not researched or explored to its fullest, the design may not be meeting the needs of the client. Skipping the communication stage could have disastrous repercussions. In today's competitive environment, just one unsatisfactory season could place many people out of work. By identifying your own design process, you will find it easier to get back on track if something goes wrong in your planning. For example, you will be able to reflect on your processes and might determine that you were not being flexible enough in the exploration stage or open to constructive criticism in the production phase.

Table 6.1 associates the design process with the creativity components presented in this book. As with every generative course of action, creativity is an integral part of the entire design process.

TABLE 6.1

Considering the Design Process and Elements of Creativity

Design Process	Creative Elements			
Stage	Environment	Cognition	Character Traits	Motivation
Inspiration	rich, varied	knowledge base exploring	optimism openness	intrinsic drive to create
Identification	rich, varied	learning researching	fantasy nonconformity	curiosity interest
Conceptualization	family, peers, society influences	divergent thinking making connections	excitement hope	freedom from constraints
Exploration/Refinement	making connections	fluency, flexibility, and elaboration	adventurousness determination	willingness to work hard
Definition/Modeling	studio or lab	convergent thinking	realistic attitude critical attitude	desire to achieve
Communication	consider garments' effect on others	feedback judging	self-confidence fear	desire for recognition
Production	sustainability ethical consideration	closure	toughness flexibility	desire for extrinsic reward

Source: Derived from Cropley, A. (2001). *Creativity in education and learning: A guide for teachers and educators. Sterling, VA: Stylus.*

Figure 6.6

The creative problem solving framework guides individuals through generating possibilities and focusing their thinking when addressing design problems. *Adapted from Isaksen, S., Dorval, K., & Treffinger, D. (2000). Creative approaches to problem solving: A framework for change, 2nd ed. Buffalo: Creative Problem Solving Group*

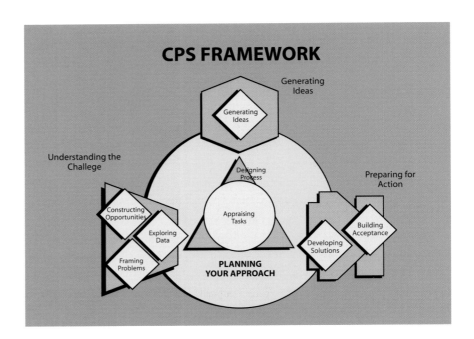

the creative problem-solving approach: design as problem solving

To design is to solve problems. Whether it is to determine what silhouette will work best on a petite figure, what color story will best represent a selected theme, or how to pattern a complex tiered dress, designers are solving problems every step from inspiration to production. **Problem solving** is a process of closing the gap between what is and what is desired (Isakson, Dorval, & Treffinger, 2000). Just as the stages of the design process can form an underpinning for creative design, so can the **Creative Problem Solving** (CPS) model assist designers looking for ways to break creative blocks and solve the complex design problems (Figure 6.6). Creative Problem Solving is intended to be a flexible process framework. It has three main purposes: (1) to generate ideas for solving problems, (2) to clarify direction and frame problems, and (3) develop plans for successful action. By one account, it takes over 50 ideas to reach one successful new product (Isakson, et al, 2000, p. 17). With such odds, individuals want to make the most of every opportunity and give themselves the best chances for success. The CPS approach includes three phases:

1. understanding the challenge

2. generating ideas

3. preparing for action (Isakson, Dorval, & Treffinger, 2000).

understanding the challenge

Sometimes we are in such a hurry to complete a challenge that we do not allocate sufficient time and effort to look closely at the way the challenge is structured or the problem is defined. If designers do not understand the nature of the challenge, they are easily sidetracked; their garments may be functional and beautiful, but they might not be what the client was hoping for. Understanding the challenge captures imagination, curiosity, and motivation.

In understanding the challenge, first select a broad goal or "opportunity." If you try to focus on an idea too soon, you may miss important opportunities. However, keep ideas brief and positive. Try to refrain from making negative statements such as "There is no way to make this garment sustainable." Instead, use starters such as: improve, invent, increase, enhance, support, and develop.

When an opportunity has been pinpointed, it is time to explore related data. This information could be found in the form of a rich knowledge base, impressions, observations, feelings, or questions. Intentionally looking at all these varied areas ensures that you consider many viewpoints and do not close off an avenue too quickly. If you want to make a sustainable collection, investigating varied data may open new ways of doing that. For example, a designer might be thinking only in terms of organic fibers, but not investigate the possibility of reusing fabric scraps.

After a good amount of varied data is collected, it is time to focus and define the challenge more clearly. Which idea stands out as workable and stimulating? Formulate that idea into a question, for example, "In what ways might I use old fabric scraps to make a fashion collection that is environmentally friendly?" The statement should be concise but not limiting. It should invite ideas (pp. 59–95).

generating ideas

This phase is focused on producing many new, varied, and unusual ideas. Again, consider fluency, flexibility, originality, and elaboration. You have explored several idea-generating tools in this book. They include brainstorming, SCAMPER, and mind mapping.

preparing for action

The third phase of CPS involves selecting tools that will allow you to formulate a workable plan. There are two stages in preparing for action. The first is developing solutions. In developing those solutions, you can use a number of evaluation matrixes to show the viability of one aspect over another. For example, options could be placed on one axis and criteria on the other and then appropriate boxes could be filled in with Xs. The concept with the highest ranks or most Xs may be the most likely choice to proceed with. **ALUO** is another tool that can be used to limit options. ALUO is an acronym for **a**dvantages, **l**imitations, **u**nique qualities, and **o**vercoming key limitations, and considering these aspects can make the path for action clearer.

The second stage in preparing for action is building acceptance. Be able to state why your idea is better that ones that have come before, advantages of your product, and what is gained by the new ideas. People are often resistant to change. They may feel a loss of control, or the change may be just too different. Designers need to be aware of and understand these reactions. It does little good to declare the client out of touch or uncreative. You should devise strategies that work with people's resistance to change. Giving people a choice can help counteract a feeling of loss of control, and sharing information and education can address uncertainty (pp. 127–168).

creative problem solving summarized

The CPS model provides basic guidelines and specific tools for using the divergent and convergent skills necessary for creativity. Open-ended and ambiguous challenges are interesting and exciting, but they will not end in creative products unless skills are

continued on page 206

Creativity-Enhancing Exercise: Force Fitting

Original ideas spring from making novel connections. Force fitting is an intentional way to make those unexpected associations. Select objects or concepts that seem to be unrelated to the challenge and force a connection. For example, if the design challenge was to create a uniform for a particular country's Olympic sports team and the word "military" was randomly drawn, epaulettes and brass trim might be added to the design.

- Identify a design challenge (Olympic team uniforms, for example).
- List a large number of seemingly unrelated concepts or objects. Make them up or choose from the following list.
- One by one, draw an idea from a hat, or close your eyes and point to a word on the page.
- Connect the concept to your design challenge.
- Sketch the resulting ideas.

Random Words

football	pocket	duck	geometry	circus
zipper	arrow	truck	horror	nut
animal	castles	tomato	windmills	money
key	hammer	circle	water	pen
book	grass	picture	rose	reptile
sun	window	egg	rug	chocolate
phone	umbrella	insects	cooking	figure
planets	purple	computer	lipstick	leaf

Design Challenge

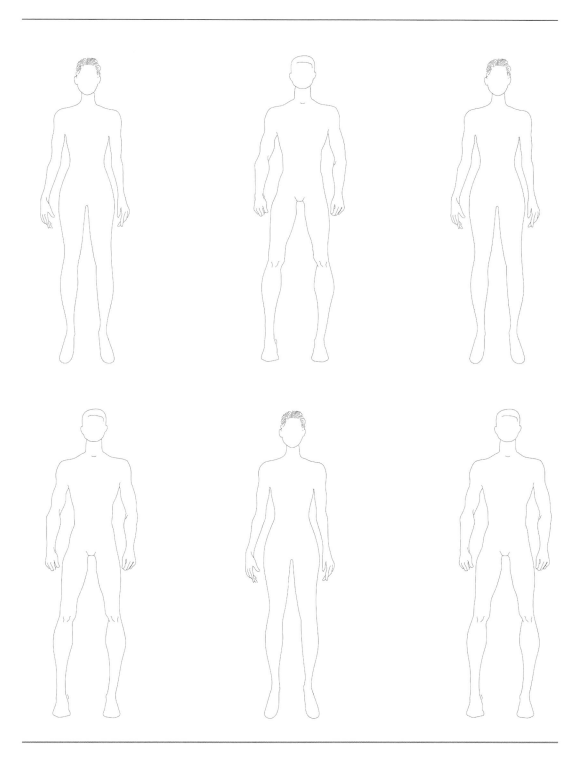

continued from page 203

used to determine the relevance of concepts derived from them. The CPS model is intended to be an extension of our naturally occurring dynamic and flexible processes.

A large portion of any design process is generating ideas. Creativity-enhancing Activity 6.2, Force Fitting, gives you practice in this part of the design process.

your design process, revisited

In considering the three ways to address design challenges introduced in this book, the holistic approach, the phase approach, and the problem-solving approach, state which elements of each one resonate with you. List how you can incorporate those aspects in your own design processes that you previously listed.

_____

_____

_____

_____

_____

pitfalls for designers

Designers have a unique calling. They are asked to lead the way in responding to change. This responsibility can be unsettling. What if they are wrong? What if the world does not accept their interpretation of the times? These are real concerns that can keep designers from acting. Lawson (1996) states that designers are not expected to write papers explaining the complexity of the current situations. Designers are expected to act. Designers not prepared to respond to an uncertain future may become victims to three common pitfalls (pp. 113–116):

- Procrastination

- Noncommittal design

- Throw-away design

Lawson also discusses the following mental "traps" that catch designers and trip up their best intentions (pp. 220–232):

- The category trap

- The puzzle trap

- The number trap

- The icon trap

- The image trap

procrastination

The procrastination approach is based on the notion that just a little more time, research, or practice will make it easier to act. The designer feels that the ideal notion for a collection is just out of reach and an additional day or week will surely solidify what should be done. The fallacy, of course, is that change will continue to occur, and a designer's course of action is always going to be indeterminate. Procrastination can also derive from a desire for the products to be perfect. The assumption is that if the designer waits until a deadline is looming, it is the fault of the deadline and not the designer if a project does not turn out as expected. Inevitably, procrastination harms, rather than enhances, a project.

noncommittal design

A second response to uncertainty is to proceed with a design but remain uncommitted to it. The fashion then becomes bland and neutral, and it does not make much of a statement at all. Designers hoping to avoid this pitfall will trust their intuition and research and formulate a concise vision.

throw-away design

A third response to uncertainty is to design clothing that is strictly meant for the moment. The closer you design to the present moment, the safer it is. Less risk is involved because you can look around to see what is currently accepted and then design within that range. Designing with an eye to the future will always contain inherent risks. Throw-away design may have worked in a time when the economy was strong and people had expendable income to buy new clothes each season. Some consumers are reacting against wasteful practices, though, and they are looking for clothing that is less transient.

the category trap

It is common for people to want to place ideas into familiar categories. Everyone has visual images of what a man's suit jacket looks like. It is often categorized as having a collar, lapels, and front pockets. Although it is true that most men's suits have these characteristics, prematurely placing the challenge of designing a man's suit into this category effectively closes off other means to solve the problem. Would a zipper closure or no lapels serve the purpose as well? Designers should look at the problem, not the category, when trying to solve a design challenge. In fact, designers looking for inspiration can intentionally place their design challenges in categories that are contrary to the usual way of doing things. A man's suit, for example, could be placed in the category of active sportswear.

the puzzle trap

Most people like the challenge of solving puzzles. Puzzles often contain a number of constraints that guide an individual to the correct answer. Fashion design problems are not so rigidly defined, however. A designer who imposes limitations where there are none may be engrossed in an interesting puzzle that is defined by pseudo-constraints. The designer may be lead astray by trying to solve a conundrum, rather than solving the real problem. For example, a designer may be interested in minimal clothing and making items with as few seams as possible. The designer could become so engaged in trying to create a garment with just a single seam, that the garment becomes unwearable in the process.

the number trap

It is easy to fall into the number trap, which is thinking that bigger numbers represent better products. This often means more beads, more embroidery, and a higher price tag. But more is not always better. Streamlined designs can be sophisticated and appealing. Designs with excessive detailing may not have a focal point, may overwhelm the wearer, and may be too costly to produce.

the icon trap

Designers are visual. Many of their sketches are beautiful works of art in their own right. Computer software makes it possible to represent garment design and fabrics realistically and elaborately. Designers can get so caught up in representing and presenting their collections that they spend more time on the trappings of presentation than they do on the actual design of the garment. Microsoft PowerPoint presentation software can illustrate the point. PowerPoint is a powerful and versatile tool. Words can be made to swoop on to the screen with sounds and animated effects. In many cases, however, all of those special effects serve to detract the viewer from the message instead of enhance the presentation. Many studies have shown that simple presentations that keep the viewer focused are the most effective. Designers should not become distracted by fancy tools. Tools should be used to serve a purpose not add extraneous flourish.

the image trap

Designers form mental images of what they want their product lines to be about. Brand image is big business today, and it is important for designers to maintain an image with their customers. This is a common and accepted way to do business. However, when adherence to an image prevents designers from looking critically at their work and testing its functional and aesthetic properties, image loyalty can become a trap. The image should not impede a solution to a design problem.

It is not just beginners who fall victim to design traps. At times, even experienced designers forget to follow good design practices. Activity 6.3 invites you to explore the design processes and discover the design successes and pitfalls of your favorite designers.

continued on page 210

ACTIVITY 6.3

Investigate Design Processes

Everyone has favorite designers. We know what kinds of fabrics they use and the styling they are known for. Most likely, you have already placed many of their designs in your *DIN* as inspiration. Do you know their processes, though? Have you heard their tricks of the trade? We know that design processes are unique to the individual, but we also know that much can be learned from experts in the field. For example, Madame Grés, well known for her structural, artistic pieces, was said to be a frustrated sculptress and artist, so she approached her design work as if they were sculptures (Mears, 2008).

- Investigate the design processes of three favorite designers. This information is not usually found on trend and style pages. You will have to look for interviews or articles in publications such as *Women's Wear Daily*, books, or online sites devoted to the designers.
- Try to identify what makes their practices special. Do they appear to use the holistic, phase, or creative problem-solving approach, or a combination of the three?
- Note these ideas, along with sketches or photos of the garments in which they are used.

Design Example	Designer _____
	Research on Favored Processes
	_____
	_____
	_____
	_____
	_____

Design Example	Designer _____
	Research on Favored Processes
	_____
	_____
	_____
	_____
	_____

Design Example	Designer _____
	Research on Favored Processes
	_____
	_____
	_____
	_____
	_____

Figure 6.7
A variety of
mushrooms were
investigated for
this design project.
© *Lothar Lenz/Corbis*
(a), © *Bernhard Kuh/*
Sodapix/Corbis (b),
and *Heidi Benser/*
Corbis (c)

continued from page 208

the design process: champignons, a case study

The challenge of this project was to identify an item found in nature, and use its structure as inspiration for design (Figures 6.7–6.15). *Champignons* is a fashion design project that looks at the relationship between fashion and sculptural forms using the mushroom as an inspiration and starting point in the design process. Champignon is the French word for mushroom. It was used here to discourage unintentional, preconceived notions of what the designer knew as morel, Portobello, and other mushrooms. Many different kinds of mushrooms were investigated. Those with interesting yet varied structures were chosen as inspiration for the project. This relates to aspects of curiosity and demonstration in da Vinci's approach and to inspiration and understanding the challenge in phase and problem-solving approaches.

To understand the structure of the organic plant, the mushroom is studied first as sculpture. Sculpture and fashion design connect via materials, construction

(patterning), form, and concept. With the mushroom as a guide, wooden sculptures were made to ascertain the essence of the three-dimensional form. This is an example of da Vinci's art/science and the identification stage. The nature of the object is examined in a format other than fashion design so inherent characteristics are discovered, but hopeful or preconceived fashion qualities are not inadvertently placed upon the piece. By avoiding fashion design for the moment, the tendency to declare that something cannot be sewn or worn is averted.

The form of the sculpture is studied to determine whether there is a connection to fashion design. A metal framework is made to test the idea. Conceptualization and exploration allow for multiple responses to the same design challenge.

Cloth is used to create fashion-inspired mushroom sculptures. With the inner edifice identified, cloth is placed on the structures to explore how the structure could translate to fashion design. Concepts are explored and refined; this is the generating ideas stage of the problem-solving approach. Da Vinci might have used the senses of touch and sight and attentiveness to detail to address this part of the design process.

At this stage uncertainty and ambiguity are common. The designer may suddenly think that the idea is ill-conceived or that the idea will never work as a fashion design. At this point the designer, free to move organically through the design process, goes back to the conceptualization stage and revisits a few more mushroom shapes. Another cloth-covered framework is constructed with added attention to detail.

Figure **6.11**
(above) A different
mushroom structure
was investigated.
© *Frontera Sur*
School/Corbis

The idea is refined to include a few workable structural shapes. The mushrooms are examined further for the physical features. Cartridge pleating was chosen to represent the mushroom "gills." Shibori dyeing and hand felting were the chosen design tactics to represent various coverings of mushroom caps.

While preparing for action, the designer considers how these elements will incorporate with the human body. Da Vinci's holistic approach considers the designer's health and well-being as an important aspect in the design process. One should consider the well-being of the wearer of the article of clothing, too. Will the person feel poise and grace while wearing the garment? The body itself is considered as the mushroom stem or stalk, so the other elements will have to relate favorably both to the concept of the mushroom inspiration and to the fashion design presentation on a person. Ideas are sketched as a part of the definition/modeling stage. Conceptual versions are visualized in exaggerated fashion illustrations.

Garments are completed and analyzed for adherence to the theme. Connections are discussed between sculpture and fashion design. The fashion design is communicated to others in a runway fashion show. At this part of the problem-solving process, the designer formulates a design statement that solidifies the thought process and communicates the advantages of the piece. Feedback is solicited.

The designer weighs the feedback and produces a collection of mushroom-inspired pieces. They, along with their sculptural antecedents, are placed in a natural context to determine the viability of the project.

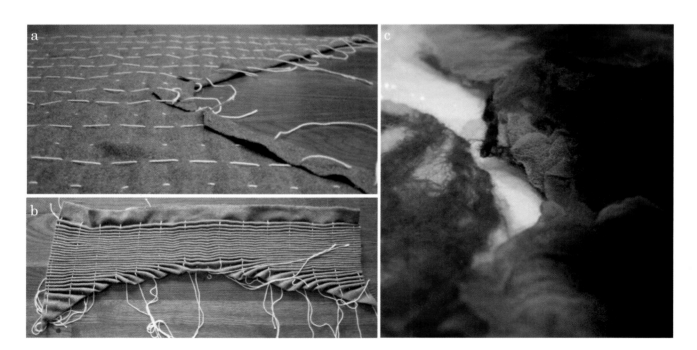

Figure **6.12**
Cartridge pleating (a and b)
and Shibori dyeing and felting
(c) are used to replicate the
mushroom characteristics.
Designer: Caroline Borucki
Courtesy of author's collection

Figure 6.13
Illustrations are used to formalize the concept, not as accurate representations of the product. *Designer: Caroline Borucki*

Figure 6.14
The finished designs are presented on the runway. *Courtesy of Percy Mui*

Figure 6.15
The sculptures (a)
and fashion designs
(b) are evaluated in
a natural setting.
Photographer:
Elieen Molony

summary

Most often, we look at garments after they have been completed. When we do, we do not consider the time, thought, and effort that goes into producing the fashion. There are a number of ways that you can go about the business of designing. You can take a holistic approach, as did da Vinci; you can consider phases of design; and you can consider fashion design as a problem-solving process. The benefit of establishing a design process is to form an underpinning for future design work. As designers, when you encounter continual problems or creators' block, you can refer to your successful processes.

KEY TERMS

product

process

holistic approach

fashion design process

creative problem solving

DIN Challenge: Designing with Your Process

Most designers do not consciously follow their design process. It is usually effortless and efficient. However, those same designers are often able to identify in good detail how they go about the business of designing. Earlier in this chapter, you identified the design process you used when you created a successful product. You took into consideration the holistic, phase, and problem-solving approaches, and refined your process. Now put it to the test!

- Identify a design challenge or start with the suggested challenge described next.

- Refer to your design process as you meet the challenge. Most likely, you will have to modify the process to accommodate the new challenge. Be sure to identify where flexibility and variability are required.

- The goal of the challenge is for you to internalize a process that works for you. It does not mean that it is inflexible—you will have to continue to make modifications—but it will be an underpinning that you can refer to.

Design Process Challenge

Your design challenge is to create a three-piece cohesive collection derived from a single vintage garment. If your school has a costume collection, select an interesting piece that you are allowed to handle. Investigate the inside and inner workings of the piece; don't select a fragile garment that cannot be touched. If you do not have access to a costume collection, purchase an intricate piece from a vintage store or resale shop.

Examine the piece carefully. Note the fabrication, texture, and silhouette. Also note the details, such as the stitching, the quality of construction, and the embellishments. Turn the garment inside out and discover the supportive materials used, such as interfacing and boning.

Now, try to ascertain the essence of the piece. What was its purpose? What do the materials and workmanship suggest? What feeling do you get while handling the item?

Sketch a three-piece collection derived from the combined elements of the vintage garment. Pattern and make up one of the designs following your design process.

Notes for Discussion

_____

_____

_____

_____

_____

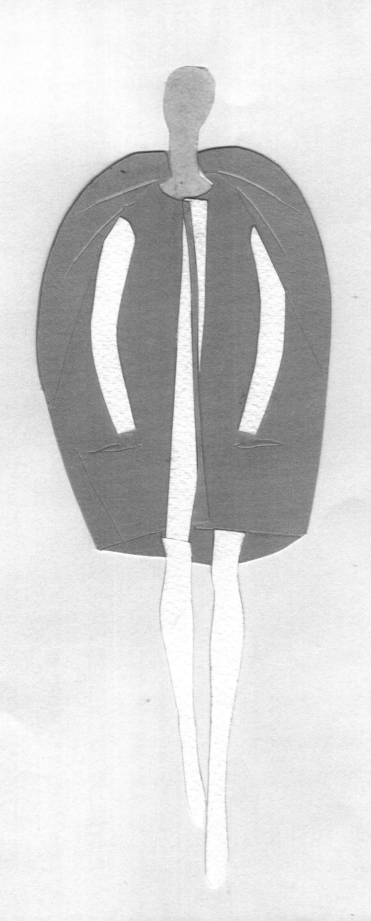

7 creativity *in* the industry

So far in this text, fashion design has been treated as a solitary activity carried out by the individual. This depiction was mostly for ease of representing certain concepts. It is apparent that the fashion designer is actually part of a social system that includes family, friends, clients, and coworkers. This intermingled web influences what designers create and how they present their design concepts.

the fashion design portfolio

It is essential that when you begin your career as a designer, you have a professional portfolio in which you can display your work. Presentation skills utilized in creating a portfolio are very similar to the skills needed as a designer. Employers want to see proficiency in both fashion design and presentation. With a résumé, you can assert that you have certain skills and abilities, but a professional portfolio provides evidence.

fashion design spreads

The fashion design portfolio should be presented as consecutive spreads. A **spread** consists of a two-page layout that presents a complete concept when the portfolio binder is laid open flat (Figure 7.1). Multiple-page spreads are always even in number so there is never more than one concept presented in an opened portfolio at one time. There is no ideal size for a portfolio, although the days of the extra large 24″ × 30″ fashion design portfolios are gone. Designers want a portfolio that is easy to transport and work with. Today, a lot of design work is done on the computer, so a standard paper size that is easily printed may be helpful. Typical portfolio page sizes are 8½″ × 11″, 9″ × 12″, 11″ × 14″, and 14″ × 17″, but 8½″ × 11″ may be too small to adequately show some concepts, such as full bridal gowns. Some concepts, such as accessories, may look lost on a large 14″ × 17″ page.

Sketch of an ensemble.
(opposite) Inspiration for fashion designer Francisco Costa for the Fall 2009 Calvin Klein clothing collection. *Courtesy of* WWD

OBJECTIVES
— To explore ways of presenting design materials

— To understand the process of creating a line from inspiration to production

— To investigate working in teams and collaboration

— To identify ethical issues in the fashion design industry

— To take stock of my own creativity

217

Figure 7.1
When the portfolio is laid open, the left and the right page together present a full and cohesive story. *Designer: Katelyn Christopher*

As a fashion design student, you should get in the habit of preparing professional spreads as you complete your school projects. Some instructors even ask for a professional portfolio presentation as a component of design assignments. *DIN* pages are great sources of inspiration, but they are for idea gathering. They are not professional presentations. Keeping up with portfolio pages during or after projects will mean that your portfolio will be nearly ready to show potential employers at any given time. It is very difficult to assemble a portfolio on short notice, so the more that can be done ahead of time, the better off you will be.

This does not suggest, however, that all spreads will be used at any one time. Portfolio pages need to be edited with the reviewer in mind. You should always research the company where you will be interviewing, and your portfolio should reflect this research. Professionals will want to see that aspiring designers have an aptitude for the kinds of tasks they will be performing on the job. For a first full-time position, you will be competing with other applicants who have experience and an educational background similar to yours. For a design position, the portfolio is one of the most important ways applicants distinguish themselves from each other. So showing versatility within a focused and edited portfolio is encouraged, but showing quantities of work that have little relevance to the open position wastes professionals' time and suggests that you did little preparation for the interview.

A designer's best work should start the portfolio. The first impression is important. Professionals may run out of time or think they've seen enough very quickly. Suggestions for inclusion in a fashion design portfolio include (Tain, 2003, p. 58):

- *An introductory page*: This is a page that says something unique about the designer. It is often personalized with the designer's personal logo or brand. Linda Tain (p. 66) suggests that a reproduction of this sheet can be left behind with the reviewer after the interview.

- *Four to six fashion-group formats*: **Group formats** are collections of coordinated pages that relate to one theme. They may include a mood/inspiration page, fabric page, color story page, design illustration page, and/or special techniques page (Figure 7.2).

- *Flats*: Most designers will need to relay technical information about their designs. **Flats** are streamlined illustrations that contain essential information about the construction of the piece. As the term suggests, they do not show the volume of the garment.

- *Awards, photos, press, etc.*: Enhance your group presentation with photos of runway exhibitions and awards.

- *Fold-out presentations*: These presentations may reflect a special project, and they may follow a different format from the rest of the portfolio.

- *Board presentation reproductions*: These are board presentations reduced to a manageable, transportable size.

- *Croquis sketchbook*: These sketches represent the versatility of your work.

  Spreads can be created on the computer using graphic design software such as Adobe Illustrator. You do not want your pages to have the look of a scrap book. Using a computer keeps text looking professional, and it avoids the need for gluing

Figure 7.2

This page is part of a six-page spread on the research, inspiration, design, and manufacture of a boys' niche market line. *Designer: Denise Headrick*

REBEL ROUSERS

The **Rebel Rousers** line exemplifies a unique style that takes boys' classic looks and puts a punk spin on them. As more parents emerge out of the 80s punk era, they continue to value those styles and want to pass them on to their children. The line offers more grown-up, edgy looks that make boys feel cool and independent.

and taping components in place. However, hand-drawn illustrations using interesting media such as charcoals or colored pencils look best when you show the original artwork. This also applies to fabrics and materials used. You can always scan in these items later if you need to present a digital version of your work.

Designers' knowledge of creativity is useful when assembling a portfolio. Those same qualities introduced in Chapter 1 that characterize creativity and fashion design can apply to design portfolios. To set your portfolio apart from the rest, assess your work for originality, effectiveness, elegance, emotion, surprise, and ethicality.

comprehensive portfolio

Gaining employment in an age of downsizing and competition requires more than just the skill set of the major. Employers are also looking for qualities including the ability to research, community involvement, ethicality, organizational skills, an ease with technology, and teamwork skills (NACE). A comprehensive or **multitasking portfolio** is planned to present a well-rounded individual who contemplates ethical issues; is comfortable drawing on history, culture, and other disciplines for inspiration; and can make useful connections from a variety of experiences. It includes spreads that detail the sometimes less tangible aspects of a student's experience (Jennings, 2009). Designers can consider adding spreads to their portfolios that cover such topics as:

- Using technology to address the needs of the field (Figure 7.3). Consider showing screen captures of computer-aided pattern design, textile design, or graphic design expertise.

- Fashion design derived from historical or cultural aspects of dress. Include a short paragraph on the relevance of the original piece and photographs showing details of accurate representations of the inspiration (Figure 7.4).

- Fashion design that demonstrates an understanding of the diverse perspectives of ethical issues of the field. Designs in this category include those using fair labor practices, fair trade fabrics, or fabrics dyed using natural dyes. A short paragraph should emphasize your understanding of the subject. The spread should also include varying viewpoints, and the design statement should articulate how your design confronts the issue.

- Connecting study abroad or service learning experiences to the major. This kind of portfolio spread can show exposure to environments outside of the classroom. Increasingly, employers want to know that you are interested and involved in community and global events. Designs inspired by trips abroad or created for those less fortunate can be included in this kind of spread.

An expanded portfolio is evidence that you are attempting to build a broad knowledge base in your major field. Employers also take clues about your work habits from your portfolio. They look for organization, presentation skills, and professionalism. Graphic designer Bill Kerr offers the following suggestions for general portfolio page layout and professional presentation:

- The portfolio reader will formulate an impression of your work in 30 seconds. Ask someone who has not seen your work to look at your portfolio, and give you his or her first impressions.

- Imagine that you will not be in the room when readers are looking at your work. Does the portfolio speak well for you, or do you desperately wish that you could be in the room explaining and clarifying the information? The portfolio is your proxy. Someone who knows nothing about you and your work should be able to get an accurate impression by looking at your portfolio spreads.

- This is the age of PDF files. Even if your portfolio is presented in physical form at an interview, employers may want a digital copy to send on to other hiring personnel. PDF files can be read on most computers, and they are a surer form of

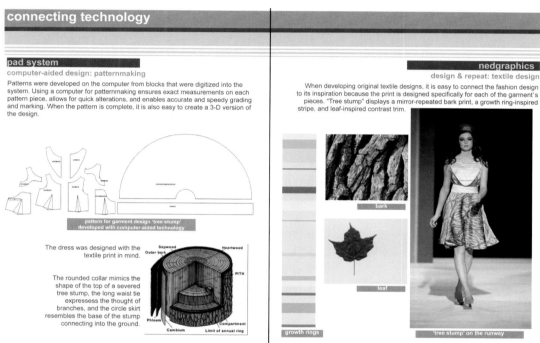

Figure 7.3

This portfolio spread indicates the designer's experience with computer-aided pattern and textile design technology. *Designer: Caroline Borucki*

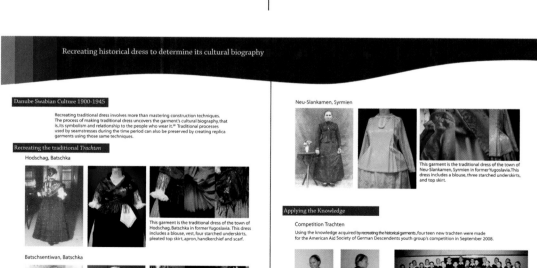

Figure 7.4

Employers look for skills that make the individual stand out. This designer is showing her aptitude for historical research and ability to accurately recreate culturally significant garments. *Designer: Erika Neumayer*

communication than specific graphic design files that cannot be opened without the corresponding software installation. Most updated software will allow files to be saved in a PDF format.

- Edit your material. When you think your portfolio is complete, intentionally take something out. This will require you to be discerning about what is included.

- Maintain a hierarchy on the page, and order content by importance.

- Go easy on special effects and flourishes on a page. You are a fashion designer, not a graphic designer. Let your creative work speak for you. Do not substitute fancy layout effects for substantive work.

In Activity 7.1 you will demonstrate your professional presentation skills by preparing a portfolio spread featuring design work done in this course.

professional presentations

Creating portfolio spreads in school is good practice for fashion designers because they will continue to prepare professional presentations during their careers. **Concept boards,** or *presentation boards,* are common tools for relaying information. They are usually presented as a physical board, but sometimes they are digital presentations. The size of the physical board depends on how it will be used, but, in general, it should be large enough that several people can congregate around it at one time and have a good view. Many times these larger boards are reproduced as smaller hand outs for distribution within the design company or to a sales force and buyers. Boards should have a central theme and be directed toward a specific market with a specific price point. Boards need to be concise and convincing. They are used to (1) present concepts and inspirations, (2) facilitate product development, and (3) relay forecast information about fabric or trends. Inspiration is usually shown as a group of images that, taken together, represent the direction fabrication and styling will take. All elements of the board should reinforce the message (Figure 7.5). If at all possible, actual fabrics, not digital reproductions, should accompany the presentation. Most people want to feel the hand and texture of fabrics so they know they are suitable for the end use. Flats are used to relay the technical information, so illustrations are often exaggerated in order to make a dramatic point. Layout is crucial in presentation boards. Sloppy boards detract from the message and severely lessen a board's impact. Guérin (2005, pp. 77 and 82) identified guidelines for creating interesting, imaginative, and exciting boards:

- Color should augment the theme.

- Balance is essential.

- Every element should reinforce the information the designer is trying to describe.

- Dimension, depth, and interest can be achieved by mounting images on small platforms.

- Boards should be simple and streamlined with no extraneous information.

- Avoid random and haphazard information.

- Edges should be clean and even.

- Creativity is paramount.

Create a Portfolio Spread

Portfolio spreads are good ways to reveal the process that goes into your work as well as show the finished product. This gives potential employers an idea of how you would take on an extended project. If you designed a tailored suit, show the pad stitching that went into creating the roll of the collar. If you created a replica of an historic garment, show the crinoline and petticoats that are giving the dress its shape.

Create a portfolio spread featuring one of the design projects you completed for this course. Give the spread a title, and label each section clearly. Make sure that the spread is professionally presented and that the text has no grammatical or spelling errors.

Include at least four aspects from the following list on your two-page spread (or add more features and make it a four page spread):

• Mood or inspiration collage

• Design statement

• Color story

• Materials used

• Design illustrations

• Flats

• Photographs of designs

• Close-up photographs of intricate detailing

• Sketches and/or explanation of special technique

Title

_____

Notes for Discussion

_____

_____

_____

_____

_____

_____

_____

dreamland sheer

inky journal scrawls reveal our innermost thoughts as sheer washed watercolor florals and inked sketching join together to tell a gorgeous tale.

Figure 7.5

This concept board from The Doneger Group shows that sheer fabric, a floral print and pastels will be prominent features in the next season. *Courtesy of the Doneger Group*

fashion design in context

Fashion designers work within the framework of product development. **Product development** encompasses the entire planning, designing, and production processes necessary to get goods to the ultimate consumer. Product development includes:

- Trend forecasting and research
- Developing line concepts
- Line presentations
- Prototype development and approval
- Production samples
- Production

trend forecasting and research

Every line begins with research. Designers look to past lines for silhouettes that sold well. Feedback is collected from the sales force and buyers. Designers also gather information by scanning the environment for events and people that may influence styling. It is very difficult for a small staff to cover a large number of events, so many product developers hire trend forecasting companies, whose sole focus is to identify emerging trends. These firms' services are expensive, but the information they provide is invaluable. In the competitive field of fashion, on-target trend information contributes to the livelihood of the company.

line concepts

With information they gather about colors, fabrics, and styling direction, designers build a concept for the season's line. The mood and feeling of the line and the direction of the styling are determined. At this time, looks, such as layers or tailored pieces, may be introduced, but actual styling is general. The concept is presented to a number of **stakeholders,** who could include company executives, additional designers, and merchandisers, among others.

line presentations

When the concept is approved, designers translate those ideas into styling appropriate for their customer base and price point. **Lines** or **collections** are designed so that there is a range of styling available that appeals to a variety of buyers. The line should look fresh and exciting each season, but it should not be so far removed from the company's image that it will lose loyal customers looking for a particular aesthetic. Most ready-to-wear lines introduce new styling each season but also bring back classic silhouettes. Styles should be consistent with the theme of the collection. To appear cohesive, they should look as though they were created by a single designer even if they were created by a design team. Styling should be different enough, however, so the buyer will decide to take all or most of the pieces instead of choosing the best of similar items. Many fabrics require minimum yardage orders, so they have to be utilized efficiently throughout the entire line.

As with the line concept, these ideas are presented to stakeholders. For many reasons, several styles may be eliminated at this time. For example, a contractor may not be available to complete the embroidery, or the cost of labor on an intricately-styled garment may be prohibitive.

Figure 7.6
The sample garment is fitted on a live model, and changes are made to the fit and design before the design goes into production. *Designer: Lydia Wawrzyniak. Model: Magdalena Zawislak*

prototype development and approval

As pieces in the line are initially accepted, patterns are developed, and a sample prototype is made in actual fabric. The **sample** is made to reflect a production garment, but it is often made in-house to save shipping time and so the designer can keep a watchful eye over the patterning and sewing. Designers involved in prototype development are often able to address problems that stem from styling early in the development process. Initial garment costing is done at this time, also. Samples are often made in the middle size of a full size range, rather than in the smaller sizes typically seen on the runway. For example, if the size run of a dress is 4, 6, 8, 10, 12, 14, 16, the sample is made in size 10. This mid-range size gives a better indication, than does a size 4, of what the garment would look like in all sizes. Selecting a median size also facilitates grading, or sizing, because the largest and smallest sizes do not deviate a great deal from the prototype. After samples are made, they are fitted on models, and styling changes are made (Figure 7.6). Designers know that changes and dropped styles are part of the product development process. Although they may fiercely fight for a style they believe has merit, they do not become defensive when a style must be dropped because it did not resonate with someone on the team or because it did not price out within allowable parameters.

production sample

After the sample fitting, the garment is repatterned with the suggested corrections, and it is usually made up once again. This **production sample** will go through another fitting to identify potential problems before the garment goes to full production. It is imperative that production problems are caught at this stage. After the garment lot is cut, it will be too late to make changes that are not costly and time consuming.

production

When the production sample is approved, multiple garments of that style are cut and sewn. This is most often done by **contractors** specializing in garment cutting and construction. Production contractors are located in many countries of the world. Usually garments are cut and sewn after orders are placed. It is too risky to produce styles on the hope that they will sell.

The development process described here is typical but not universally followed. Every design house has its preferred process. Mass marketers often skip some of the initial production steps by reworking existing styling and allocating more responsibility to contracted manufacturers. This saves them time and money in the development process.

creative collaborations

A review the product development process tells you that designing is a collective activity. Designers work with other designers, line merchandisers, buyers, the sales force, and others to ensure the line will attract the target customer. Teamwork and collaboration are important aspects of fashion design.

creativity in a group setting

Creativity flourishes when new associations and connections are made. One of the greatest advantages of teamwork and collaboration is the exchange of ideas it provides. The concept of brainstorming was introduced in Chapter 1. This technique asks the participant to think of as many ideas as possible for a given challenge. When brainstorming is done in a group, many more ideas are introduced. This yields more possible combinations and probable solutions than is possible from a single person. For this reason, collaborative teams can be innovative and, in many cases, the adage is true: the whole is greater than the sum of its parts.

creative teams

Probably the most important component of a team is diversity. If everyone on a team thinks the same, additional persons are redundant. However, if a diverse group is assembled, each person contributes an independent perspective and offers opportunities for fresh connections. In the fashion industry, examples abound of fashion designers who have created successful alliances with persons who have abilities that complement, rather than duplicate the designer's character traits. One example of a creative pairing is Calvin Klein and Barry Schwartz. During their long partnership, Klein is said to have attended to the design aspects of the Calvin Klein enterprise, whereas Schwartz concentrated on the business side. Activity 7.2 allows you the opportunity to work in a team and learn from another's perspective.

I always find it helpful to be in a group setting and work on my own, like in fashion classes. We all have our individual projects, and we're all working on our own thing, but if I need help with something, or if something doesn't seem right, I have all of these people I can go to. —*Fashion Design Student*

Teamwork

Until now, all of the entries in your *DIN* have been made by you. Collaborating with others can bring to your attention ideas and themes that you may have overlooked.

- Choose a partner, and trade your *DIN* with that person.
- Allow your partner to peruse the contents of your *DIN*, and do the same with your partner's *DIN*.
- Partners should record their perceptions on *Ideas* pages in each other's books.
- Partners should record (1) what they see as obviously present, (2) what they perceive to be missing, (3) developing themes, and (4) feelings as they look through the contents.
- This is not a critiquing exercise. It is to take advantage of another's perspective. Partners should not pass judgment on the contents. They should only record what is notable, and notable by its absence, about each other's *DIN*s.

Your Reaction to Your Partner's Observations

_____

_____

_____

_____

_____

_____

_____

_____

There is a difference between a group and a team. A **group** is simply an assemblage of people. They do not necessarily have common goals or shared values. A **team** is gathered in order that people may accomplish goals bigger than what they could accomplish on their own. They have common goals, a shared vision, and ownership in the process. Characteristics of an effective team include:

- Complementary skills
- Shared responsibility for decision making
- Trust in other's motives and skills
- Mechanisms to resolve conflict
- Commitment to the project
- Constant communication

continued on page 230

Margaret Hayes President of Fashion Group International

> I think
> that most
> designers
> continually
> strive for
> creativity.
>
> —Margaret Hayes

Creativity is . . . a process, and everybody brings a different perspective to it. If a product is innovative and also has consumer appeal, that is the trick. It is originality and scale, materials and design elements, and whether it makes the grade from a salability perspective.

I'm president of Fashion Group International, across the United States and on multiple continents. We have about 5,000 members, and the organization is over 80 years old now. Worldwide, it's a mix of all of the classifications of the business—apparel, accessories, beauty, and interior design professions. From apparel design to product development to product marketing to advertising to merchandising, public relations, and manufacturing—it's a broad mix of professionals. It was founded in 1930. It was the first non-profit organization founded by and for executive women, but now our membership encompasses both men and women. We focus on the business end of the fashion design industries at large. We're not a designer organization; we're a business organization. My background is retailing.

Our mission is focused on the professional and executive ranks of the business. Secondary to that, we have foundations in many states that do focus on career development for students and scholarship programming. Career Day is a program with multiple speakers; students attend, and there is philanthropic direction obviously. Supporting those in school is secondary, though. You have to be a professional or executive in the business in order to become a member. Fashion Group has an event that they put together each year called the Rising Star. Many of the regions have a similar event. It is a competition for new and emerging design talent that has already graduated from school and has been in business from one to six years. They generally recognize a mix of these talents in different forms, but it is usually a competition that is voted on by the members of Fashion Group. There is a nominating process, followed by a voting process. We have criteria in the nomination process. It's a series of three questions that focus on the designers' creativity, innovation, where and when they have a retail outlet, and what they have learned in this brief one- to six-year period that will help them in their business. They have to submit product, and they have to submit a paper on the criteria questions. And they have to be nominated. The nominating process is usually focused within each of the cities. The process is broader even than the membership base itself. We have a creative committee that we bring in for that, which allows us to seek out specialists who might not be members but can help us identify potential young designers. The committee is looking for quality of the product, the design element, uniqueness, and innovative textile. The support system is not only apparel. It is men's and women's apparel, accessories, fine jewelry, interior design home products, new retail concepts, and beauty and fragrance. The program brings some recognition to the designers and a lot of publicity. It generally helps to market their skills.

Creativity is a very amorphous word and it's an overused word to some degree. It spans everything, really, in terms of how you view what a woman should look like

wearing a garment. Is it important? Yes, it's important to have a vision. Bringing innovation to that vision is creativity. It's a very esoteric word and probably the one that everybody uses the most. It's in the eye of the beholder, and I would not be too finite about it. Workmanship has a lot to do with a product as well. You can be really creative but shoddy in terms of workmanship. The craft itself is equally as important.

I think that most designers continually strive for creativity. They have to reinvent themselves two, three, four times a year, and then they have to reinvent themselves each year after that. So, it's the ability to reinterpret existing ideas and give a fresh or innovative approach to a silhouette or a fabric. A lot of design tends to cycle. These looks cycle in and out of fashion unless we resort to wearing transparent bubbles— you never know, that could happen. A lot of the interest is certainly in the technology of the textiles. They have textiles now that are treated so that they change color. Creativity is reinterpreting history with a new perspective. It is working with new technological breakthroughs in textiles. This says a lot about the importance of creativity.

Today's young designers need to work for someone first and not attempt to go into business on their own. It is very important to have a work platform to learn from because too many young people are totally unrealistic about what it is all about. The business aspect of a design house is extraordinarily important. The second step, after they've worked four or five years with different companies, is to get a business partner and research a demographic and a psychographic so they are not all over the place. There are a limited number of people who can afford high-end design products, so they should find a good niche. This will get them a solid start.

Fashion Group President Margaret Hayes (center) with New York City Mayor Michael Bloomberg (left) and Sandy Weill (right). *Photography: Courtesy of Fashion Group International*

continued from page 227

Effective teams also need stated objectives and clearly defined challenges. This keeps distractions to a minimum and allows participants to stay on target. For innovation, these guidelines and the participants should be flexible.

Creative teams can be adversely affected by even one noncontributing member. Members who do not contribute show lack of respect for those who are doing the work, and they can drain the motivation from the entire group.

networking

Designers work within a company and also an industry. They find alliances through trade associations and industry organizations. Many of these organizations are not for profit, and their mission is to simply serve their members. They are usually established so people can easily exchange ideas, expertise, and information. They are great repositories of resources for hard-to-find items and information. Often, the organizations provide financial support to students and/or those just starting out in the field. Through **networking** opportunities offered by the organizations, designers can meet with others who are going through, or have went through, what they are now attempting. See Table 7.1 for a partial listing of apparel organizations and associations. Spaces are left blank, so you can add to the list as your network grows.

Networking is an important aspect of being a designer. It is one more avenue for keeping informed. Online sites, such as LinkedIn, Facebook, and Twitter, provide opportunities for up-to-the-minute communication with others in the industry and also with clients.

the ethical designer

Today's new designers are entering the field at an uncertain time. Recent headlines have brought to light ethical lapses in the fashion design industry. It is easy to become discouraged with headlines of labor abuses and irresponsible environmental practices. Some designers are taking on these challenges head on, however, by creating lines and companies that specifically address ethical issues. American Apparel (2009) has built its reputation on paying fair wages to its employees, all of whom are located within the United States (Figure 7.7). Patagonia (2009) has made it its mission to do no harm to the environment and to inspire and implement solutions to the environmental crisis. You can turn the tables on poor ethical practices by finding

Figure 7.7
In an effort to be transparent about its sweatshop-free labor practices, American Apparel posts images of its Los Angeles factories on its website. *Courtesy of American Apparel*

TABLE 7.1

Apparel Organizations

Space is left at the end of the table for you to add your networks.

Organization	Mission	Website address
American Apparel and Footwear Association	Represents apparel, footwear, and other sewn product companies and suppliers that compete in the global market	www.apparelandfootwear.org
American Association of Textile Chemists and Colorists	Not-for-profit professional association supports the textile design, materials, processing, and testing industries	www.aatcc.org
American Sewing Guild	Supports sewing enthusiasts	www.asg.org
American Wool Council	Works to improve the wool industry and promote the usage of American wool	www.sheepusa.org
Apparel Industry Board	Promotes the apparel and sewn products industry and assists its members in developing professional skills and identifying business opportunities	www.aibi.com
Arts of Fashion Foundation	Non-profit organization links academics and professionals; fosters international cultural exchange, and supports creativity and design in fashion and the arts linked to it	www.arts-of-fashion.org
Color Association	Forecasts, researches, and archives color	www.colorassociation.com
Color Marketing Group	Creates color forecast information for professionals who design and market color	www.colormarketing.org
Costume Society of America	Advances the global understanding of dress and appearance; stimulates scholarship and encourages study in costume	www.costumesocietyofamerica.com
Cotton Incorporated	Ensures that cotton remains first choice among consumers in apparel and home products	www.cottoninc.com
Council of Fashion Designers of America	Not-for-profit trade organization recognizes top talent and supports professional development	www.cfda.com
Ethical Fashion Network	Network focusing upon social and environmental sustainability in the fashion industry.	www.ethicalfashionforum.com
Fashion Group International	Global, non-profit professional organization supports apparel, accessories, beauty, and home	www.fgi.org
The Global Fashion Association	Unifies, organizes, and enhances member's Fashion Weeks by aggregating collective strength of its members	http://globalfashionassociation.com
International Textile and Apparel Association	Advances excellence in education, scholarship, and innovation and their global applications	www.itaaonline.org
National Retail Federation	Advances and protects the interests of the retail industry; world's largest retail trade organization	www.nrf.com
National Textile Association	Supports fabric-forming industry	www.nationaltextile.org
United States Small Business Administration	Aids, councils, assists, and protects the interests of small business concerns	wwwsba.gov

creative ways to design and promote your line within socially responsible guidelines. Ethical issues that fashion designers face today include:

- Unfair and discriminatory labor practices

- Environmental abuses

- A culture of disposable fashion

- Promotion of an unrealistic body type

- Pervasive copying and counterfeiting

- Mistreatment of animals

unfair and discriminatory labor practices

Competition keeps apparel prices low. This is good news for consumers who are struggling to make ends meet in an uncertain economy. However, tight competition can drive business people to do whatever it takes to keep costs low and stay in business. This includes exploiting the labor of those who have no recourse. Workplace violations include unpaid labor, forced overtime, low wages, and child labor. Many times labor abuses take place in underdeveloped countries where labor laws are lax, but sweatshop practices have also been found in the United States. Illegal immigrants, desperate for work, are sometimes paid below minimum wage. The work is often done clandestinely in homes with poor lighting and ventilation, overcrowding, and no regulatory oversight. These workers rarely complain, though, because they do not want to be deported.

Many individuals and organizations are confronting the exploitation of workers. For example, United Students Against Sweatshops (USAS) is a grassroots organization run entirely by youth and students with the goal of building power for working people (Figure 7.8). Its supporters believe in a pluralistic approach to addressing

Figure 7.8
United Students Against Sweatshops is an organization that uses diverse tactics to bring attention to labor issues in the apparel industry. *Time & Life Pictures/Getty Images*

complex labor issues. One of the organization's notable campaigns focuses on college and university apparel contracts and abuses of workers in factories that supply apparel, such as sports teams' sweatshirts and t-shirts, to schools.

environmental abuses

The textile industry was a large component of the Industrial Revolution. Progress was the mantra at that time, and environmental issues were rarely considered. Chemicals and pesticides used in crop production, consumption of crude oil to manufacture fibers, and excessive water and chemical usage in fabric dyeing and finishing are just a few of the environmental offenses perpetrated by the textile industry. In fragmented fields such as the apparel industry, where development and production occurs all over the globe, sweeping changes toward sustainability will not happen quickly, but incremental changes are taking place throughout the apparel product development cycle. Sustainable practices include incorporating renewable natural resources, developing effective waste treatment practices, and recycling.

culture of disposable fashion

In the United States, clothing is abundant and available at all price points. This has contributed to a culture of disposable fashion. The purchase of new styling each season may be good for the fashion industry in the short term, but it may not be good for landfills or the long-term vitality of the field. Huge amounts of clothing are disposed of each year. Refocusing an industry that delights in the newest innovations and latest technologies is a large and maybe even unwelcome task, but utilizing creativity may allow the industry to have it all. The newest innovations can certainly apply to sustainable product development, and the latest technologies can be employed to connect existing products and textiles to futuristic applications.

Many textile materials can be recycled. Recycled fibers can be used to create new apparel items, and knitted items can be unraveled and reknitted into new products. Apparel items can also be reused. Enterprising designers are creatively cutting clothing, such as jeans, and piecing them back together into new configurations (Figure 7.9)

promotion of an unrealistic body type

The fashion industry has been accused of promoting an unrealistic ideal body type. Tall, ultra-slim models seen on the runway and in print perpetuate the notion that women should be thin and lithe. This imposed ideal may be unattainable for some women, and it can provoke self-consciousness, eating disorders, and poor body image.

Several segments of the apparel industry are moving away from using only the slimmest models in their runway shows and print advertising. The regional government of Madrid, Spain was one of the first entities to ban overly thin models from the runway. Its actions were both praised for setting the standard for a healthy body mass index and criticized for suggesting that the fashion industry is culpable for such complex conditions as anorexia and bulimia.

Many companies are recognizing a more diverse consumer profile. For example, the Dove company's "campaign for real beauty" focuses on freeing people from beauty stereotypes.

Figure 7.9
Designer Martin Margiela is a master at using whatever resources are available. His fashions incorporate 33rpm records, paper towels, hair combs, gift wrap ribbon, pen caps, plastic bags, balloons, twisted sleeves from old shirts, and cut-up leather jackets, vintage jeans, and trenchcoats (shown here). *Courtesy of WWD/Giovanni Giannoni*

pervasive copying and counterfeiting

Copying has been pervasive in the fashion industry for decades (see Chapter 5). It has been a tolerated, if not accepted, practice. The concept of fast fashion has brought this issue to the fore. Today, knockoffs are available in stores at nearly the same time as the originals, and the original design then has to compete for sales with the knockoff. As problematic as this practice is, it is legal to knock off fashion designs. Some advocate for laws to regulate against copying and knockoffs, but others believe that design piracy acts would be hard to enforce and cause as many problems for designers as they solve.

Counterfeiting is the blatant use of other's intellectual property, and the practice hurts legitimate designers. In some instances, counterfeited goods are produced in such large quantities that consumers end up purchasing more counterfeit than real goods (Jimenez, 2010, p. 27). Laws exist that prohibit counterfeiting, but the practice is difficult to monitor because many countries may be involved in production of the goods, and street and Internet operations can spring up and dismantle again very quickly before being caught.

Consumers bear some of the responsibility for curbing counterfeiting practices. Poor quality of materials and construction often suggest that the item is a fake, but a too-good-to-be-true low price is a nearly sure indicator that it is a counterfeited product, and the consumer should not condone the practice by purchasing it.

treatment of animals

Leather and animal skins have been used as body covering since prehistoric times. Skins and hides of animals are used in coats, shirts, pants, bags, and shoes. Some believe that it is not ethical to use animals for fashion purposes. They assert that, unlike our prehistoric ancestors, consumers now have better alternatives. Faux fur and faux animal skins are authentic-looking and beautiful, and these products have negated the functional need for actual hides and skins. However, aesthetic and expressive needs are often met with products made from animals, so designers still must take their own educated stance on the subject.

creative approaches to ethical issues

Ethical issues are always complex and two-sided. However, today's consumers expect companies to integrate a decisive socially responsible stance into their corporate structure. A panel of corporate executives interested in social responsibility admitted that "consumers increasingly expect companies to be actively engaged in these issues, while revealing more about the processes involved in bringing their goods to store shelves." Some of these programs are a challenge to implement in an economic environment that also prioritizes slashed prices and cost cutting, though. Regardless, those able to implement a program of corporate social responsibility will gain a competitive advantage (Tucker, 2009). Utilizing conviction, transparency, and creativity, designers can address some of these difficult issues while carving out their market niche.

Creativity-enhancing exercise Activity 7.3 asks you to consider a controversial issue faced by fashion designers, and decide how you might use creative design to approach the challenging question.

continued on page 237

Creativity-Enhancing Exercise: Six Thinking Hats

Six Thinking Hats is a tool that can be used effectively individually or in a group setting. The technique was created by Edward de Bono, who also promoted the idea of lateral thinking. Most people have a tendency to think in a linear fashion. This is logical and analytical, but it does not allow for multiple perspectives and taking a lesser path. Lateral thinking is fluid, malleable, and generative. The Six Thinking Hats technique encourages us to look at challenges from a number of different perspectives. It is intended to push us out of thinking ruts into understanding the full complexity of a situation. It allows necessary skepticism and logical thinking, but does not allow thinking to get bogged down in a single mode.

The Six Thinking Hats Exercise:

- Identify a problem that needs to be solved or a challenge that needs to be addressed. (You might consider one of the ethical issues facing the fashion design industry presented in this chapter, and use it to formulate the design challenge. For example, how can a new designer confront a culture of disposable fashion?)
- Divide a group into six smaller groups (at least one member per each subgroup).
- Assign a color, or thinking hat, to each group. (The blue hat can be given to a single person to keep the process moving. The person with the blue hat can also be part of another subgroup.)
- Within the smaller groups, address the challenge using your assigned mode of thinking. Sketch what your design would look like when using the properties assigned to a single thinking hat.
- Come back together as a group, and discuss and show your ideas. Or allow each group to experience each thinking hat and then come together as a group. Contrast the merits of designs inspired by a single focus with those created with input from all aspects.
- Illustrate the design.

The roles of those "wearing" each of the following "hats" are described as:

- *White Hat*: With this hat, you will focus on the data that is available. Analyze past trends. Look at what is known and what also what information is still needed.
- *Red Hat*: With this hat, look at the challenge using your intuition and emotion. Take your gut reaction seriously. Most issues are emotionally charged, so incorporate those feelings. Also, consider the emotional reaction that others may have to the problem.
- *Black Hat*: With this hat, look at the problem pessimistically, cautiously, and defensively. Try to think of reasons why ideas will not work.
- *Yellow Hat*: With this hat, think positively and optimistically. Find the value in ideas. Look for opportunities.
- *Green Hat*: This hat stands for creativity. Use a free and open approach to problem solving. Look at possibilities, connections, and alternatives.
- *Blue Hat*: The blue hat is used to manage the thinking process. It is worn by the person chairing the meeting and directing activities. This person will move the process along and keep the groups moving forward with ideas.

continued on page 236

continued from page 235

Design Problem

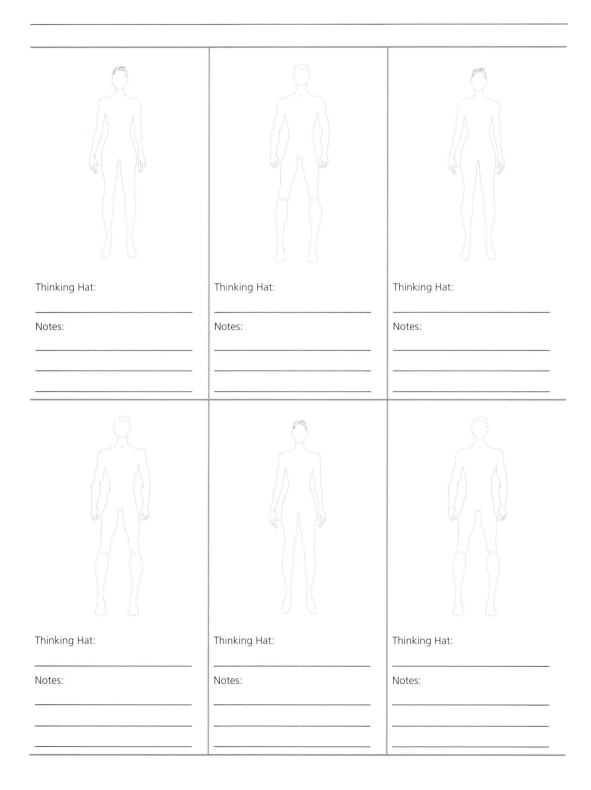

Thinking Hat:

Notes:

Thinking Hat:

Notes:

Thinking Hat:

Notes:

Thinking Hat:

Notes:

Thinking Hat:

Notes:

Thinking Hat:

Notes:

continued from page 234

the future of fashion

Teri Agins (1999) identified four megatrends that changed the trajectory of fashion. She stated that women let go of the idea of fashion. Women in the workplace wanted an authoritative look, not one of a fashion groupie (Figure 7.10). Agins also noted that people stopped dressing up. Casual Fridays became the norm and jeans and t-shirts were ubiquitous. Also, people's values changed with regard to fashion. Fashion was no longer placed on a pedestal. Consumers of high-end merchandise began to be seen in mass-market apparel. The label was not so important as fabric, workmanship, and value. Lastly, Agins suggested that top designers stopped gambling on fashion. Big-name designers now produce a variety of merchandise at a variety of price points. Publicly traded companies cannot be beholden to the whims of fashion. Today's big designers are grounded in reality, even if they still indulge in outlandish runway shows. Average consumers are now looking for clothes that fit their lives and lifestyles.

Writer and market consultant Ted Polhemus (1998) suggests that people buy clothes on the basis of what the products say, rather than for aesthetic reasons. "The more packed with reference, allusion, and symbolism, the more valuable and desirable the product" (p. 78). In the past, a look relayed a simple message of "I'm rich" or "I'm sexy." Polhemus states that a look today is intended to impart the many nuanced ways in which the wearer is interesting. Layered, juxtaposed, and multi-faceted clothing denotes that the wearer is unique and authentic. Designers are no longer needed to dictate an entire look. Today's designer is important in another way. The designer is the visionary who creates the fantasy that the consumer wants to buy into. This vision is compressed into a logo that radiates a lifestyle message. Polhemus suggests that it is important for designers to recognize what people want from their clothes. The post-modern world is pluralistic and heterogeneous, and consumers want authentic items that cut through the confusion and allow them to say "I'm here."

preparing for change

If history is any indication, fashion means change. The changes that Agins and Polhemus note will surely evolve into new and different trends. Other perceptive individuals will identify additional progressions in fashion. Fashion is uncertain. The skills and design tactics we know today will be usurped by newer methods. Flexibility, the ability to adapt, and tolerance for ambiguity are becoming increasingly necessary if designers are to acclimate to a changing world. Not coincidentally, these are the same qualities inherent in creativity. A review of creativity reminds us that it transcends ordinary experiences by making unusual connections. It asks many questions and considers many interrelated alternatives before deriving at a surprising and surprisingly elegant solution. Designers equipped with an arsenal of creativity tools are prepared to meet the changes and challenges of an ambiguous future of fashion.

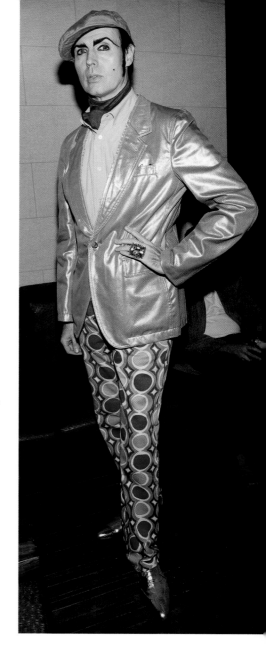

Figure 7.10
Patrick McDonald demonstrates an individualized approach to dressing.
Getty Images

I want to be a designer, and I want to have my own clothing line. It's a big dream, I know, but I think I'm making progress towards it, and I'm taking all the necessary steps. I want to take it as far as it goes, as far as it will take me. —*Fashion Design Student*

trend forecasting

As a fashion designer, you are expected to feel the pulse of the industry and recognize the forces of change. Trends do not just pop into existence; there are always plenty of clues that point toward major changes in fashion. Those indicators include (Burke, 2008, p. 79):

- Silhouettes and styling
- Textiles
- Colors
- Current trends
- The youth market (Figure 7.11)
- The arts and lifestyles
- Historical and cultural references
- Technical developments

This information can, of course, be gathered through your own research and observation, but a number of sources exist that can assist you in identifying trends. Information can be found through forecasting publications and online services such as Doneger Creative Services and Trend Report; trade shows, such as Magic and Premier Vision; trade papers and journals, such as *Women's Wear Daily*; and a plethora of Internet resources. Actually, there is so much information available today that even the keenest designers need help in keeping apprised of global conditions. Table 7.2 gives a partial list of resources. Internet sources grow and change daily. You are encouraged to update this list often with new, valuable sources that you find.

Not every trend has to be acted on. Some may not apply to a particular niche market. Good designer's intuition plays a part in knowing which trends to invest in.

my creative potential: a stocktaking

What is the best way to influence your creativity as a fashion designer? Make creative fashion designing your goal. Purpose is an essential step in inspiring design and enhancing personal creativity. **Purpose** is a "deep and abiding intention to develop one's creative potential—a long term interest in some form of creative expression" (Nickerson, 1999, p. 408). With the purpose of enhancing our creativity, we can take stock and assess our growth in those traits associated with creativity. Some tactics are challenging to address, but others are relatively easy to influence. Some factors are internal and within control of the designer. Others are external and require change that is not currently within the power of the individual (Table 7.3). You can act with purpose and take control of your growth with the many varied aspects of creativity. Activity 7.4 gets you started.

As asserted throughout this book, numerous components contribute to creativity. Environmental, cognitive, and motivational aspects and character traits all intermingle to encourage creativity. People are creative in different ways, at different times, and any attempt to turn creativity into a step-by-step process has the potential to trivialize and mechanize it. However, investigating the components of creativity can cause us to think differently, and this can inspire design.

By all accounts, creativity is a powerful, positive force that can enhance one's personal and professional life. Everyone is creative, so make the most of your creative potential.

Figure 7.11
Trend resources look at a variety of environmental conditions to identify fashion direction. This image shows the influence of lifestyle on design. Singer Alicia Keys sports sweatpants in a color that shows fashion consciousness, and the top is not the average jacket of a sweat suit. It has been modified to fit her lifestyle and make a fashion statement. *FilmMagic*

TABLE 7.2

Trend Resources

Resource	Description	Website Address
The Color Association of the United States	Global influences of color	www.colorassociation.com
Cotton Incorporated's Lifestyle Monitor	Consumer research	www.cottoninc.com/lifestylemonitor
Design Options	Los Angeles-based trend and color forecasting	www.design-options.com
Dexinger	Cataloging and tracking the latest designs, innovations, and trends in apparel, trim, labeling, and packaging	www.dexinger.com
Fashion Forecast Services	International focus on color and trends	www.fashionforecastservices.com
Fashion Mall	International fashion directory	www.fashionmall.com
Fashion Net	Research site with hyperlinks to other sites	www.fashion.net
Fashion Snoops	Daily online trend reports from London, Paris, Amsterdam, Berlin, Tokyo, New York, and Los Angeles	www.fashionsnoops.com
Fashion Windows	Listing of fashion trends, runway shows, and calendar of events	www.fashionwindows.com
Global Color	Inspiration for colors and trends	www.global-color.com
Iconoculture	Monitors pop culture and trends	www.iconoculture.com
Le Book	Good inspiration for fashion designers	www.lebook.com
Moda Italia	Fashion from Italy plus more on textiles and beauty	www.modaitalia.com
Pantone Color Institute	Color services	www.pantone.com
Peclers Paris	Trend forecasting and consultancy services	www.peclersparis.com
Promostyl	International design agency reporting on trends	www.promostyl.com
Snap Fashun, Inc	Interactive fashion libraries of women's men's and children's wear	www.snapfashun.com
Style.com	Site linked with Vogue and W; contains video and photo coverage of designer shows and breaking fashion news	www.style.com
Stylesight	Provides fashion research and business tools for designers and merchandisers	www.stylesight.com
Trend Bible	Forecasting service for the home, gift, and packaging industry	http://trendbible.wordpress.com
Trend Report	Separates hype from reality and give factual editorial information	www.thetrendreport.com
Tobe Report	Respected fashion and merchandising publication for retailers	www.tobereport.com
Trendease International	Lots of images from trade fairs, runway shows, and exhibits; also includes interviews and articles	www.trendease.com
Trend Stop	Fashion forward reporting including street style, store photos, and runway images	www.trendstop.com
Trendwatching.com	Global trendspotting editorials	http://trendwatching.com
Trends West Los Angeles	Started for Los Angeles retailers; allows for zeroing in on specific niches and needs	http://trendswest.com
Trendzine	Detailed insight into fashion trends from a unique perspective	www.fashioninformation.com

continued on page 240

continued from page 239

TABLE 7.2

Trend Resources

Space is left at the end of the table for you to add your own resources.

Worth Global Style Network (WGSN)	Research and trend analysis that includes textile, retail, and business information	www.wgsn.com
U.S. census	Statistics on population including information on age, marital status, income, and so on in the United States	www.census.gov
Zandl Group	Trendforecasting focusing on the youth market; publishes the HOT SHEET report on the 8-24 age group	www.zandlgroup.com

TABLE 7.3

Creativity Assisters and Blockers

	Easy to Modify		
	Easy to Encourage	Easy to Remove	
Creativity Assisters (fostering creativity involves strengthening these concepts)	Positive attitude to creativity Increased self-confidence Willingness to consider alternatives Willingness to break boundaries Varied environments and experiences Play	Negative attitude toward creativity Fear of being laughed at Narrow range of interests Extrinsic factors that take focus from task Rigid sanctions against harmless mistakes	**Creativity Blockers** (fostering creativity involves weakening these concepts)
	Difficult to Encourage	Difficult to Remove	
	Openness Unconventionality Inner directedness Tolerance for ambiguity Social attitudes toward creativity Allowing time for reflection and incubation	Social emphasis on instant gratification Strict sex roles Long-embedded stereotypes Focus on grades Emphasis that there is one best answer to a challenge	
	Difficult to Modify		

Source: Adapted from Cropley, A. (2001). *Creativity in education and learning: A guide for teachers and educators.* Sterling, VA: Stylus, p. 130.

Purposeful Creativity

You can influence your creativity. You can practice those aspects that foster creativity and avoid those that hinder it. Under each main category, highlight the qualities that you would like to address. Use the space in the box to state how you will accomplish that goal. Space is left at the end of the table for you to add more ideas for enhancing your creativity.

Ways to Influence My Personal Creativity

Environmental	Cognitive	Character Traits	Motivation
Stimulate exploration *Example: Try a new ethnic cuisine each week.*	Build basic skills used in the field *Example: Take that tough fashion design class I have been avoiding*	Be willing to take risks *Example: Enter a design into a wearable art competition*	Remove extrinsic rewards that take focus away from the task *Example: Design for myself and not for praise from others*
Provide opportunities for choice and discovery	Acquire a broad and deep knowledge base	Develop self-management skills	Build intrinsic motivation
In an environment that requires specialization, find balance	Focus on mastery; learn to do things well	Build self-confidence	Cultivate determination, persistence, and drive
Operate close to the edge of social rules	Practice divergent thinking skills: fluency, flexibility, originality, elaboration	Try for independence and autonomy	Focus on self-competition
Remove sanctions against harmless mistakes	Practice convergent thinking skills	Aim for complexity	Work hard
Cultivate a congenial environment and supportive family and peers	Practice problem solving	Build tolerance for ambiguity	Find challenges that have meaning
Relish in diverse settings	Practice problem finding	Address fears	Build a positive attitude toward furthering my creative potential
Practice non-conformity	Utilize technology	Discover meanings of dress	Be willing to play and imagine
Shape my space	Practice non-linear thinking	Cultivate a positive attitude toward learning	Make time for incubation and relaxation
Take charge of my schedule	Look at problems from many viewpoints	Develop freedom from stereotypes and functional fixity	Choose projects that I am curious about and interested in

continued on page 242

continued from page 241

ACTIVITY 7.4

Purposeful Creativity

Ways to Influence Your Personal Creativity			
Environmental	Cognitive	Character Traits	Motivation

Source: Adapted from Nickerson, R.S. (1999). *Enhancing creativity,* in R. J. Sternberg (Ed.), *Handbook of creativity* (pp. 392–430). New York: Cambridge University Press; Cropley, A. (2001). *Creativity in education and learning: A guide for teachers and educators.* Sterling, VA: Stylus; and Csikszentmihalyi, M. (1996). *Creativity: Flow and the psychology of discovery and invention.* New York: HarperCollins.

summary

Students transitioning from school to their careers will want to create a relevant portfolio. Presentation skills used in making a portfolio are similar to those needed in a fashion design career. Neither creativity nor fashion design is a solitary endeavor, and teamwork can make both more interesting, productive, and rewarding. In the industry, designers work with a number of production, development, sales, and marketing professionals. Creativity principles can be applied in industry and group settings as successfully as in solitary design projects. Creativity can also be used to address ethical issues and to confront the uncertainty inherent in a career in fashion.

KEY TERMS

spread	concept boards	collection	group
group formats	product development	sample	team
flats	stakeholders	production sample	networking
multitasking portfolio	line	contractors	purpose

DIN Challenge: The Future of My Creativity

If you faithfully contributed to your *DIN* during this course, you have accumulated a large number of pages. Review those pages and the *Ideas*, *Themes*, and *Connections* you discovered. Identify the concepts that resonate with you. Prioritize and reorder the contents. Delete pages that no longer show your voice or aesthetic. Your new *DIN* challenge is to continue to make entries into your *Dynamic Inspiration Notebook* as you complete your education and move into your designing career.

Notes for Discussion

_____

_____

_____

_____

_____

_____

_____

_____

references

Abling, B. (2007). *Fashion sketchbook* (2nd ed.). New York: Fairchild.

Agins, T. (2005). The body in cultural context. In M. L. Damhorst, K. Miller-Spillman, & S. Michelman (Eds.), *The meanings of dress,* (2nd ed.), (pp. 421–428). New York: Fairchild.

Agins, T. (1999). *The end of fashion: How marketing changed the clothing business forever.* New York: William Morrow and Company, Inc.

American Apparel. (2009). www.americanapparel.net

AOBA. (2009). *Alpaca Owners and Breeders Association.* www.alpacafashion.com

Aspelund, K. (2010). *The design process* (2nd ed.). New York: Fairchild.

Binkley, C. (2010, Jan. 21). What's out: The fashion trend. *Wall Street Journal,* p. D8.

Bollier, D. & Racine, L. (2003, September 9). Control of creativity: Fashion's secret. *Christian Science Monitor.* www.csmonitor.com

Braddock Clarke, S. & Mahony, M. (2005). *Techno textiles: Revolutionary fabrics for fashion and design.* New York: Thames & Hudson.

Burke, J. (1996). *The pinball effect: How renaissance water gardens made the carburetor possible—and other journeys through knowledge.* New York: Little, Brown and Company.

Burke, S. (2008). *Fashion entrepreneur: Starting your own fashion business.* Burke Publishing. www.burkepublishing.com

Calasibetta, C. & Tortora, P. (2003). *The Fairchild dictionary of fashion* (2nd ed.). New York: Fairchild.

Cameron, J. (2002). *The artist's way: A spiritual path to higher creativity.* New York: Tarcher/Putnam.

Cattell, R. & Butcher, H. (1968). *The prediction of achievement and creativity.* New York: Bobbs-Merrill.

Chicago spire. www.thechicagospire.com

CFDA. Council of Fashion Designers of America. www.cfda.com

Cole, K. (2003). *Footnotes.* New York: Simon & Schuster.

Crace, J. (2007, October 23). Walk on the wired side: Jacket that lets parents keep track of children. *Guardian.* www.guardian.co.uk

Cropley, A. (2001). *Creativity in education and learning: A guide for teachers and educators.* Sterling, VA: Stylus.

Csikszentmihalyi, M. (1996). *Creativity: Flow and the psychology of discovery and invention.* New York: HarperCollins.

Dacey, J. & Lennon, K. (1998). *Understanding creativity: The interplay of biological, psychological, and social factors.* San Francisco: John Wiley & Sons.

DeCarlo, J. (2007). *Fair Trade.* Oxford: One World.

Design Museum. (2009). Hussein Chalayan. www.designmuseum.org

Dove. www.campaignforrealbeauty.com

Ericson, S. (2009, March). The golden rule of proportions. *Threads,* 141, pp. 37–41.

Fair Trade Federation. http://fairtradefederation.org

Fehrman, K. & Fehrman, C. (2004). *Color: The secret influence,* (2nd ed.). Upper Saddle River, N.J.: Prentice Hall.

Fletcher, K. (2008). *Sustainable fashion and textiles.* London: Earthscan.

Florida, R. (2002). *The rise of the creative class and how it's transforming work, leisure, community, and everyday life.* New York: Basic Books.

Foley, B. (2009, May 04). Here's the good news: Designers and execs see positive points. *Women's Wear Daily.*

Gardner, H. (1993). *Creating minds: An anatomy of creativity seen through the lives of Freud, Einstein, Picasso, Stravinsky, Eliot, Graham, and Gandhi.* New York: Basic Books.

Gardner, H. (1991). Creating the future. Intelligence in seven steps. *New horizons for learning.* www.newhorizons.org

Gardner, H. (1983). *Frames of mind: The theory of multiple intelligences.* New York: Basic Books.

Gelb, M. (2004). *How to think like Leonardo da Vinci: Seven steps to genius every day.* New York: Delta.

Goff, K. & Torrance, E. P. (2002). *Abbreviated Torrance test for adults manual.* Bensenville, IL: Scholastic Testing Service, Inc.

Greenberg, A. G. (2009, July, 15). Hilfiger named Chicago's lead designer. *Chicago Tribune,* p. 3–2.

Heinelt, G. (1974). *Kreative lehrer/creative schuler* [Creative teachers/creative students]. Freiberg: Herder.

Henderson, B. & DeLong, M. (2000). Dress in a postmodern era: An analysis of aesthetic expression and motivation. *Clothing and Textiles Research Journal,* 18 (4), 237–250.

Hunter, V. (2007). *The ultimate fashion study guide: The design process.* Pasadena, CA: Hunter Publishing Corporation.

Isaksen, S., Dorval, K., & Treffinger, D. (2000). *Creative approaches to problem solving: A framework for change,* (2nd ed.). Buffalo: Creative Problem Solving Group.

Jennings, T. (2009). The multitasking portfolio: Integrating learning goals into the student capstone. Proceedings of the *International Textiles and Apparel Association.* www.itaaonline.org

Jennings, T. (2007). Pattern/Patron. *Clothing and Textiles Research Journal,* 25, (3), 275–276.

Jennings, T. (2006). *Investigating creativity: Understanding the perspectives of teachers and students.* Doctoral dissertation, Northern Illinois University, Dekalb, IL. (UMI Microform No. 3205101.)

Jimenez, G. (2010). *Fashion Law.* New York: Fairchild.

Jones, S. J. (2005). *Fashion design,* (2nd ed.). New York: Watson-Guptill.

Kaiser, S. (1997). *The social psychology of clothing: Symbolic appearances in context.* New York: Fairchild.

Kallal, M. & Lamb, J. (1994). Apparel product development: Meshing a consumer needs model with industry practice. *Proceedings of the International Textile and Apparel Association*, 141.

Keiser, S. & Garner, M. (2008). *Beyond design: The synergy of apparel product development* (2nd ed.). New York: Fairchild.

LaBat, K. & Sokolowski, S. (1999). A three-stage design process applied to an industry-university textile product design project. *Clothing and Textiles Research Journal*, 17 (1), 11–20.

Lamb, J. & Kallal, M. (1992). A conceptual framework for apparel design. *Clothing and Textiles Research Journal*, 10 (2), 42–47.

Language study in the age of globalization. (2009). Modern Language Association. www.mla.org/pdf/adfl_brochure.pdf

Lawson, B. (2006). *How designers think: The design process demystified*, (4th ed.). Burlington, MA: Architectural Press.

Leaner, meaner green. (2009). *Lifestyle Monitor.* www.cottoninc.com/lsmarticles/?articleID=615

Leland, N. (2006). *The new creative artist: A guide to developing your creative spirit.* Cincinnati: North Light Books.

Levine, F. & Heimerl, C. (2008). *Handmade nation: The rise of DIY art, craft, and design.* New York: Princeton Architectural Press.

Malone, T. & Lepper M. (1987). Making learning fun: A taxonomy of intrinsic motivation for learning. In *Aptitude, learning, and instruction: Cognitive and affective process analyses*, pp. 255–286. Hillsdale, NJ: Lawrence Erlbaum.

Maslow, A. (1954). *Motivation and personality.* New York: Harper.

McDonald, M. (2009, May 20). Some high-tech swimsuits banned. *New York Times.* www.nytimes.com

Mears, P. (2008). *Madame Gres: Sphinx of fashion.* New York: Yale University Press.

Mikalko, M. (2001). *Cracking creativity. The secrets of creative genius.* Berkeley: Ten Speed Press.

Miller-Spillman, K. (2005). The body in cultural context. In M. L. Damhorst, K. Miller-Spillman, & S. Michelman (Eds.), *The Meanings of Dress,* (2nd ed.), (pp. 13–28). New York: Fairchild.

Mindtools. (2009). www.mindtools.com

Myers-Briggs. MBTI Basics. www.myersbriggs.org

NACE. (2008). Job Outlook 2009. *National Association of Colleges and Employers.* www.naceweb.org

Nickerson, R. (1999). Enhancing creativity. In R. J. Sternberg (Ed.), *Handbook of creativity* (pp. 392–430). New York: Cambridge University Press.

Osborn, A. (1963). *Applied imagination: Principles and procedures of creative problem solving,* (3rd ed.). New York: Charles Scribner's Sons.

Pantone. www.pantone.com

Patagonia. www.patagonia.com

Piirto, J. (2004). *Understanding creativity.* Scottsdale, AZ: Great Potential Press.

Polhemus, T. (1998). Beyond fashion. In G. Malossi (Ed.), *The style engine: Spectacle, identity, design, and business* (pp. 78–79). New York: Monacelli Press.

Quinn, B. (2002). *Techno fashion.* New York: Berg.

Random House Dictionary. (2009). http://dictionary.reference.com/technology

Red Campaign. www.joinred.com

Reiss, S. (2004). Multifaceted nature of intrinsic motivation: The theory of 16 basic desires. *Review of general psychology*, 8 (3), pp. 179–193.

Roach-Higgins, M. E. & Eicher, J. B. (1992). Dress and identity. *Clothing and Textiles Research Journal*, 10 (4), pp. 1–8.

Rossman, G. & Rallis, S. (1998). *Learning in the field: An introduction to qualitative research.* Thousand Oaks, CA: Sage.

Runco, M. (2003). Creativity, cognition, and their educational implications. In J. C. Houtz (Ed.), *The educational psychology of creativity* (pp. 25–56). Cresskill, NJ: Hampton Press.

Ryan, R. & Deci, E. (2000, January). Self-determination theory and the facilitation of intrinsic motivation, social development, and well-being. *American Psychologist*, 55, pp. 68–78.

Sanchez, J. (2007, September 14). Thou shalt not knock off. *The American.* http://american.com

Solomon, M. & Rabolt, N. (2004) *Consumer behavior in fashion.* Upper Saddle River, NJ: Prentice Hall.

Sternberg, R.J., & Lubart, T.I. (1999). The concept of creativity: prospects and paradigms. In R.J. Sternberg (Ed.), *Handbook of Creativity* (pp.3–15). New York: Cambridge University Press.

Sternberg, R. & Lubart, T. (1996). Investing in creativity. *American Psychologist*, 51, pp. 677–688.

Still green and growing. (2008, Fall). *Lifestyle Monitor Trend Magazines.* www.cottoninc.com/lifeStyleMonitor/LSM-Fall-2008/?Pg=2

Stolberg, S. (2009, January 28). White House unbuttons formal dress code. *The New York Times,* p. A1.

Tain, L. (2010). *Portfolio presentation for fashion designers* (3rd ed.). New York: Fairchild.

The shifting paradigm: Rules being redefined for fashion and retail. (2009, April 13). *Women's Wear Daily*, pp. 1, 8–10.

Thiry, M. (2009, January). Smart fabrics for today and tomorrow. *AATCC Review.*

Tortora, P. (1996). *Fairchild's dictionary of textiles.* (R. Merkel, Ed.). New York: Fairchild.

Tortora, P. G. & Eubank, K. (2009). *Survey of Historic Costume* (5th ed.), New York: Fairchild.

Treffinger, D. J. (1996). *Creativity, creative thinking, and critical thinking: In search of definitions.* Sarasota, FL: Center for Creative Learning.

Tucker, R. (2009, April 28). Social responsibility aids survival strategies. *Women's Wear Daily*, p. 10.

USAS. United students against sweatshops. www.usas.org

Vivometrics. http://www.virtualworldlets.net/Shop/ProductsDisplay/VRInterface.php?ID=49

Von Stamm, B. (2008). *Managing innovation, design, and creativity* (2nd ed.). London: John Wiley & Sons, Ltd.

Wallas, G. (1926). *The art of thought.* New York: Harcourt Brace.

Women's Wear Daily. (2003, March 5). Courting gen-y: Forget the hype, find street cred. *Women's Wear Daily.*

appendix

male template

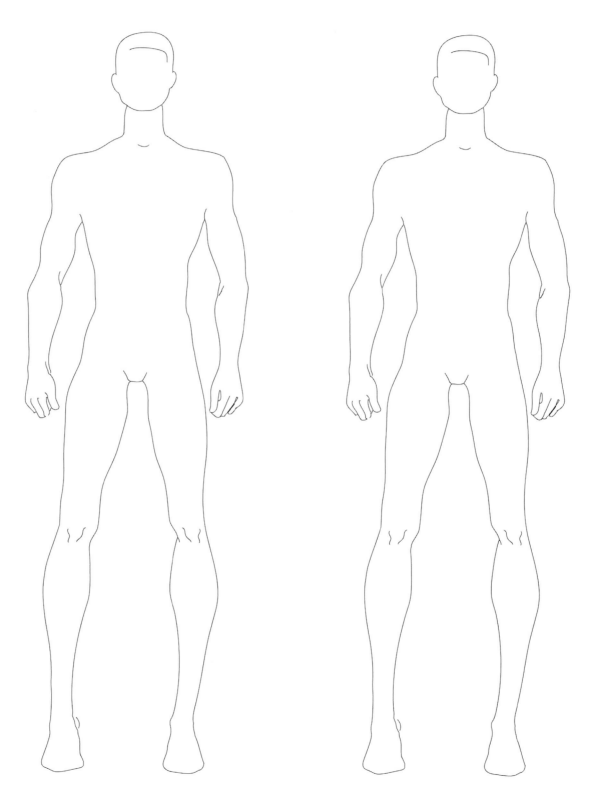

female template

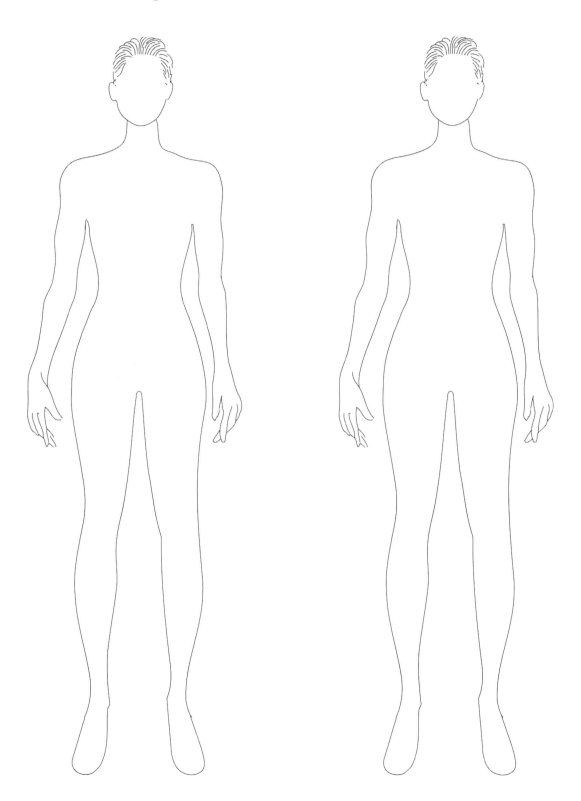

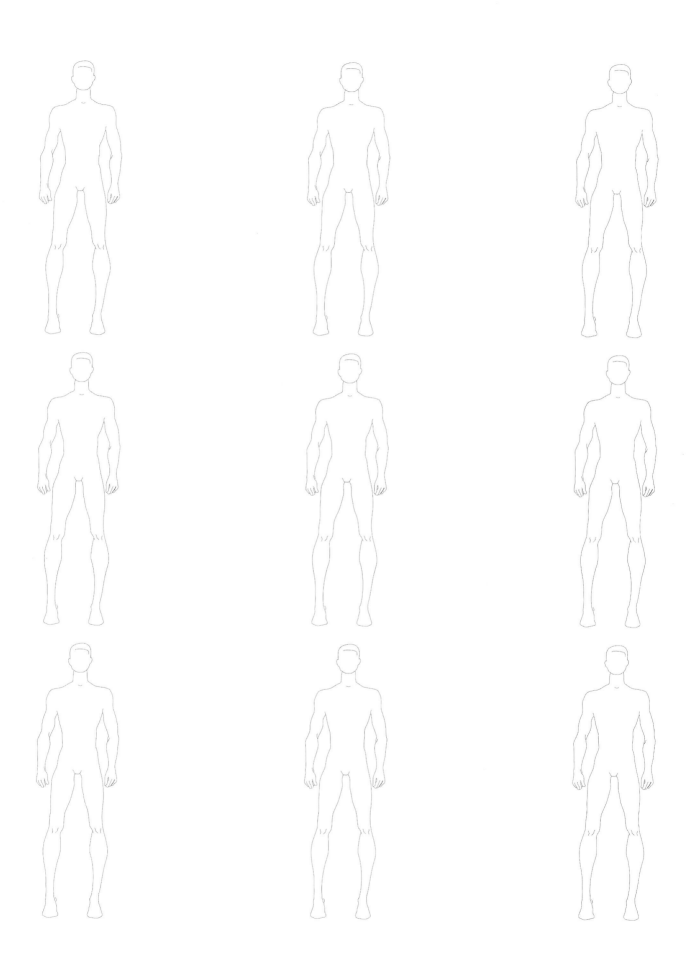

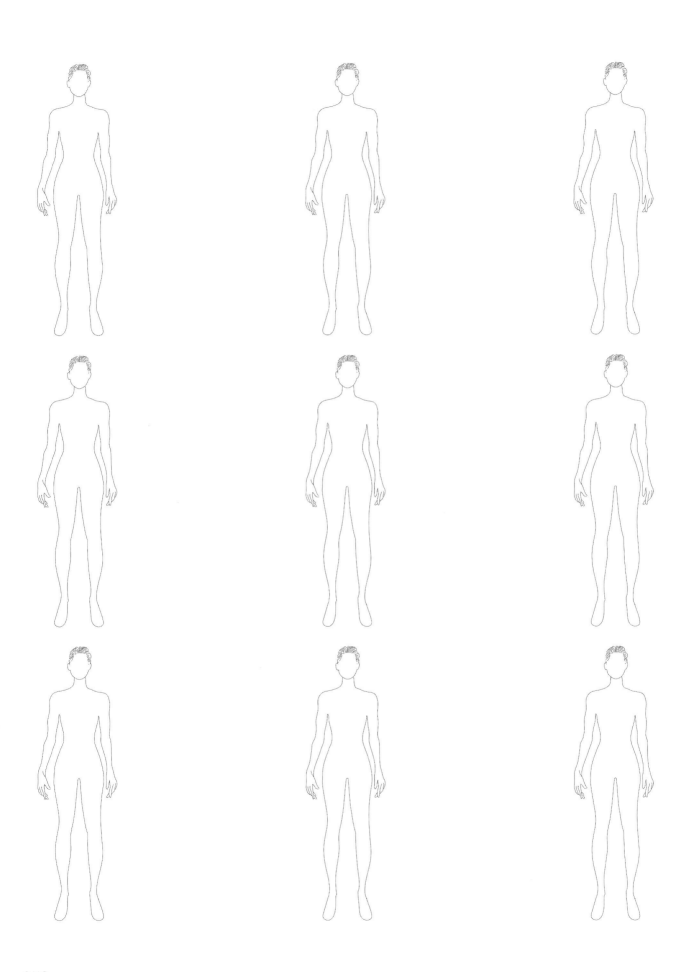

IDEAS

List as many words as you can that embody the ideas on the spread.

Attach concepts in the space below.

1. _____
2. _____
3. _____
4. _____
5. _____
6. _____
7. _____
8. _____
9. _____
10. _____
11. _____
12. _____
13. _____
14. _____
15. _____
16. _____
17. _____
18. _____
19. _____
20. _____
21. _____
22. _____
23. _____

THEMES

Revisit your IDEA spreads.
Group similar ideas and create a corresponding THEME

List like Ideas

1. _____
2. _____
3. _____
4. _____
5. _____
6. _____
7. _____
8. _____
9. _____

Combine ideas into a THEME
and give it a title:

List like Ideas

1. _____
2. _____
3. _____
4. _____
5. _____
6. _____
7. _____
8. _____
9. _____

Combine ideas into a THEME
and give it a title:

List like Ideas

1. _____
2. _____
3. _____
4. _____
5. _____
6. _____
7. _____
8. _____
9. _____

Combine ideas into a THEME
and give it a title:

List like Ideas

1. _____
2. _____
3. _____
4. _____
5. _____
6. _____
7. _____
8. _____
9. _____

Combine ideas into a THEME
and give it a title:

List like Ideas

1. _____
2. _____
3. _____
4. _____
5. _____
6. _____
7. _____
8. _____
9. _____

Combine ideas into a THEME
and give it a title:

List like Ideas

1. _____
2. _____
3. _____
4. _____
5. _____
6. _____
7. _____
8. _____
9. _____

Combine ideas into a THEME
and give it a title:

CONNECTIONS

Combine *similar* THEMES to add details and embellishment to inspiration OR
Combine *dissimilar* THEMES for novel inspiration

List three similar OR three dissimilar THEMES:

1.

2.

3.

Combine THEMES into a CONNECTION and give it a title:

Sketch your CONNECTION:

index

Page numbers in italics refer to images.

achromatic color scheme, 37

activities

    art and fashion, 64–65

    associations, 91; style associations,
        139–40

    brainstorming, 44

    bulletin boards, 53

    change of scenery, 78

    creativity assisters and blockers, 240

    creativity components, 18

    creativity sphere, 20

    cultural traditions, 74–75

    design processes, 208–9

    design rubric, 47

    design tools, 57

    divergent thinking, 93

    elements and principles of design, 33–34

    emotions, 134–35

    the five senses, 121

    force fitting, 204–5

    golden ratio, 29–30

    imagination, 159–60

    mindmapping, 95–96

    multiple intelligences, 99

    music and poetry as muses, 136–37

    online databases, 25–26

    origami-inspired design, 100

    play, 164

    portfolios, 223

    purposeful creativity, 241–42

    SCAMPER, 70–72

    special needs apparel, 176

    stripes, 191–92

    taking time, 167

    tattoos, 146–47

    teamwork, 227

    thinking hats, 235–36

affective, 16

"aha" moment, 168

ALUO, 203

ambiguity, 122

American Apparel, 230

analogous color schemes, 37

anatomy/human form, 24, 27

apparel

    categories, 173

    organizations, 231

    special needs, 173–75, 176

arbiters of fashion, 40

art and fashion, 63–65

audience, 24

balance, 32

body type, unrealistic, 233

brainstorming, 44

bulletin boards, 53

Butter dress, *81*

Calatrava, Santiago, 93

Calvin Klein , *12*, 13

Cameron, Julia, 127

Carlson, Miriam, 60, 61

Cave, Nick, 162–63

Chalayan, Hussein, *90*, 112–13

Chanel, Gabrielle "Coco," *23*

Chow, Cat, *122*

chroma, 36

cognition and creativity, 89–116

collaboration, 226–27, 230

color, 28, 35–39, 138, 141–44

    black, 141

    blue, 142–43

    color story, 37

    color wheel, *35*

color, *(cont.)*
  green, 143–44
  hue, value, and chroma, 36
  red, 142
  schemes, 37, 38–39
  theory, 35–39
  white, 141–42
  yellow, 144
communication, 16
complementary color schemes, 37
concept boards, 222, *224*
congenial creativity environments, 51
contractors, 226
convergent thinking, 90
corporate social responsibility (CSR),
    180–82
Costa, Francisco, *216*, 217
cotton gin, 102
counterfeiting, 176, *177*, 178, 234
courage, 124
Creative Problem Solving (CPS), 202–3, 206
creativity
  and character traits, 119–50
  and cognition, 89–116
  components/characteristics, 14; com-
    munication, 16; effectiveness, 15–16;
    elegance, 16; emotion, 16–17; ethical-
    ity, 17; novelty, 14; surprise, 17
  creativity sphere, *20*
  definitions, 2, 13
  and the design process, 187–215; consid-
    ering the design process and elements
    of creativity, *201*
  and the environment, 51–87; *see also*
    design environments
  and fashion design, 13–48
  knowledge base, 19, 21–24, 27
  and motivation, 153–84
  as multifaceted, 19
  pseudocreativity, 17
  quasicreatvity, 17
  as a social process, 58–59, 62
  subjective nature of, 40
  traits important to creativity, 119–20,
    122–28; ambiguity, 122; courage, 124;
    disorder, 123; fear, 125–28; freedom,
    122–23; goal setting, 126; passion, 128;
    perseverance, 123; polarities of traits,
    124–25; risk taking, 123; self control,
    124; visualizing success, 126–27
  see also design
creativity sphere, *20*

creativogenic, 51
criticism, 45
critiques, 45–46
culture, 145, 148
cut-make-trim stage, 82

Dacca boots, *86*
Da Vinci, Leonardo, *94*, 193, 197–98,
    210–12
demographics, 62
design
  affective dimensions of, 128–29, 132
  critiquing, 40–41, 45–46
  design statements, 132, 136
  elements, 27–34; color, 28, 35–39; line,
    28; patterns, 32; shape, 31; texture, 28,
    31
  globalization, *83*
  inspiration sources, 63–69; architecture,
    63; art, 63–65; cinema and TV, 66; cur-
    rent events, 66; graphic and industrial
    design, 66; nature, 67; popular culture,
    67; print and online media, 67–68;
    sports, 68; subcultures, 68; technology,
    68–69; zeitgeist, 69
  knowledge-base, 22
  pitfalls, 206–8
  portfolios, 217–22
  presentations, 222
  principles, 32–39; balance, 32; color,
    35–39; emphasis, 32; harmony, 32;
    proportion, 32; repetition, 32
  skills of the discipline, 24
  sustainable design, 76–77, 79–82, 84–86
  see also creativity; design process
design environment, 51–59, 62
  environmental scanning, 62
  physical aspects, 52–56
  psychological aspects, 57–59, 62
  tools and equipment, 54–55
  workspace, 54
Design Piracy Prohibition Act, 178
design process, 187–215
  case study (champignons), 210–12
  Da Vincian principles, 193, 197–98,
    210–12
  with elements of creativity, *201*
  phase approach, 198–200
design statements, 132, 136
Dickinson, Emily, 136–37
disposable fashion, 233
divergent thinking, 90, 93

Doo Ri, *118*, 119
Dove's "campaign for real beauty," 233
dress, 144–45, 148–49
  cultural aspects, 22
  historical aspects, 22
dress form, 56
Dynamic Inspiration Notebook (DIN), 3–9
  articulating your style, 128
  challenges, 49, 87, 117, 151, 185, 215,
    243
  connections, 8
  ideas, 5–6
  themes, 7

effectiveness, 15–16
eco-fashion, 76
  see also sustainable design
elaboration, 92
elegance, 16
emotions, 16–17, 129, 132, 134–35
emphasis, 32
environment. *See* design environment;
    sustainable design
environmentally friendly design. *See* sus-
    tainable design
environmental scanning, 62
ethics, 17, 230, 232–34

fabrics, traits of, 138
fair trade, 180–82, *183*
fashion arbiters, 40
fashion design. *See* design
fashion figure, 27
Fashion Research Institute, 108–11
fast fashion, 175
FEA Consumer Needs model, 172
fear, 125–26
  strategies to overcome, 126–28
Fibonacci series, 29
flats, 219
flexibility, 92
flow, 166, 168
fluency, 90
full-cycle sustainability, 76

Gamble, Melissa, 60–61
Gaultier, Jean Paul, *63*
Gernreich, Rudi, *70*
gestalt theory, 168–69
globalization, *83*
goal setting, 126
golden ratio, 27–28, 29–30

greenwashed, 84–85
group formats, 219

harmony, 32
Hayes, Margaret, 228–29
hierarchy of needs, 169–71
holistic approach, 193
hue, 36
human figure, 24, 27

imagery, 158
imagination, 158, 159–60
incubation, 165
The Incubator, 60–61
information sources, 24
intuition, 166

J. Mendel, *xx*
journaling. *See Dynamic Inspiration Note-book (DIN)*

kilts, *62*
kimonos, *23*
knockoffs, 176, *177*, 179
knowledge base, 19, 21–24, 27
Kors, Michael, 42–43

lab, 52
labor practices, 232–33
Lam, Derek, *50*, 51
line, 28
lines/collections, 225
Long, James, *186*, 187

Macroenvironment, 51
mannequin, 56
Marigiela, Martin, *233*
Maslow, Abraham, 169–70
masstige, 178
McDonald, Patrick, *237*
McQueen, Alexander, *31*, *188*
Mendel, Giles, *xx*
metamerism, 36
micro-encapsulation, 104–5
microenvironment, 51
microfibers, 104
mindmapping, 94, 95–96
Miyake, Issey, 114
monochromatic color schemes, 37
mood boards, 132, *133*
mores, 51
Moss, Kate, *177*

motivation, 153–58, 161, 164–66, 168–76
    the Cs of motivation, 155–57
    extrinsic, 153, 157
    gestalt theory, 168–69
    intrinsic, 153–57
multiple intelligences, 97–98, 99
multi-use apparel, 80–81
Myers-Briggs Type Indicator (MBTI), 129

Nadia, *81*
nanotechnology, 104
needs, 169–72
networking, 230
niche markets, 172–73
notebook. *See Dynamic Inspiration Note-book (DIN)*
novelty, 14
no-waste designing, 80

Obama, Michele, *66*
online databases, 25–26
origami, 100
originality, 90, 92
organization, laws of, 169
Orta, Lucy, 113
Owens, Rick, *62*

passion, 128
Patagonia, 230, 232
patterns, 32
perseverance, 123
personality, 129
play, 161, 164
portfolios, 217–22, *223*
    multitasking portfolios, 220
presentations, 222
problem finding, 92, 94, 190
problem solving, 92, 94, 190
    Creative Problem Solving (CPS), 202–3, 206
procrastination, 206–7
product development, 224–26
Project Runway, 42–43
proportion, 32
pseudocreativity, 17
psychographics, 63
purpose, 238

quasicreatvity, 17

Raya, Agga B., 194–96
recycling, 79

(RED) campaign, 180, *181*, 182
reference sources, 24
reflection, 165
repetition, 32
rhythm, 32
risk taking, 123
rubrics, 45, 47
Rucci, Ralph, *88*, 89

samples, 225
SCAMPER, 70
Scott, L'Wren, *50*, 51
Second Life, 106, 109–110
self control, 124
self esteem, 148–49
sewing machines, 103
shade, 36
shape, 31
silhouette, 31
slow fashion, 115
smart textiles, 104
special needs attire, 173–75, 176
spread, 217, *219*
stripes, 191
studio, 52
subcultures, 148, *149*
surprise, 17
sustainable design, 76–77, 79–82, 84–86
    and consumers, 84–85
    customization, 81
    manufacturing of apparel, 82
    multi-use apparel, 80–81
    no-waste designing, 80
    packaging and shipping, 84
    post-consumer use, 85–86
    recycling, 79
    retail outlets, 84
    textiles and fibers, 77, 79
    see also corporate social responsibility (CSR)
sustainable fashion. *See* sustainable design

Takara, 130–31
taking time, 166, *167*
talent, 19
tattoos, 146–47
teamwork, 226, 227
technology, 98–99, 101–7, 112–16
    ancient world, 101
    athletics, 105–6
    baroque and rococo, 102
    communication, 106

technology *(cont.)*
 contemporary innovations, 104–5
 home-grown technology, 115–16
 innovators, 112–14
 medical field, 105
 middle ages, 101
 nineteenth century, 103
 renaissance, 102
 twentieth century, 104
 virtual design, 106–7, 112
textiles, 23
 smart textiles, 104
texture, 28, 31
Timberland, *85*
tint, 36
tools and equipment, 54–55
traits important to creativity, 119–20,
 122–28
 ambiguity, 122
 courage, 124

disorder, 123
expressing through fashion design, 132,
 141–44
fear, 125–26; strategies to overcome,
 126–28
freedom, 122–23
goal setting, 126
passion, 128
perseverance, 123
polarities of traits, 124–25
risk taking, 123
self control, 124
visualizing success, 126–27
trends, 237
 forecasting, 224, 238
 resources, 239–40
triadic color schemes, 37

unconscious mind, 165
upcycling, 86

value, 36
Versace, Gianni, *15*
Vibskov, Henrik, *152*, 153
virtual fashion, 106–7, 112
visualizing success, 126–27
VivoMetrics Life Shirt, *105*

Wardrobe surgery, 86
Warhol, Andy, *17*
Winkler, Shenlei, 108–11
workroom, 52
workspace, 54
 see also design environment
Worth, Charles, *22*

Xiaofeng, Li, 132

zeitgeist, 1, 69
Zucchelli, Italo, *12*, 13